C++

Programming with

CodeWarrior™

Beginning OOP for the
Macintosh® and Power Macintosh®

D1737961

C++

Programming with CodeWarrior™

Beginning OOP for the Macintosh® and Power Macintosh®

Jan L. Harrington

AP PROFESSIONAL

Boston San Diego New York
London Sydney Tokyo Toronto

Copyright © 1995 by Academic Press, Inc.
All rights reserved.
No part of this publication may be reproduced or
transmitted in any form or by any means, electronic
or mechanical, including photocopy, recording, or
any information storage and retrieval system, without
permission in writing from the publisher.

All brand names and product names mentioned in this book
are trademarks or registered trademarks of their respective companies.

AP PROFESSIONAL
1300 Boylston St., Chestnut Hill, MA 02167

An Imprint of ACADEMIC PRESS, INC.
A Division of HARCOURT BRACE & COMPANY

United Kingdom Edition published by
ACADEMIC PRESS LIMITED
24–28 Oval Road, London NW1 7DX

Harrington, Jan L.
    C++ programming with CodeWarrior : beginning OOP for the
Macintosh and the Power Macintosh / Jan L. Harrington.
        p.   cm.
    Includes bibliographical references and index.
    ISBN 0-12-326420-0 (acid-free paper)
    1. Macintosh (Computer) --Programming. 2. C++ (Computer program
language) I. Title.
QA76.8.M3H359 1995
005.265--dc20   95-20134
                                                                 CIP

Printed in the United States of America
    95 96 97 98 IP   9 8 7 6 5 4 3 2 1

Contents

Preface

So you've decided it's time you learned how to program! Programming is fun, challenging, frustrating, infuriating, and satisfying—all at the same time. The fun and the challenge come as you puzzle through the logic of a program to make it work exactly the way you want; the frustration and fury come when a problem is seemingly unsolvable. And the satisfaction? That comes when you solve that unsolvable problem and end up with a working program. If you enjoy working through puzzles and find satisfaction in the problem-solving process, you're really going to love programming.

This book is targeted primarily at two audiences. The first is readers who have little or no programming background. If you fall into that group, you'll spend a lot of time with the first 12 chapters, which present programming concepts from the beginning. You'll move on to the more advanced material in Chapters 13 through 17 as you develop your programming skills. However, if you are relatively fluent in a language other than C++, you will be able to skim some of the first 12 chapters and then spend more time with the advanced material in the later chapters.

Teaching Macintosh programming presents a bit of a dilemma. Because of the Macintosh's user interface and the support for both the interface and the operating system found in the computer's ROM, learning to program the Macintosh presents a special challenge. You must first learn programming concepts. Once you understand how programs are written, you can learn to work with the programs in the ROM's ToolBox. All of this is just too much for one book. In fact, it generally takes two good-sized volumes to teach someone who already knows how to program to work with most of the features of the ToolBox.

This book has therefore been written to teach you programming concepts, using object-oriented C++ from the ground up. You will learn how object-oriented programs are constructed and how to write them in C++. To make it easy for you to get started, you will be working with a text interface. In this way you can focus on the concepts of the programming without worrying about the added complexities of the ToolBox.

The C++ you will learn in this book is based on the emerging C++ standard as described by the American National Standards Institute (ANSI). ANSI C++ can be used with many C++ development environments. For the purposes of this book, you will be using Metrowerks's CodeWarrior, an integrated software development environment that is the most widely used platform for PowerMac software development. CodeWarrior also creates programs for 680x0 Macintoshes. If you have a PowerMac, the software will run in native PowerPC code; if you have a 680x0 Macintosh, it runs in native 680x0 code.

How to Use This Book

The way in which you use this book depends on your programming background. This section of the Preface contains some suggestions as to how you might use each chapter. However, regardless of your background, you'll want to take advantage of the "programming challenges" scattered throughout the book.

THE PROGRAMMING CHALLENGES

To help you develop your own programming skills, you'll find a number of "programming challenges" throughout this book. Each programming challenge asks you to modify one of the sample programs, adding functionality that gives you practice with the concepts taught in a given chapter. These challenges make it possible for you to work with the CodeWarrior software that comes on the CD-ROM that accompanies this book.

FOR READERS WITH LITTLE OR NO PROGRAMMING BACKGROUND

If you have little or no programming background, you will probably use the chapters in this book in the following way:

- Chapter 1: This chapter covers computing concepts that provide a foundation for programming. You should read carefully before you proceed further into the book. You should also pay attention to where specific ideas are discussed so that you can refer back to it later as those ideas become important in your study of C++.

- Chapter 2: This chapter introduces the concepts of object-oriented programming. You should read and study it in depth.

- Chapter 3: This chapter provides an overview of the CodeWarrior programming environment. If you are new to CodeWarrior, you should work through the chapter carefully, performing the hands-on exercises in the chapter.

- Chapter 4: This chapter teaches you how to write the building blocks of an object-oriented program (a class). You will learn about variables and functions. The concepts in this chapter are fundamental to everything you will be doing in the rest of the book. You should therefore make certain that you understand the material in this chapter before moving on.

- Chapter 5: In this chapter you'll learn how to transfer data from the keyboard into a program and from a program to the keyboard. You'll also learn how to write to a file and read from a file. It's essential that you master keyboard input and screen output before moving on. However, if file I/O seems a bit mysterious, you can leave it for now and return to it when you're a bit more comfortable with C++.

- Chapter 6: In Chapter 6 you will be introduced to how computers perform arithmetic. This is another chapter you should study in depth.

- Chapter 7: This chapter introduces you to how computer programs tell the computer to make choices between alternative sets of actions. Like Chapter 6, the material in this chapter is fundamental to your programming skills. If you skipped file I/O in Chapter 5, you may also want to leave the last section of this chapter for later.

- Chapter 8: This chapter introduces you to how computer programs tell the computer to repeat groups of actions. This material, as well as that in the preceding two chapters, forms an essential foundation for any program. You should learn the material in this chapter thoroughly.

At this point you will have been introduced to the basic elements of C++ programming. Before moving on, you should work through the programming challenges so that you begin to have some confidence in what you have learned so far. Use the "blank" project provided on the CD-ROM to write programs of your own. (More on this blank project later.) When you feel confident, move on to a study of Chapters 9 through 12:

- Chapter 9: In this chapter you will learn about a way to group data together and handle the group as a unit. You should study the first section of the chapter (the part that covers one-dimensional arrays) thoroughly. You can skip the last part of the chapter (two-dimensional arrays) if you find it a bit daunting.
- Chapter 10: Chapter 10 focuses on character strings (more than one character handled as a unit). Because much of what computers do today deals with character strings, you should study this chapter thoroughly. However, because C++ strings are implemented as arrays, you shouldn't move on to this chapter until you are comfortable with one-dimensional arrays.
- Chapter 11: This chapter teaches you how to use C++ to access main memory directly. You may need to read the chapter several times. However, perseverance pays off. When you master Chapter 11, you'll have learned an essential part of C++ programming.
- Chapter 12: Chapter 12 pulls together everything you've read about to this point. It presents a long program that demonstrates all the concepts covered in the first part of the book.

After reading through and understanding Chapter 12, you will have mastered the basics of C++ programming. This is another point at which you will probably want to stop and make certain that you are comfortable with everything you've learned. In fact, you may want to spend some time practicing your programming before moving on to the remainder of the book.

The remaining five chapters of the book cover more advanced material that can make your programs more efficient:

- Chapter 13: In this chapter you'll learn how to give operators (for example, the addition operator, +) more than one meaning. The material in this chapter is a bit tricky, so you should work all three programming challenges at the end of the chapter for practice. If you find this chapter a bit daunting, you can skip it. However, the concepts developed in this chapter are used in sample programs in the rest of the book.
- Chapter 14: Chapter 14 takes another look at arrays, to which you were first introduced in Chapter 9. In many ways, this material is easier than Chapter 13. If

you're comfortable with everything up through Chapter 12, this chapter won't be difficult.

- Chapter 15: In this chapter you'll learn a technique for dealing with multiple objects by chaining them together in a list. Although this is a different way of looking at objects, it doesn't require any new language elements. However, you should be familiar with Chapter 14 before you tackle Chapter 15.

- Chapter 16: This chapter presents the final piece of the object-oriented model (inheritance). The topic isn't particularly difficult, but it does use concepts from Chapters 14 and 15.

- Chapter 17: This final chapter provides an overview of Macintosh ToolBox programming. You should read through it to find out what comes next in your programming education. At the very end you'll find a bibliography of books that can take you beyond what you've learned in this one.

FOR READERS WHO ARE FLUENT IN A LANGUAGE OTHER THAN C++

If you are fluent in a language such as Pascal, Modula-2, C, structured BASIC, or COBOL, you will probably use the chapters in this book in the following way:

- Chapter 1: Skim this chapter to be certain that you are familiar with the programming foundation material covered. Read in depth sections that are new to you.

- Chapter 2: This chapter introduces the concepts of object-oriented programming. If you've never worked in an object-oriented environment before, you should read and study the chapter in depth.

- Chapter 3: This chapter provides an overview of the CodeWarrior programming environment. If you are new to CodeWarrior, you should work through the chapter, performing the hands-on exercises in the chapter.

- Chapter 4: This chapter introduces C++ variables and functions in the context of classes. If you've never programmed in an object-oriented language, you should pay special attention to the way in which classes are declared. You should also focus on the C++ syntax for declaring variables (it's different from just about every other language except C) and the syntax for function prototypes.

- Chapter 5: C++ supports several types of I/O, the easiest of which to use is stream I/O. Because stream I/O isn't widely used by other languages, you should work through this chapter thoroughly, delving into both screen and keyboard I/O, as well as file I/O.

- Chapter 6: This chapter covers C++ arithmetic. You can skim most of the material, but you should pay attention to the C++ arithmetic operators, some of which are different from those found in other languages. Pay special attention to the sections on the increment and decrement operators, typecasting, and math library functions.
- Chapter 7: This chapter covers `if/else` and `switch` (`case`) constructs. You should skim the chapter to discover the C++ syntax for these language elements. You should also focus on the ? operator (a shorthand for `if/else` unique to C and C++) and on verifying file operations.
- Chapter 8: This chapter covers iteration. You should skim it to discover the C++ syntax for `while` and `for` loops.
- Chapter 9: Chapter 9 covers both one- and two-dimensional arrays. If you are comfortable with arrays, skim this chapter to discover the C++ syntax. If arrays give you problems, you may want to read this chapter in more depth.
- Chapter 10: Chapter 10 deals with strings. Unless you are fluent in C, you should pay special attention to this chapter. C++ handles strings differently from every language except C, and insensitivity to these differences can have unwanted effects on Macintosh main memory while your program is running.
- Chapter 11: This chapter covers pointers. You can't do anything sophisticated in C++ without using pointers. If you're fluent in C, you can skim the first major sections of this chapter ("Pointer Variables" and "Pointers and Parameter Passing"). However, the rest of the chapter contains material unique to C++ and should be read carefully. If you're experience is in a language other than C, you should study this chapter carefully.
- Chapter 12: Chapter 12 provides a summary of the preceding 11 chapters. In it you will find a long program that uses all the concepts discussed so far. Before proceeding, skim the chapter and read through the source code, just to make sure that you're comfortable with the structure of an object-oriented program and with C++ syntax.

The remainder of the book covers more advanced material, some of which is unique to C++ and some of which provides a new twist on old concepts:

- Chapter 13: This chapter presents a way to give operators (the assignment operator, arithmetic operator, and so on) new meanings. Known as operator overloading, it's one of the trickiest parts of C++. You'll want to work through this chapter carefully.
- Chapter 14: In this chapter you'll read about the "object-oriented" way of handling arrays. It's not difficult, but it is important nonetheless because it provides an introduction to object-oriented data structures. Even if you've worked with

data structures in another language, you'll want to pay special attention to this chapter. The object-oriented way is considerably different from the way arrays are handled in structured languages.

- Chapter 15: This chapter extends the coverage of object-oriented data structures by looking at linked lists. Again, the material isn't particularly difficult but does give you added insight into how object-oriented programs are constructed.

- Chapter 16: The final piece to the object-oriented model is inheritance, which is covered in this chapter. You'll find that the toughest part of inheritance is recognizing when inheritance is appropriate and when it isn't. However, using inheritance where applicable can greatly simplify your programming tasks and clarify the organization of your program. You should therefore study this chapter in some detail.

- Chapter 17: Chapter 17 provides a springboard for further study of Macintosh programming. It discusses the structure of Macintosh ToolBox programs and presents some sample ToolBox access so that you can get a flavor for what is involved in supporting the Macintosh user interface. The chapter concludes with a bibliography to help you extend your Macintosh programming knowledge. You should read through this chapter. Ideally, you'll be excited enough when you finish to pick up one of those books that teaches ToolBox programming so that you can write sophisticated, user-friendly Macintosh applications.

What You Need to Know

This book assumes that you have a good working knowledge of the Macintosh and its operating system. You should be familiar with using the Macintosh user interface (opening, closing, and copying files, working with windows, using menus, and so on). You should also be comfortable with using a text editor (for example, Simple-Text or TeachText) or a word processor. In other words, you should consider youself a knowledgeable user. However, you don't need to have any background in computer programming.

About the CD-ROM

The CD-ROM that accompanies this book contains a fully functional copy of CodeWarrior C++. That copy, however, is limited in a significant way: It will compile and run only the projects that are on the CD-ROM. You will therefore find two types of projects. The first type includes all the sample code from the book. You will be using those projects and their source code files for the book's programming challenges.

The second type of projects are two "blank" projects. In other words, empty files have been added to the projects so that you can add your own code to those files. The first blank project is for use in the exercises in Chapter 3. The second is for you to use to create your own programs from scratch. Because each blank project has only two source code files (one for the main program and one for class functions), they are suitable only for very small programs that you can use to practice.

Acknowledgments

No book of this kind springs from just one person. It wouldn't have happened without the help of some very great folks at AP Professional and Metrowerks. I would therefore like to take some space to thank them properly:

- Chuck Glaser, Executive Editor at AP Professional, who has seen this project all the way through.
- David Hannon, Editorial Assistant at AP Professional, who keeps everything running smoothly.
- Mike Williams, Production Editor at AP Professional, who shepherded the book into print.
- Evelyn Pyle, the copyeditor.
- Jean Belanger, Greg Galanos, and the rest of the Metrowerks team.
- Carole McClendon, my agent, who knows how to find great people for me to work with.

JLH

Some Basic Concepts

Regardless of the language in which you are programming, there are some underlying concepts that are common to all types of programming. This chapter looks at a variety of programming fundamentals, including a description of exactly what a program is, how it is prepared, the impact of the type of microprocessor on programming, storing and measuring things using the binary numbering system, some basic operations on binary numbers, and how a computer organizes its main memory. If these topics seem somewhat unrelated, don't worry—you'll use the knowledge you gain here over and over again as you work through this book.

The Anatomy of a Program

A computer program is a series of detailed steps that a computer follows. In fact, a computer without programs is nothing but an expensive paperweight; it can't do anything unless a program gives it the proper instructions. These instructions are drawn from the computer's *instruction set*, the native language that the microprocessor can understand. Each type of microprocessor has its own instruction set. Of particular concern to the Macintosh programmer is the fact that the instruction set for 680x0 (the microprocessor family found in Macintoshes other than the Power Macs) is different from that of the PowerPC (found in Power Macs). This means that without special help, a program prepared for one type of microprocessor won't run on a computer with a different type of microprocessor.

NOTE

A PowerMac is able to execute 680x0 programs by emulating the 680x0 instruction set. The 680x0 emulator, which is in the PowerMac's ROM, intercepts 680x0 instructions, translates them into the equivalent PowerPC instruction, and then passes them to the PowerMac's CPU for execution. SoftPC and SoftWindows, which allow Windows and MS-DOS programs to run on Macintoshes, work in the same way, by translating instructions originally in the language of one of Intel's x86 CPU family into Macintosh instructions (either 680x0 or PowerPC, whichever is appropriate for the computer).

A microprocessor's instruction set is coded in *binary* (base 2) as a sequence of 0s and 1s. Each instruction has its own code that the computer can understand without any further translation. Programs in this form are said to be in *machine language* or *object code*. Unfortunately, it's difficult for humans to write programs using what appear to us as meaningless sequences of binary digits.

People therefore write programs using languages that are more understandable. The first step above machine language is *assembly language*, a type of programming language in which each binary instruction code is replaced by a two- to five-letter mnemonic code. For example, an instruction to move a piece of data from one place to another might be represented by MOV. A good assembly language program runs very fast and makes efficient use of main memory. However, to program in assembly language you need to be familiar with the internals of a computer's CPU and the specific actions of each instruction in the CPU's instruction set. In addition, an assembly language program can be used only on the microprocessor for which it was written. If you want to write programs for more than one type of CPU, you need to learn a separate assembly language for each one.

Early in the history of computing, programmers realized that they needed programming languages that were less closely related to the type of CPU. The group of languages that arose from that need were the *high-level languages*, languages that are more English-like than assembly language and somewhat independent of the type of computer for which a program is written. Among the first high-level languages were FORTRAN (good for mathematical and scientific programming) and COBOL (used primarily for business programming). Also in that category are BASIC (used primarily for amateur programming efforts but currently making a comeback in business), Pascal (used for teaching programming and for a lot of Macintosh programming), and C and C++ (used widely for commercial software development).

LANGUAGE TRANSLATION

The problem with using assembly language or a high-level language is that a microprocessor can't understand the program unless it is first translated into machine language. The development of assembly language and high-level languages therefore also required the development of programs that could perform the required translations. Assembly language programs are translated by *assemblers*; high-level language programs are translated by *interpreters* or *compilers*.

An interpreter, which translates a program line by line as the program is being run, is usually found with the BASIC programming language. Most other high-level languages (and some versions of BASIC) are translated by compilers, which perform their translation before the program is run. Compiled programs run faster than interpreted programs because the computer doesn't need to spend time performing language translation when the program is running.

Because a compiler generates machine language, it is specific to one microprocessor. For example, it requires different compilers to generate both 680x0 and PowerPC machine language. However, you do not necessarily need to have both types of computers to create both types of programs. Programming environments like CodeWarrior provide *cross-compilers* that generate both 680x0 and PowerPC output on a single Macintosh, regardless of the type of CPU on which the programming is performed. In practical terms this means that you can write and test your Macintosh program on one type of Macintosh and, when the program is complete, cross-compile it for the other platform without needing access to another computer.

In most programming environments you use a text editor to write a program. The file containing the program (the *source code*) is submitted to the assembler or compiler for translation. The language translator scans the source file for errors in the structure of the language statements (*syntax errors*) and reports the errors it finds.

A program can't be run until it assembles or compiles without error. However, it is important to recognize that just because a program passes the language translator without a problem, the program doesn't necessarily work properly. As you will discover as you work through this book, the most significant program errors are logical errors, errors in the way in which you have given the computer instructions.

LINKING

In almost every case, the object code produced by compiling a single source code file isn't a program that can be run. Unless a program is very small, the source code is usually stored in several files. In addition, the source code that you write isn't enough; some parts are missing. These parts are found in *libraries*, collections of pre-written object code that you can use. Libraries contain a wealth of useful programs, including code to perform I/O, perform mathematical functions (for example, taking a square root), manipulate strings of text, and support the Macintosh user interface. Throughout this book you will be introduced to the contents of a number of libraries, some of which are standard with virtually every C++ compiler and others that are specific to CodeWarrior.

The step that combines your object code modules with the libraries you have used, producing an executable application, is known as *linking*. Although some program development environments require separate compilation and linking steps, CodeWarrior automates the process for you. To manage the process, you create a *project* that tells CodeWarrior which files should be linked together. As an example, consider Figure 1.1. The names of the libraries used by the program appear in boldface; the source code file names are in plain text. This particular project is used on a PowerPC; the libraries used in a 680x0 project are somewhat different.

Figure 1.1　A CodeWarrior project window

File	Code	Data		
Checkbook PPC				
▽ Group 1	184K	18K	• ⊟
ANSI C++.PPC.Lib	132200	5130	🔳
ANSI C.PPC.Lib	49268	12193	🔳
MVCRuntime.Lib	3492	810	🔳
account.cpp	984	40	• 🔳
main.cpp	1804	343	• 🔳
trans.cpp	1352	67	• 🔳
▽ Group 2	0	0	⊟
InterfaceLib	0	0	🔳
▽ Group 3	16K	1K	⊟
SIOUX.PPC.Lib	16568	1449	🔳
MathLib	0	0	🔳
9 file(s)	200K	19K	

Libraries (in boldface)

Source code (in plain text)

When you give the command to run your program, CodeWarrior compiles all source code files in the project that have been modified since they were last compiled. If the compilation is successful (no errors were detected), CodeWarrior then links all files in the project.

Errors can occur during linking. If your program has made reference to code contained in a library and the library isn't part of the project, linking will be unsuccessful. Figuring out which library to add can sometimes be a bit tricky, because occasionally the missing library isn't used by your program directly but by one of the other libraries used by your program. This book will help you avoid such problems by specifying exactly which libraries you will need to use.

Introducing Binary Numbers

Although you certainly don't have to be a math whiz to write great computer programs, you can avoid some frustrating errors in your programs if you understand something about the binary numbering system and how it's used by a computer. Most of us were introduced to alternative base number systems in grade school. However, like any other math concept, it's one of those things you forget quickly if you don't use it every day. This section therefore presents a review of binary numbers in light of their application to computer programming.

Binary, like the base 10 numbering system we use every day, is a place value system. Each position in a binary number presents the value of the digit occupying that position multiplied by a power of 2. To make this a bit clearer, let's first look at the base 10 number 256:

$$256 = (2 \times 10^2) + (5 \times 10^1) + (6 \times 10^0)$$

This equation works correctly when we realize that any number raised to the 0 power is 1 and that any number raised to the 1 power is the number itself.

A binary number, which uses only the digits 0 and 1 (each known as a *bit*), can be written in the same way:

$$256 = (1 \times 2^8) + (0 \times 2^7) + (0 \times 2^6) + (0 \times 2^5) + (0 \times 2^4) + (0 \times 2^3) + (0 \times 2^2) + (0 \times 2^1) + (0 \times 2^0)$$

The key to understanding the decimal equivalent of a binary number is knowing powers of 2. Then just add up the value of those places that contain a 1. (Zero times any number is zero.) In Table 1.1 you can see that the powers of 2 are generated by simply multiplying the value of the preceding power by 2.

One of the most common things you will need to do with binary when you are programming is figure out the maximum value that can be stored in a given number

Table 1.1   Some useful powers of 2

2^0	1	2^{30}	1,073,741,824
2^1	2	2^{31}	2,147,483,648
2^2	4	2^{32}	4,294,967,296
2^3	8		
2^4	16		
2^5	32		
2^6	64		
2^7	128		
2^8	256		
2^9	512		
2^{10}	1,024		
2^{11}	2,048		
2^{12}	4,096		
2^{13}	8,192		
2^{14}	16,384		
2^{15}	32,768		
2^{16}	65,536		
2^{17}	131,072		
2^{18}	262,144		
2^{19}	524,288		
2^{20}	1,048,576		

of bits. For example, assume that you need to know the maximum value that can be stored in seven bits. That is equivalent to the following:

$$(1 \times 2^6) + (1 \times 2^5) + (1 \times 2^4) + (1 \times 2^3) + (1 \times 2^2) + (1 \times 2^1) + (1 \times 2^0)$$

Adding up the place values gives you:

$$64 + 32 + 16 + 8 + 4 + 2 + 1 = 127$$

Notice that this value (127) is one less than the value of the next highest power of 2 (128, or 2^7). In every case, if n represents some number of bits (assuming the bits are numbered beginning with 0), the maximum value that can be stored in those n bits is $2^{n+1} - 1$.

Binary and Data Storage

A computer uses the binary numbering system for just about everything, including organizing main memory, storing characters, and storing numbers. Understanding how binary is used in each of these situations will help you become a successful programmer.

ORGANIZING AND ACCESSING MAIN MEMORY

As you have read, a program must be in main memory before it can run. While it is running, a program moves instructions and data between the CPU and main memory. In addition, data are written from main memory to external devices (for example, disk drives, tape drives, and printers) and read from external devices into main memory (for example, the keyboard, disk drives, and tape drives).

NOTE

The CPU may or may not play a direct role in I/O operations. If you have a PowerMac, a Mac IIfx, or any other Macintosh equipped with a Direct Memory Access (DMA) expansion board, your Macintosh can transfer data directly to and from memory. All the CPU needs to do is to give the command to start the transfer. However, other Macintoshes must transfer all data directly to the CPU, from where it is then transferred to main memory.

A computer's main memory is organized into groups of eight bits, known as a *byte*. The bits in a byte are numbered from right to left—beginning with 0—so that each byte contains bits 0 through 7, as in Figure 1.2.

Figure 1.2   Numbering the bits in a byte

	1	**0**	**0**	**1**	**1**	**1**	**0**	**0**
Bit number:	7	6	5	4	3	2	1	0

Because a computer's memory is made up of a large quantity of bytes, it's convenient to speak about thousands of bytes (*kilobytes*, or K), millions of bytes (*megabytes*, or M, Mb, or meg), and billions of bytes (*gigabytes*, or G or Gb). To be completely accurate, a kilobyte is 2^{10} (1024) bytes, a megabyte 2^{20} (1,048,576) bytes, and a gigabyte 2^{30} (1,073,741,824) bytes. The next highest grouping, which is bound to confront us sooner rather than later as storage capacities continue to grow, is 2^{40} (1,099,511,627,776) bytes—a *terabyte*.

Each byte in main memory is numbered to identify it. This number, a byte's *address*, is used by a program to reference the storage location and its contents. A program can therefore use main memory to store temporary data that are used while the program is running. However, this doesn't mean that you need to write main memory addresses as part of a program. In fact, doing so wouldn't be very practical.

A Macintosh running System 7.x (or System 6.x with MultiFinder) can have many programs in main memory at the same time. This means that when a program is run, there is no guarantee that it is given access to the same range of main memory addresses it used during a previous run. If the program references specific addresses, they might well be in use by another program. Writing to those addresses would disrupt the other program. As a programmer, you therefore can't predict exactly what addresses your program will use. In addition, it's difficult for a human programmer to specify addresses in binary.

High-level programming languages handle the memory addressing problem by using two related strategies. First, a programmer doesn't need to work with binary addresses at all, but instead assigns a word to each storage location to be used. Such labeled storage locations are called *variables*. When the program is assigned, the compiler assigns a binary address to each variable.

The second part of the solution deals with which addresses the compiler uses. Rather than using specific addresses, the compiler generates address that are relative to the start of the program. In other words, a storage location is identified by the number of bytes it is displaced from the beginning of the program. Then, when the program is run, the CPU adds each relative address to the address where the program begins to generate each complete address as needed.

POINTERS

Although a programmer doesn't need to work with binary addresses directly, there are circumstances under which it is useful to refer to the address where data are stored. A C++ program does this with a *pointer*, the address at which some form of data storage begins in main memory. There are two primary ways to get a pointer. The first is to use one of the features of C++ that produce a pointer as a result. The second is to ask C++ for the address assigned to a variable. In either case, the pointer can be saved in a variable set aside for that purpose. Therefore even though your program is using main memory addresses, you never have to write the binary as part of your program.

Pointers and the addresses of variables are essential tools for C++ programs. You will therefore find a great deal about using them throughout this book, beginning with the discussion of arrays in Chapter 11.

VARIABLES AND DATA STORAGE

When you use a variable to set aside storage space, you specify the type of data to be stored in the variable. Some types of data, such as individual characters, take up one byte. Other types of data, such as numbers, require more than one byte.

Storing Characters

A computer really doesn't understand characters (letters, numbers, punctuation marks, and so on). In fact, because everything in a computer must be represented in binary, the only way to represent characters is to give each character a code. The most commonly used character coding scheme is the *American Standard Code for Information Interchange*, or more familiarly, *ASCII* (pronounced "ass-key").

The original ASCII coding scheme used seven bits for each character. Unfortunately that provides only 128 distinct codes (127 codes consisting of 0s and 1s and the code 0000000). The Macintosh, with its special characters, such as °, π, and é, needs many more codes. The Macintosh therefore uses an extended eight-bit ASCII that provides 256 codes (255 codes consisting of 0s and 1s and the code 00000000).

The ASCII codes for the letters and numbers in a typical Macintosh font can be found in Table 1.2. There are two important things to notice about these codes. First, look at the digits 0 through 9: Their ASCII codes aren't the same as the values of the digits. For example, if you translate the ASCII code for 1 (0011 0001) into decimal, you get 31 rather than 1. If you attempt to use this in an arithmetic operation, you'll get an inaccurate result because the computer will interpret the ASCII code as a number. In other words, the computer doesn't "understand" the meaning of the digit when it is stored as an ASCII code. This means that you shouldn't attempt to use a digit stored in a character storage location in arithmetic operations. Although C++ will usually allow you to do so, the result will be wrong.

The second important feature of ASCII codes is the difference between upper- and lowercase letters. When a computer compares characters, it does so by evaluating the numeric equivalence of ASCII codes. This means that as far as a computer is concerned, "a" isn't the same as "A," "b" isn't the same as "B," and so on. You often will need to take this into account when evaluating the data manipulated by a program.

Table 1.2   Sample ASCII codes

Character	Code	Character	Code	Character	Code
0	0011 0000	A	0100 0001	a	0110 0001
1	0011 0001	B	0100 0010	b	0110 0010
2	0011 0010	C	0100 0011	c	0110 0011
3	0011 0011	D	0100 0100	d	0110 0100
4	0011 0100	E	0100 0101	e	0110 0101
5	0011 0101	F	0100 0110	f	0110 0110
6	0011 0110	G	0100 0111	g	0110 0111
7	0011 0111	H	0100 1000	h	0110 1000
8	0011 1000	I	0100 1001	i	0110 1001
9	0011 1001	J	0100 1010	j	0110 1010
		K	0100 1011	k	0110 1011
		L	0100 1100	l	0110 1100
		M	0100 1101	m	0110 1101
		N	0100 1110	n	0110 1110
		O	0100 1111	o	0110 1111
		P	0101 0000	p	0111 0000
		Q	0101 0001	q	0111 0001
		R	0101 0010	r	0111 0010
		S	0101 0011	s	0111 0011
		T	0101 0100	t	0111 0100
		U	0101 0101	u	0111 0101
		V	0101 0110	v	0111 0110
		W	0101 0111	w	0111 0111
		X	0101 1000	x	0111 1000
		Y	0101 1001	y	0111 1001
		Z	0101 1010	z	0111 1010

Storing Numbers

Numbers are stored in two different general formats: as floating point numbers and as integers. Floating point numbers are decimal fractions, often multiplied by 10 raised to some power, such as 2.45689×10^{56}. The Macintosh uses a special binary format to store floating point numbers. The details of that format are generally not important for high-level language programmers. Unless you are writing scientific or high-resolution graphics applications, your programs are unlikely to deal with values that are too large or too small for the Macintosh's floating point format.

Integers are whole numbers with nothing to the right of the decimal point. Integers are stored in a special binary format known as *2's complement*. The leftmost bit in the storage location is set aside for the sign of the number (0 = positive, 1 = negative). The rest of the bits are used for the magnitude of the number. The possible values are evenly divided between positive and negative numbers.

By default, the Macintosh uses two bytes (16 bits) for integers, providing a range from -32,768 to 32,767, a total of 65,536 values. (Don't forget that 0 is a positive value.) If a program stores a number in an integer storage location that is either too small or too large, the computer won't warn you. Instead you'll get an incorrect value.

If there is any chance that a value won't fit in an integer storage location, you can use a long integer instead. Although a long integer consumes 32 bits of space, it also expands the range of possible values to -2,147,483,648 to 2,147,483,647.

Binary and Hexadecimal

The amount of main memory in today's Macintoshes is measured in megabytes. Each one of those bytes has its own identifying address. However, if we express those addresses in binary, they will be very, very long and difficult to work with. The solution is a shorthand for binary: *hexadecimal* (also known as *hex*), or base 16.

Writing hexadecimal presents a bit of a problem. Each place in a hexadecimal number must be able to hold a single digit for the values 0 through 15. Unfortunately our decimal numbering system has only 10 digits, not 16. We therefore use the letters A through F to represent the additional digits needed by hexadecimal (A = 10, B = 11, C = 12, D = 13, E = 14, F = 15). If you see a number with letters in it, it is almost certainly hexadecimal.

The relationship between binary and hexadecimal appears when you take a look at some powers of 16 and equivalent powers of 2. Notice in Table 1.3 that each power of 16 is equal to four powers of 2. This means that each hexadecimal digit can take the place of four binary digits, making the hexadecimal representation of a number one-quarter of the size of the binary representation.

Table 1.3   Powers of 16 and equivalent powers of 2

Power of 16	Power of 2	Value
16^0	2^0	1
16^1	2^4	16
16^2	2^8	256
16^3	2^{12}	4,096
16^4	2^{16}	65,536
16^5	2^{20}	1,048,576
16^6	2^{24}	16,777,216
16^7	2^{28}	268,435,456
16^8	2^{32}	4.294,967,296

As an example, consider the binary number in Figure 1.3. To convert it to hexadecimal, you divide the binary number into groups of four, beginning at the right edge of the number. Then you substitute the equivalent hexadecimal digit for each group of four binary digits. As you can see, the 28-digit binary number has turned into a 7-digit hexadecimal number, a value that is much easier to handle.

Figure 1.3   Using hexadecimal to Represent a binary number

If a hexadecimal number doesn't contain any letters, it might be difficult to know whether you are dealing with base 10 or base 16. Most computer software and documentation therefore use one of two techniques to identify hexadecimal values. The first is to place a dollar sign in front of the hex value (for example, $E30F5A4). The second is to precede the value with the characters 0x (for example, 0xE30F5A4).

You will see this latter notation used in CodeWarrior's debugger to indicate the location in main memory where some types of data are stored.

How a Program Executes

A computer is really a very single-minded piece of equipment. Unless it's given very specific instructions, it can't do anything. Even when it is given instructions, it will do exactly what it's told, even if what the program tells it to do isn't exactly what the programmer had in mind.

When you double-click on a program icon to launch the program, the Macintosh copies the program into main memory, allocates space in main memory for the program's variables, and then begins execution with the first statement in the program. The program executes program statements in order, one after the other, until it encounters a statement that tells it to do otherwise.

There are three basic ways in which a program can change the order of program statement execution:

- Tell the computer to repeat a series of actions for a specified number of times or until some condition is met. This type of program logic is covered in depth in Chapter 8.

- Tell the computer to go directly to another part of the program and begin executing statements at that point. There are many circumstances under which this occurs. You will be introduced to them throughout this book.

- Tell the computer to choose between two or more sets of alternative actions, based on some logical criteria. This type of program logic is covered in depth in Chapter 7.

The statements you use to give a computer these types of instructions make up the *structured* portion of C++. The way in which you organize the data and the actions the data know how to perform make up the *object-oriented* portion of C++. Because you need to use the structured portion to make the object-oriented portion work, you will be learning both types of programming throughout this book.

Introducing OOP

2

The most difficult part of writing a program is developing the logic of the program. (The syntax of a specific programming language is the easy part; you can always look up syntax details in a manual if you forget.) The reason is that a program must give rather specific instructions to a computer, such as "add these two numbers" or "ask the user to enter a number." These instructions must be assembled in such a way that the computer encounters them in the correct order to produce a working program. There are several general ways to arrange the logical structure of a program; object-oriented programming (OOP) is a method that is currently very widely used.

C++ is a programming language that lets you write object-oriented programs. This chapter looks at exactly what that means. You will be introduced to the basic building blocks of an object-oriented program and how those elements work together to produce a complete application. It will be your first look at putting together the logic of a computer program.

Why OOP?

In the past few years there has been a significant migration from older high-level programming languages, such as COBOL, Pascal, and C, to object-oriented languages. Why has this occurred? Why should you bother to learn an object-oriented language like C++ rather than Pascal or C?

There are several answers to both of these questions, which together have provided compelling reasons for software developers to invest in object-oriented technologies. Object-oriented programming brings the following advantages:

- Object-oriented programs are easier to write because the logic of the program is encapsulated into small modules that interact with one another in a consistent manner.
- Object-oriented programs are easier to modify because the structure of the program is easier to understand, even if a programmer hasn't looked at a program for months.
- Object-oriented programs make it easier to use the same module of code in many programs, saving programming time.
- Object-oriented programs simplify and bring consistency to the way in which programmers interact with program elements, speeding program development time.

As a beginning programmer, you will find learning object-oriented programming no more difficult than learning to use one of the older high-level languages. At the same time, it is also easier to learn object-oriented programming from the beginning, rather than first learning other ways of structuring program logic and then having to relearn the OOP. This is why you are reading about the concepts of object-oriented programming first, rather than jumping right into writing code.

The type of program logic used by such languages as COBOL, Pascal, and C is known as *structured programming*. One of the ironies of C++ is that although the overall structure of the program is object-oriented, the details of program behavior have to be written using structured programming logic. This means that you will be learning structured programming techniques throughout this book, along with the object-oriented concepts.

NOTE

The syntax of the structured programming elements of C++ is very similar to C syntax, and C++ programs can use many of the elements of a C environment. However, C++ is a distinct language from C rather than simply a superset of the older language.

Classes

The fundamental building block in an object-oriented program is a *class*. In this section you will learn about the purpose of classes and how they provide an overall framework for program logic. Among the examples you'll see will be a first look at the checkbook management program that we'll be developing throughout this book.

CLASSES AND OBJECTS

A class is a description of an entity that is used by a program. A class might represent a customer, an order placed by a customer, a game that is being played, a dialog box, or a menu. A class doesn't need to represent something that has a physical existence; it represents anything in the programming environment that has properties that describe it (data).

Once defined, a class provides a template from which a program can create *objects*, which are instances of classes that a program manipulates. To make the relationship between an object and a class a bit clearer, let's consider one of the classes used by the checkbook program—Account. The Account class has variables to hold data that describe a checking account, such as the account number, the bank name, and the current balance. However, the class itself doesn't contain any data, but rather just the declarations of variables that will hold data. When the program is run, each new account is created by stamping out an Account object from the Account class and filling in data for the variables. The program manipulates one Account object for each account. Although there is only one Account class, there may be many Account objects.

MEMBER FUNCTIONS

Along with variables that contain the data that describe an object, a class also has declarations of the operations that an object knows how to perform. For example, a menu object knows how to draw itself when a user presses the mouse button with the mouse pointer on the menu's title in the title bar. The menu object also knows how to highlight menu options as the mouse pointer moves down the menu and how to report which option is chosen back to the program using the menu. These operations are sometimes called *methods*, but with C++ are more commonly known as *member functions*.

A C++ *function* is a self-contained block of program code. Member functions are therefore functions that are declared as part of a class. In fact, a C++ program is nothing more than a collection of functions, some of which are member functions and others that aren't. Every C++ program must include a function named `main`. The program begins execution with this function. However, the remaining functions that make up a C++ program are under the control of the programmer.

The `Account` class's member functions include the following:

- A function to place data into variables when a new account is created (a *constructor*)
- A function to read account data from a file into main memory
- A function to reconcile a checking account
- Functions to search the transactions (checks, deposits, and so on) made against an account, using a check number or the transaction date and payee/source
- A function to display an account's transactions

Some member functions are obvious to a programmer when the class is written initially. It is not unusual, however, for member functions to be added to a class declaration as a program is under development, as the programmer discovers during program development that additional member functions are required.

COMMUNICATING WITH OBJECTS

A function communicates with an object by passing the object a *message*. The message tells the object which member function it should execute and includes any data the object needs. For example, if the checkbook program sends an `Account` object a message to find a specific transaction, the program must also include data to identify the transaction. If the transaction is a check, the program can supply a check number; if the transaction is other than a check, such as a deposit, the program can supply the date and source of the deposit.

When any function sends a message to a member function, we say that the function *calls* the member function. A function can also call a function that isn't a member function. The function sending the message is the *calling* function. A calling function can be another member function or a function that isn't part of a class.

INFORMATION HIDING

The details of how a member function does its job and the specific variables that make up a class are usually hidden from functions that call the member function. The calling function knows only the name of the object, the name of the member function, and how data should be sent to the member function. The combination of a function's name and data requirements are known as the function's *signature*.

The idea that all that is publicly known about a class is the way in which its member functions are called is known as *information hiding*, a principle that brings with it one major benefit: As long as a member function's signature remains the same, a programmer can change a class's variables and the details of how the function operates without having to change any programs that use the function. This can greatly simplify program modification. It means that less code will need to be changed and that there are fewer chances for errors caused by changes that weren't propagated through an entire program.

FUNCTION OVERLOADING

To help simplify the interface that a class's member functions provide to a programmer, object-oriented languages support *function overloading*, which allows two or more member functions in the same class to have the same name, as long as they have different signatures. This makes programming easier because functions that perform the same action on different types of data can have the same name.

You might, for example, have member functions that are designed to search through all objects of the same class. One find function might search based on an account number; the data used as input to the function would be the account number for which you were searching. A second find function might search on a customer's name; the data used as input to the function would therefore be the customer's name. The two find functions have different signatures because one expects a number and the other, text. When the program is compiled, the compiler identifies the correct member function by matching function signatures, not just function names.

Inheritance

The classes in an object-oriented program don't necessarily exist as unrelated entities. They can share variables and member functions in a hierarchical structure. To get a feeling for how objects can be related, assume that you will be writing a program that stores and retrieves data about a variety of motor vehicles that are purchased by individuals. Such vehicles include motorcycles, cars, and small trucks. (The program doesn't deal with trucks used in business.)

As you think about the variables that might be used to describe the three types of motor vehicles, you realize that there are some pieces of data that apply to only one type of vehicle. For example, a maximum payload describes only a truck, and side cars are available only on motorcycles. On the other hand, the number of passengers a vehicle can carry, the manufacturer of a vehicle, and the name of a vehicle are variables that can be used to describe any of these vehicles.

Rather than create three classes—one for motorcycles, one for cars, and one for trucks—that contain many duplicated variables, an object-oriented program can use *inheritance* to share variables the classes have in common. To get a feeling for how this works, take a look at Figure 2.1. Each rectangle represents a class. Next to each class is a list of variables that describe objects created from that class.

Figure 2.1   A class hierarchy

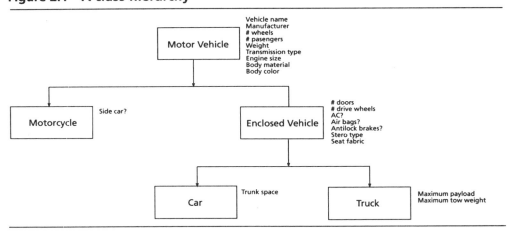

If you consider each class in isolation, no single class is complete. For example, the Motorcycle class seems to have only one variable (Side car?, which indicates whether the motorcycle has a side car). However, the Motorcycle class also has all the variables that are defined for the Motor Vehicle class, the class above in a hierarchy of classes. We say that the Motorcycle class *inherits* the variables from the Motor Vehicle class. By the same token, the Enclosed Vehicle class inherits all the variables of the Motor Vehicle class; the Car and Truck classes each inherit all the variables of the Enclosed Vehicle class, which in turn also gives them all the variables of the Motor Vehicle class.

Each class that inherits from another class is known as a *derived class*; the class from which it is derived is a *base class*. The Motor Vehicle class is only a base class; Motorcycle, Car, and Truck are only derived classes. However, Enclosed Vehicle is both a base class and a derived class, depending on whether you are viewing it from the Motor Vehicle class's perspective or from the Car and Truck classes' perspectives.

As well as inheriting variables, classes can inherit member functions. Often a base class contains just a declaration of the message that needs to be sent to a member function when the function is used. The program code that defines how the member function operates appears in the derived classes. This feature of object-oriented programs is known as *polymorphism*. It permits different classes to respond to the same message in a way that is appropriate to the specific class.

> **NOTE**
> *Polymorphism can be easy to confuse with overloading. Keep in mind that overloading refers to member functions in the same class with the same name but different signatures. Polymorphism refers to member functions in different classes with the same signature.*

If the class hierarchy in Figure 2.1 were to be used as the basis for a program, it is likely that objects would be created only from the Motorcycle, Car, and Truck classes. Whether it is possible to create objects from the Motor Vehicle class and the Enclosed Vehicle class depends on the way in which the classes are declared.

Inheritance brings several benefits to a programmer:

- It avoids duplicating variables between classes.
- It clarifies the logic of a program by formalizing the relationships between classes.
- Through polymorphism, it helps provide a consistent function interface to the programmer.

The most difficult part of using inheritance is deciding under which circumstances inheritance is appropriate. You will therefore learn a great deal more about it in Chapter 16.

Using CodeWarrior

3

Metrowerks's CodeWarrior provides an easy-to-use environment for developing Macintosh applications. In this chapter you will be introduced to how you can use that environment to create source code files and projects, run a program, and work with a debugger to help you identify logical errors. To begin, you will get an overview of some of the issues surrounding the structure of a C++ program.

Putting Together a C++ Program

Any C++ program is a collection of functions. Some of these functions you will write yourself (both class member functions and program functions that aren't part of a class). Others will have been written by the developer of your compiler and provided in libraries, to which you were introduced in Chapter 1. Although you always have great discretion in naming and choosing functions, there are rules that govern the way in which you put together a program.

THE MAIN FUNCTION AND FUNCTION STRUCTURE

As you have just read, a C++ program is nothing more than a collection of functions. That being the case, the computer needs to know exactly which function represents the starting point of the program. To make it easy, every C++ program must contain a function named `main`. Program execution always begins with this function.

Like any other C++ function, the `main` function begins with its function signature; the body of the function is surrounded by braces:

```
void main ()
{
        body of function goes here
}
```

The `void` that precedes the function's name is the data type of the value returned by the function. All C++ functions must have a return value. However, if the function doesn't send anything back to the function that called it, the function can use `void` as a placeholder to indicate no value.

The parentheses following the name of the function are used to hold the data that are sent into the function. These data are known as a function's *formal parameters*. Because the `main` program has no formal parameters, the parentheses have no contents.

NOTE

It is possible to have input data to a main function. However, in the Macintosh environment that is very rare. Sending data to a program as it is launched is much more common in command-line environments, such as the UNIX or MS-DOS operating systems.

FUNCTION PROTOTYPES AND HEADER FILES

For the C++ compiler to accept a function, it must first encounter a *function prototype*. A function prototype contains just the function's signature; the body of the function is defined elsewhere. Any time your program calls a function, the compiler verifies that a prototype for that function exists. This is one way the compiler can ensure that functions are being called correctly.

A prototype has the following general format:

```
return_data_type function_name (formal_parameters);
```

If you look back at the skeleton for the main function in the previous section, you'll notice that the prototype format is very similar to the first line of a function. The only difference is that the prototype ends with a semicolon.

Assume, for example, that you want to write a function that sums several values and then returns the sum to another function. A prototype for the function might be written as:

```
float addThemUp (float []);
```

The float that precedes the function name indicates that the function will be sending a floating point value (a value with digits to the right of the decimal point) back to the calling function. The name of a function is completely arbitrary, but in most cases it is chosen so that it conveys some information about what the function does. In this particular example the formal parameter list contains a group of floating point values. (The [] indicates an array, or list, of values; you will learn about arrays in Chapter 10.)

Functions from the Macintosh, C, and C++ libraries must have prototypes, just like any function you write yourself. Library function prototypes are found in *header files*, files that typically contain only data definition statements (for example, class declarations and function prototypes). To gain access to a header file, you use the *compiler directive* include to merge the contents of header file with your source code file.

A compiler directive is a command to a compiler that is processed during compilation. It isn't executable code; it has no effect on your program once compilation is finished. To differentiate them from C++ code, compiler directives begin with a pound sign.

There are two syntax variations of the include directive:

```
#include <header_file_name>
#include "header_file_name"
```

Which variation you use depends on where the header file is stored. CodeWarrior, like most C++ compilers, keeps track of the folders in which it expects to find header files (the compiler's default access path). If the header file is in the default access path, you can use the first syntax, surrounding the header file name with < and >. However, if the header file is located elsewhere, you must put the file's path name in double quotes.

NOTE

The idea of a path name is foreign to most Macintosh users because the Macintosh automatically searches all mounted disks to find an application that matches a file that has been double-clicked. However, in programming you often need to specify the exact sequence of folders in which a file is nested. The folders in a Macintosh path name are separated by colons. For example, a file named sales.cpp stored in a folder named Program1, which is nested in a folder named C++, which rests on the disk named Development, has the path name Development:Program1:sales.cpp.

CodeWarrior's default access paths are set in the Access Paths preferences panel. To get to it, click the Preferences button in the button bar or choose Preferences from the bottom of the Edit menu. As you can see in Figure 3.1, the Preferences window has a scrolling list of icon switches at the left, each of which displays a different preferences panel. Scroll to the bottom of the list and click on the Access Paths icon.

Figure 3.1   Setting access paths

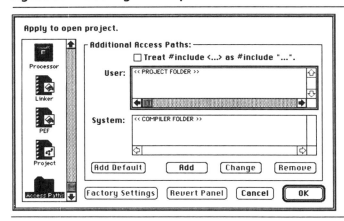

There are two access paths, one for system files and one for files you create yourself. By default, CodeWarrior will search the folder in which your project file is contained for header files; it will also search the file in which the compiler is stored. If you install CodeWarrior using the Installer application and always store header files you write yourself in the same folder as the program's project file, the compiler will have no trouble locating your header files.

By convention, header file names are given an extension of *.h*. This makes it easy to distinguish them from source code files. If, for example, you want to use the I/O function to which you will be introduced in Chapter 5, you will need to include the header file *iostream.h*:

```
#include <iostream.h>
```

Notice that there is no semicolon at the end of this statement. Only C++ statements require semicolons. Because compiler directives aren't part of the language, but instead are instructions to the compiler, semicolons aren't needed.

How do you know which header files you need? The documentation of the C and C++ libraries includes that information. Each function in the libraries is documented with at least its prototype and the name of the header file in which that prototype appears. In many cases, the documentation also includes an example of using the library function.

The CodeWarrior Environment

CodeWarrior is often described as an "integrated" software development environment because it provides a text editor for creating source code files, compilers, and a *debugger* (a program that helps you find logic errors in your programs), all accessible from within the same application shell.

To launch the integrated development environment, double-click on the MW C/C++ 68K icon (to generate code for 680x0 Macs) or MW C/C++ PPC icon (to generate code for PowerMacs). Alternatively, you can double-click on any file that was created with CodeWarrior's text editor.

Once running, CodeWarrior displays its button bar directly under the menu bar. As you can see in Figure 3.2, placing the mouse pointer over a button in the button bar displays the button's function below the bar. All of the functions in the button bar are, of course, available from CodeWarrior's menus. However, three of the buttons at the right edge of the bar are particularly useful when you are writing programs. These buttons simplify checking the syntax of a program, creating an executable application file, and running a program.

Figure 3.2 The CodeWarrior button bar

During the program development process, you will be using primarily the Run command to compile, link, and execute programs. If you hold down the Option key when you click the Run button, the program will run through the debugger, giving you a chance to execute the program one line at a time, as well as to see the values stored in objects and variables as the program is running.

The Compile command checks the syntax of the files in a project without linking or running the program. This can be useful when you don't have enough source code available to test a program but want to catch syntax errors as you work. The Make command compiles and links, creating an executable application, but doesn't run the program.

Creating Source Code Files

CodeWarrior's text editor is very similar to such editors as TeachText or SimpleText. You open file, save file, and enter and edit text just as you would with any other text editor. However, the editor has some additional features that make it particularly well suited to working with program source code. These features are configured through two of CodeWarrior's preferences panels.

COLOR TEXT

One of the nicest features of CodeWarrior's text editor is its use of color. Keywords, those words that form part of the C++ language and that can't be used for variable names, appear in one color; comment statements appear in another. The rest of the text is in a third color. Although this might seem to be trivial, it can help you avoid some troublesome errors, particularly those that occur when you accidentally use a keyword as a variable name (confuses the living daylights out of the compiler) or when you accidentally include executable code in a comment (produces all sorts of unexpected errors).

Text colors are set in the Editor preferences panel. By default, main text is black, comments are red, and keywords are blue. To change these colors, double-click on the color you want to change. A color wheel appears from which you can choose the new color.

Figure 3.3   Setting Editor preferences

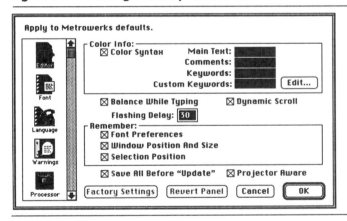

AUTOMATIC BALANCING

Throughout a C++ program, you will be grouping parts of your source code with parentheses ( ) and curly braces { }. Whenever you use an opening parenthesis, you need to match it with a closing parenthesis somewhere in the program; the same it true for braces. The *Balance While Typing* checkbox controls whether the editor shows you the opening partner for each closing parenthesis or brace you type. The *Flashing Delay* value determines how long the opening parenthesis or brace will flash after you type the closing character. Because all parentheses and braces must be balanced (one close for every open), this feature can help you see the opening parenthesis or brace to which a closing parenthesis or brace applies.

FONT PREFERENCES

The font in which source code appears is controlled by the Font preferences dialog box (Figure 3.4). It's generally easier to read source code when it appears in a monospaced font (a font in which all characters occupy the same width). On the Macintosh this includes Monaco and Courier. Monaco is the easier of the two to read on the screen and is therefore usually the font of choice for source code.

Figure 3.4   Setting Font preferences

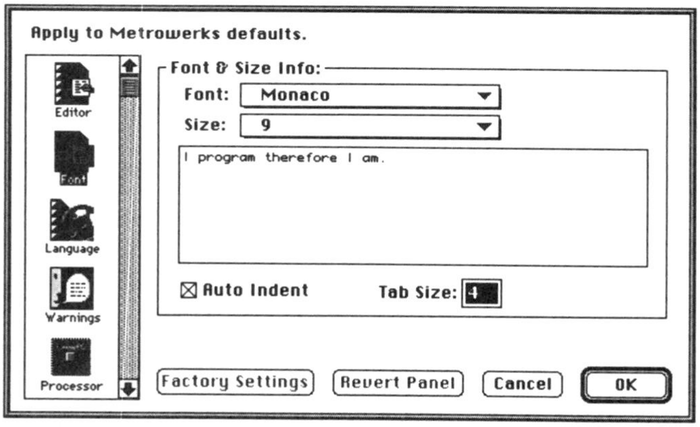

NOTE

Monaco is a TrueType font. However, if you have Font Substitution turned on in the Page Setup dialog box when you print a source code file on a PostScript printer, the text prints in a PostScript font rather than Monaco. To get around this, you can turn off Font Substitution. Nonetheless, the TrueType version of Monaco that prints looks a bit different from the bit-mapped version that appears on the screen.

AUTOMATIC INDENTING

Another one of the CodeWarrior editor's useful features is automatic indentation. If Auto Indent is turned on in the Font preferences panel, CodeWarrior "remembers" the number of times you pressed Tab to indent a line. When you press Return to move to the next line, the insertion point automatically appears at the starting indent of the preceding line. You can backspace if necessary to move farther to the left.

Why is this so useful? As you will see throughout this book, one of the ways that programmers make their source code easier to read is to use indentation to set off blocks of code that are part of the same logical unit. Automatic indentation simply means that you don't have to have press the Tab key so often.

Notice also in Figure 3.4 that the Font preferences panel can be used to set the number of spaces that are to be inserted whenever you press Tab.

EDITOR WINDOW CONTROLS

The three pop-up menus in the lower-left corner of a CodeWarrior editor window can at times make working with files easier. The rightmost of these three, which appears in Figure 3.5, controls whether syntax coloring is active (the top option in the menu) and the type of file. By default, CodeWarrior treats source code files as Macintosh files. However, if you are importing a file from or exporting a file to either an MS-DOS or a UNIX environment, use this pop-up menu to let CodeWarrior know how to treat end-of-line and end-of-file markers.

Figure 3.5   Controlling file type and syntax coloring

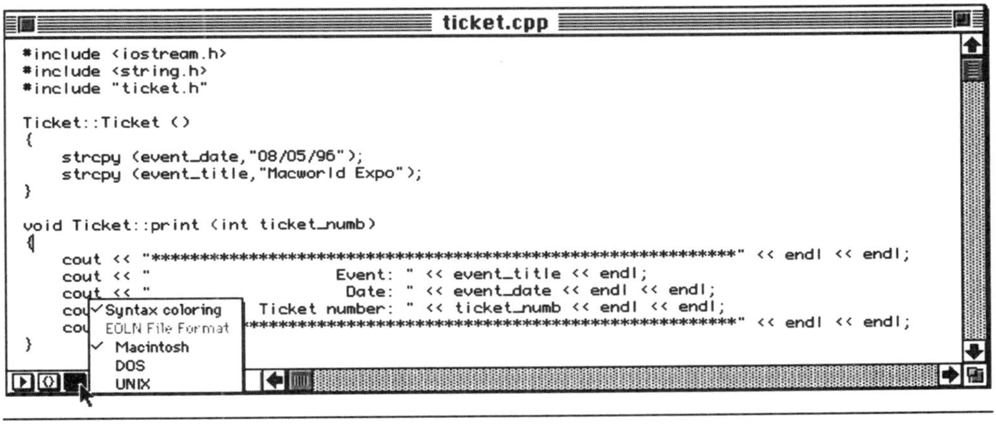

The middle pop-up (Figure 3.6) displays a list of all functions that are defined in the source code file. To move quickly to a function, select its name from the pop-up. (This comes in particularly handy for large source code files.)

Figure 3.6   Moving directly to a function definition

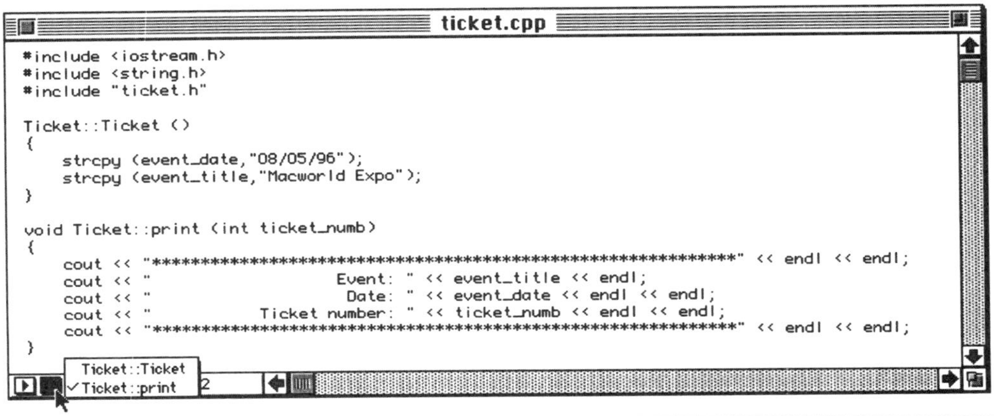

```
┌─────────────────────────── ticket.cpp ───────────────────────────┐
│ #include <iostream.h>                                              │
│ #include <string.h>                                                │
│ #include "ticket.h"                                                │
│                                                                    │
│ Ticket::Ticket ()                                                  │
│ {                                                                  │
│     strcpy (event_date,"08/05/96");                                │
│     strcpy (event_title,"Macworld Expo");                          │
│ }                                                                  │
│                                                                    │
│ void Ticket::print (int ticket_numb)                               │
│ {                                                                  │
│     cout << "********************************************" << endl << endl; │
│     cout << "                    Event: " << event_title << endl;  │
│     cout << "                     Date: " << event_date << endl << endl; │
│     cout << "            Ticket number: " << ticket_numb << endl << endl; │
│     cout << "********************************************" << endl << endl; │
│ }                                                                  │
│        ┌──────────────────┐                                       │
│        │   Ticket::Ticket │                                       │
│ [▶][■] │ ✓ Ticket::print  │ 2   [◀][▦]                            │
│        └──────────────────┘                                       │
└────────────────────────────────────────────────────────────────────┘
```

The leftmost pop-up (Figure 3.7) contains a list of header files used by the current project. Many of the header files declare functions used by the C and C++ libraries; others are specific to a given application program. You will be using and writing header files throughout this book.

Working with Projects

A project file provides a way of telling the linker which files should be combined into an executable application. The first step in creating a new program is therefore to create a project file.

Figure 3.7   Accessing header files

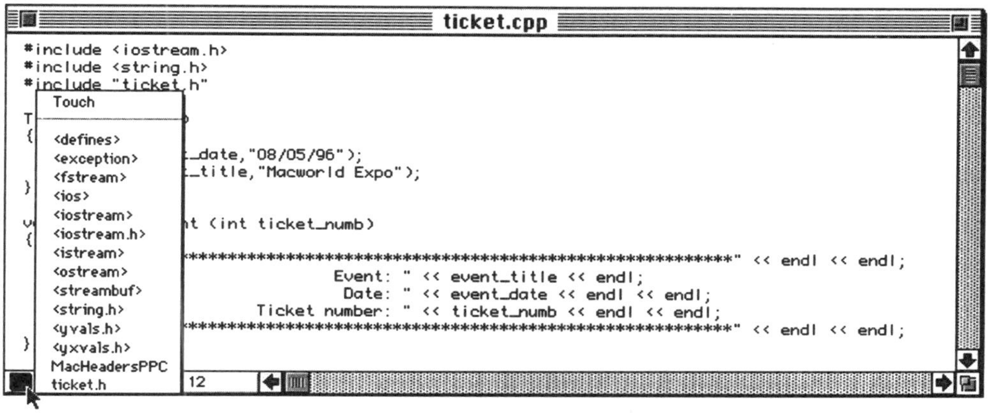

Project Templates

The easiest way to start a new project is to use one of the project templates supplied with CodeWarrior. These templates already contain the libraries that need to be linked into a program.

As you can see in Figure 3.8, there are three general types of projects. The first are "Mac" projects, those that use ToolBox functions. The "PowerPlant" projects are for use with CodeWarrior's PowerPlant, an application framework that can simplify creating Macintosh applications. (To use PowerPlant successfully, you need to first be familiar with programming using the ToolBox.) The final group of projects includes those that are written using the ANSI standard version of C or C++.

If you look carefully at the ANSI project template files, you'll notice that there is just one template for PowerPC C programs (ANSI PPC C) and one for PowerPC C++ programs (ANSI PPC C++). If you are working on a Power Mac, you should use the latter file whenever you are creating a new ANSI C++ project.

However, the situation for 68K Macintoshes is somewhat more complex. There are four C project templates and four C++ project templates. The difference in these projects resides in amount of storage you want allocated for integers and floating point values. Those projects whose names include *2i* use two-byte (16-bit) integers; those whose names include *4i* use four-byte (32-bit integers). As you read in Chapter 1, the number of bytes allocated to integer storage directly affects the size of the value that can be stored in a given storage location. The 32-bit integers take up more space in RAM, producing a larger program. You must therefore decide whether

Figure 3.8   Project stationery

```
▤▤ (Project Stationery) ▤▣▤
 20 items     747.1 MB in disk    269.7 MB a▼
─────────────────────────────────────────────
          Name                         Size
─────────────────────────────────────────────
   📄 About Project Stationery         16 ⇧
   📄 Mac C app-68K                    32
   📄 Mac C app-PPC                    32
   📄 Mac C XCMD-68K                   32
   📄 Mac C++ app-68K                  32
   📄 Mac C++ app-PPC                  32
   📄 Mac C++ XCMD-68K                 32
   📄 PowerPlant 68K                   32
   📄 PowerPlant PPC                   32
 ▷ 📁 Stationery Support Files          -
   📄 ~ANSI 68K (2i) C                 32
   📄 ~ANSI 68K (2i) C++               32
   📄 ~ANSI 68K (2i/F/8d) C            32
   📄 ~ANSI 68K (2i/F/8d) C++          32
   📄 ~ANSI 68K (4i) C                 32
   📄 ~ANSI 68K (4i) C++               32
   📄 ~ANSI 68K (4i/F) C               32
   📄 ~ANSI 68K (4i/F) C++             32
   📄 ~ANSI PPC C                      32
   📄 ~ANSI PPC C++                    32 ⇩
 ←▐▓▒░░░░░░░░░░░░░░░░░░░░░░░░→ ▣
```

it is more important to save memory or to have more space available for integer storage.

NOTE

Using two-byte integers doesn't prevent you from obtaining a four-byte integer storage location. You can always define a "long" integer to double the size of a regular integer.

The projects whose names include *8d* indicate the number of bytes you want to use for the Macintosh's medium-sized floating point storage. (There are three floating point formats.) If a program will be using extremely large or small numbers, the extra space needed for the longer numbers is worth the trade-off in main memory space.

Projects whose names include *F* produce programs that take advantage of a *floating point unit* (FPU), circuitry designed to speed operations on floating point numbers. If you happen to be writing code on or for a 68000, 68020 or 68030 without an external FPU installed or for a 68LC040 Mac, you should avoid these projects. (The full 68040 and the PowerPC have their FPUs integrated into the CPU.)

For the purposes of this book, two-byte integers and standard-sized floating point numbers are sufficient for ANSI 68K projects. However, any of the ANSI C++ project templates will work. If you want to take advantage of an FPU, be sure to pick one with an *F* in its name.

CREATING A NEW PROJECT

When you begin working on a new program, you will usually create a new project for that program. Creating a new project means creating the project file, adding the libraries needed for the program, and adding the source code files used by the program.

Opening and Saving the Project File

To set up a new project, double-click on the project template that represents the type of project you want to create. CodeWarrior asks you to name the project and then opens and saves a copy of the project file. (If necessary, the Macintosh launches CodeWarrior first.) To distinguish project files from other files that make up a program, project files are often named using the convention *program_name* π, as in *Checkbook* π. (The π symbol is generated by pressing Option-p.)

NOTE

In most cases the easiest way to manage all the files used by a program is to put them together in their own private folder. Should you choose to do so, you can either create the folder before you create the project file or use the New Folder button in the Save File dialog box that appears when you create the new project.

As you can see in Figure 3.9, the new project (in this case, an ANSI C++ PowerPC project) contains all the libraries needed to run the project, as well as a file named *main.ANSI.cp*. By convention, the file that contains a program's `main` function is stored in a file whose name begins with *main*. The *ANSI* is to remind you of the type of program; the *cp* represents the language, C++. (You will also see C++ source code files using the file name extension *cpp*.)

To open any source code file in the project, double-click on the file's name in the project window. The *main.ANSI.cp* file contains executable code (see Figure 3.10). If you run it, you will see a CodeWarrior SIOUX window containing the text *Hello World*. Throughout the history of the C and C++ languages, this has traditionally been the first program new programmers learn to write.

Figure 3.9   A project file created from a template

```
╔══════════════════ test ══════════════════╗
║  File                    Code   Data ▣ ☘  ║
║ ▽ source                   0│    0   • ▽ ⇧ ║
║      main.ANSI.cp          0│    0   • ▶  ║
║ ▽ libraries                0│    0       ▽ ║
║      InterfaceLib          0│    0       ▶ ║
║      MWCRuntime.lib        0│    0       ▶ ║
║      ANSI C.PPC.Lib        0│    0       ▶ ║
║      ANSI C++.PPC.Lib      0│    0       ▶ ║
║      SIOUX.PPC.Lib         0│    0       ▶ ║
║      MathLib               0│    0       ▶ ⇩ ║
║    7 file(s)               0     0        ║
╚═══════════════════════════════════════════╝
```

Figure 3.10   The default main.ANSI.cp file

```
╔════════ main.ANSI.cp ════════╗
║ #include <iostream>          ⇧ ║
║                              ║
║ void main (void)             ║
║ {                            ║
║                              ║
║     cout << "Hello World\n"; ║
║                              ║
║ }                            ⇩ ║
║ ▶◁▣    Line: 1    ←▥▶ ▤       ║
╚══════════════════════════════╝
```

Adding Files

A C++ program is generally stored in more than one file. There will be at least one
header file containing class definitions, a source code file containing the member
functions for the classes, and the file containing the `main` function. Large programs
are often split into many files, including one header for each class, one source code
file for each class, and multiple files for functions used by the `main` function. In addition, if you are writing code for the Macintosh user interface, you may also have
resource files (files that contain definitions of portions of the Macintosh user interface). You certainly can't get away with having just the *main.ANSI.cp* file!

Only source code files are added to project files. Header and resource files are used
directly by source code files; they aren't compiled and linked separately. To add a
source code file, first create the file and save it to give it a name. Then, choose Add
Files from the Project menu. The Add Files dialog box (Figure 3.11) appears.

Make the folder that contains the source code files you want to add the current
folder. Then double-click on each file you want to add; the files are moved from the

Figure 3.11   Adding files to a project

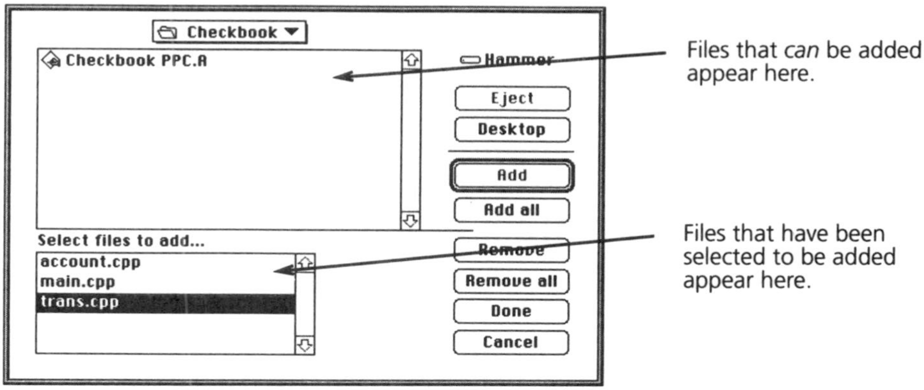

list at the top left of the dialog box to the list at the bottom left. When all files are in the lower list, click the Done button.

NOTE

If you want to add all the files in the current folder, click the Add all button to transfer them directly to the list at the bottom left of the dialog box.

You can add files to a project at any time. This means that you don't have to be able to create every source code file a program will use at the time you begin writing the program.

Running a Program

When you are developing a program, you will run the program repeatedly to see if it is working the way you intend. The easiest way to do this is to use CodeWarrior's Run command. However, before you run a program for the first time, you need to give CodeWarrior some information about the nature of the application file you want to produce.

SETTING PROJECT PREFERENCES

The Project preferences panel (Figure 3.12) sets three very important characteristics of the application file that is generated when you run a program. The first is the name of the file. By default, CodeWarrior names an application file *Test*, followed by extensions that indicate the platform and type of project. In most cases, you will want to replace *Test* with a more meaningful application name. In Figure 3.12, for example, the application file produced for the checkbook program will be named *Checkbook PPC*.

Figure 3.12   The Project preferences panel

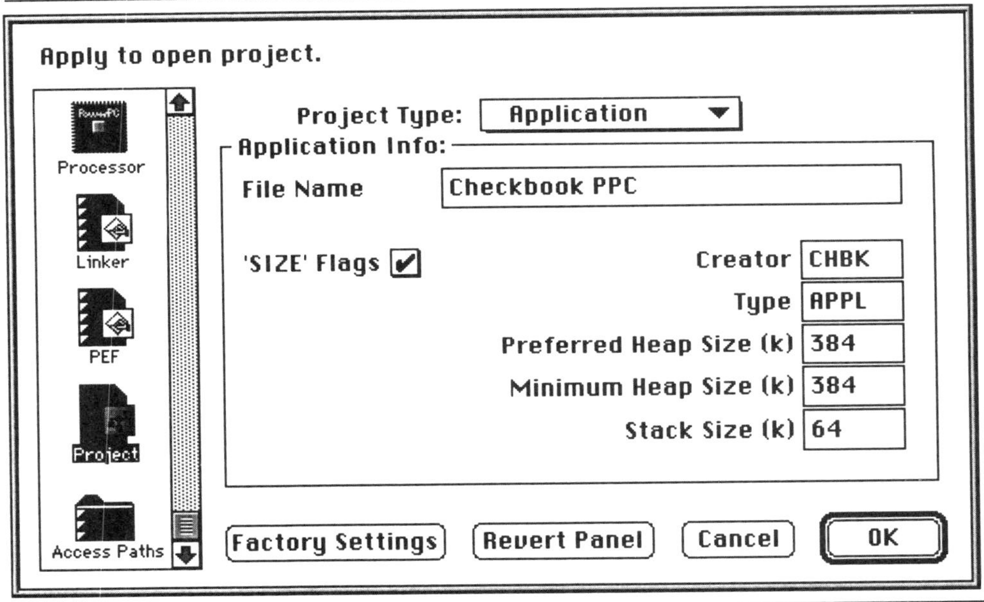

The second and third important pieces of information are the file's *type* and *creator*. Both are four-character strings that affect the behavior of the application file and any document files it may create. Any file that can be launched from the Finder by double-clicking on its icon must have a type of APPL. CodeWarrior enters this as the default file type; you shouldn't change it.

An application's creator string identifies the specific application. When a program creates a document file, it can use a ToolBox routine to set the document file's creator to match the application's creator. Then double-clicking on the document file's icon opens the file using the correct application, launching the application if necessary.

In Figure 3.12 the creator has been set to CHBK as an example. However, you can't arbitrarily decide on a creator string; it might match the creator used by another application. Creator strings must therefore be cleared with Apple Developer Services, which maintains a registry of all creator strings in use.

WORKING WITH THE SIOUX WINDOW

When you are ready to test an ANSI C++ application, choose Run from the Project menu or click the Run button in the icon bar. CodeWarrior compiles all source code files that have been modified since the last time the program was run and links the program. Then it draws a SIOUX window and places the two SIOUX menus in the menu bar (Figure 3.13).

Figure 3.13   The SIOUX execution environment

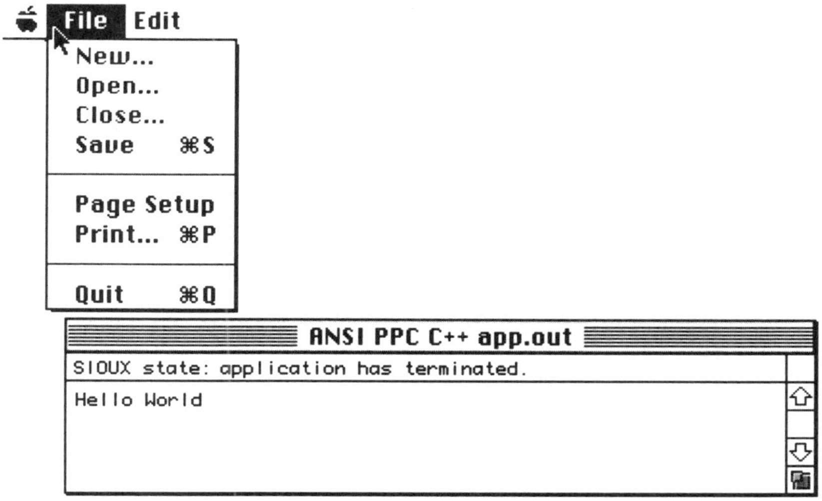

The top line of the SIOUX window (the "SIOUX state" gives you information about the application (whether it is running or terminated). The rest of the window displays the output of the ANSI C++ program. When the program terminates naturally, as it has in Figure 3.13, you are still within the SIOUX environment. To return to the CodeWarrior environment, choose Quit from the File menu or press ⌘-Q.

NOTE

One of the handiest things about the SIOUX window is that it scrolls. When a program terminates, the SIOUX window contains a transcript of the entire program run's output. You can then scroll to look at the output, save the contents of the window as a text file, or print the contents of the window.

Creating Your First Program

In this section you will get a chance to create a working program from scratch. The program—Profiler—asks you for your name, favorite color, and age. It stores that data in an object and then displays the contents of the object. Just for practice, you will enter source code, add files to a project, and run the program. To get started, locate the folder named *Profiler (empty)* on the CD-ROM that came with this book. Copy that folder onto your hard disk. Then do the following:

1. If you are working on a PowerPC, double-click on the file *Profiler PPC π*. If you are working on a 68K Macintosh, double-click on the file *Profiler 68K π*.
2. Open the file *profiler.h*. This file will hold the class declaration for the program.
3. Enter the contents of Listing 3.1. Be sure to type all punctuation exactly as it appears in the listing.

Listing 3.1   Header information to type into profiler.h

```
typedef char string50[51];

class Profiler
{
    private:
        string50 name, color;
        int age;
    public:
        Profiler();
        void init (string50, string50, int);
        void display ();
};
```

4. Save the file.

5. Open the file *profiler.cpp*. This file will hold the class's member functions.

6. Enter the contents of Listing 3.2. Be sure to type all punctuation exactly as it appears in the listing.

Listing 3.2   Source code to type into profiler.cpp

```
#include <string.h>
#include <iostream.h>
#include "profiler.h"

Profiler::Profiler() // use two colons for ::
{
    // For "", type two double quotes right next to each other
    strcpy (name,"");
    strcpy (color,"");
    age = 0;
}

void Profiler::init (string50 iname, string50 icolor, int iage)
{
    strcpy(name,iname);
    strcpy(color,icolor);
    age = iage;
}

void Profiler::display ()
{
    // Be sure to use double quotes
    cout << "\nYour name is " << name << "." << endl;
    cout << "Your favorite color is " << color << endl;
    cout << "You are " << age << " years old.";
}
```

7. Open the file *main.cpp*. This file will hold the `main` function that controls the program's actions.

8. Enter the contents of Listing 3.3. Be sure to type all punctuation exactly as it appears in the listing.

9. Run the program. CodeWarrior will compile the two source code files and then link the program.

Listing 3.3   Source code to type into main.cpp

```
#include <iostream.h>
#include <stdio.h>
#include "profiler.h"

void main ()
{
    Profiler you; // create Profiler object
    string50 iname,icolor;
    int iage;

    cout << "\nWhat is your name? ";
    gets (iname);
    cout << "What is your favorite color? ";
    gets (icolor);
    cout << "How old are you? ";
    cin >> iage;
    you.init (iname, icolor, iage);
    you.display ();
}
```

DEALING WITH SYNTAX ERRORS

If you have entered the program correctly, it will run and conduct a dialog with you like that in Figure 3.14. However, if you've made a typing error, CodeWarrior will in all likelihood report a syntax error.

Figure 3.14   The output of the Profiler program

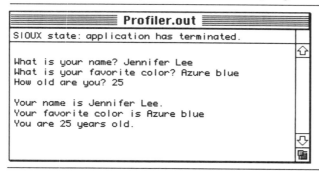

Syntax errors appear in the message window (Figure 3.15). The three types of messages that can appear in the message window are represented by icons just under the window's title bar. The leftmost icon represents errors (usually syntax errors) that prevent the program from compiling. The middle icon represents warnings, errors that indicate problems that won't necessarily keep the program from running but that might generate significant problems with the program. The rightmost icon represents informational messages. By default, the compiler reports errors and warnings. You can, however, control which type of messages appear with the check boxes to the left of each icon. If the box contains a check, messages appear; if the box has no checks, no messages appear.

Figure 3.15   The message window

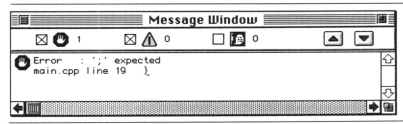

In Figure 3.15 the compiler has detected one error. The error message contains a statement of the error, the name of the file in which it was found, and the line on which the error was detected.

It is important to realize that the line on which the error was detected may not be the line that in fact contains the error. In this particular example, the error is in the line above: It's missing a semicolon at the end. It isn't unusual to discover that a syntax error is caused by something preceding the line on which the error is detected. If you can't find an error on the line reported in the message window, be sure to look above.

To move quickly to the line on which an error was detected, double-click on the error message in the body of the message window. However, if you want to step through the errors one by one, click on the up or down arrow at the right edge of the region just under the title bar.

Introducing the Debugger

As you have read, *debugger* is a programming tool that helps you ferret out logical errors in a program by letting you execute a program one line at a time, look at the values in variables as the program is running, and even change memory locations while the program is running. It is an invaluable tool is the program development process.

A debugger is by its nature a powerful and somewhat complex program. In this section you will be introduced to the basic features of the CodeWarrior debugger. You can use the skills you learn in this section throughout this book. As you gain proficiency as a programmer, you will be able to tap some of the more advanced features that are covered in the debugger's documentation.

> **NOTE**
>
> *If you are using a Power Mac with RAMDoubler, then be sure that you have at least version 1.5.2 of RAMDoubler. The Power Mac debugger is incompatible with earlier versions.*

ENTERING THE DEBUGGER

To run a program using the debugger, hold down the Option key and either click the Run button in the button bar or choose Run with Debugger from the Project menu. CodeWarrior compiles and links the program and then launches the debugger. The program is loaded in memory, but execution is halted before the program's first statement.

In one corner of the screen, you will see debugger's control palette (Figure 3.16). The second button from the left—Halt—is depressed, indicating that the program is stopped. The Kill button aborts program execution at any point. The Go button executes the program without pausing until it reaches either the end of the program or a place in the program that you have marked as a stopping point.

The three Step buttons let you run a program one line at a time. Click the Step Over button to execute the next line of the program; if the program statement being executed contains a function call, the debugger executes the function but doesn't show you the statements in the function. In other words, you "step over" the function. However, if you want to see that actions of a function, use the Step In button. It "steps into" a function to show you how a function operates. On the other hand, if you find yourself tracing through a function unnecessarily, you can use the Step Out button to return to the part of the program that called the function.

Figure 3.16 The debugger's control palette

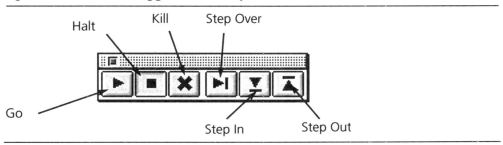

The debugger screen also contains two windows. You won't be using the one with the *SYM* extension. The other, which takes on the name of the program, contains a listing of the source code in the bottom portion of the window (see Figure 3.17). An arrow in the left margin of the source code listing indicates the next line to be executed.

The top left of the window maintains a scrolling list of all functions used by the program. The top right of the window contains a list of the variables in the current function, along with each variable's current contents. As you execute the program, the display in the variables list is updated to reflect changing variable contents.

STEPPING THROUGH A PROGRAM

One of the most useful things you can do with a debugger is step through a program one line at a time. This makes it very easy to see if you are giving the computer instructions that you didn't intend. It can, for example, help you determine whether you are repeating actions the wrong number of times or whether you are making the wrong choice at a particular point in the program.

To see how this works, try doing the following to use the debugger with the Profiler program you created earlier in this chapter:

1. Open the Profiler project file.
2. Hold down the Option key and click on the Run button in the button bar.
3. Click the Step Over button five times. This will bring you to the first `gets` function call. The debugger lets you know that the program is waiting for input by displaying the message in Figure 3.18.
4. If the SIOUX window is visible, type your name and press Enter. If you can't see the SIOUX window, choose Run from the Control menu or press ⌘-R. This

Figure 3.17 The debugger's source code window

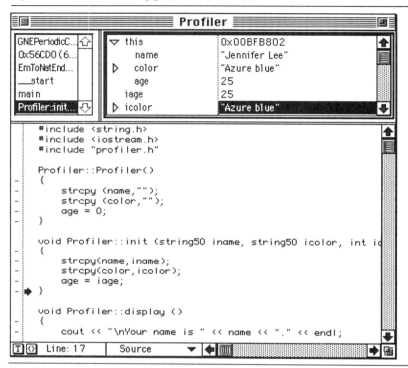

brings the SIOUX window to the front so you can type data to respond to the
gets.

NOTE

*Developing software is a lot easier if you have a large amount of monitor real estate.
Using a debugger, for example, if much simpler if you can place the debugger and
SIOUX windows so they don't hide each other.*

5. Continue to click the Step Over button and respond to the input prompts for your
   favorite color and your age.

6. When the arrow in the left margin of the listing points to the you.init function
   call, click the Step In button. Notice that the source code changes to show you the
   source code of the init function.

Figure 3.18 Debugger status when waiting for keyboard input

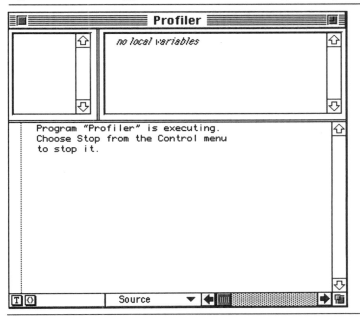

7. Use the Step Over button to step through the `init` function. Notice that when you come to the last line of the function, you are automatically returned to the place in `main.cpp` where you clicked Step In.
8. Click the Go button to let the program run to completion.

If you click Step In on a line that contains a call to a library function, the debugger will be unable to display source code for that function: Library functions exist only as compiled binary code. You will therefore see a listing of the assembly language version of the function (Figure 3.19). In this particular example, the listing shows PowerPC assembly language. If you end up looking at an assembly language listing, use the Step Out button to return you to your previous location.

VIEWING VARIABLES

As you step through a program, the list of variables at the top right of the window change as the values in the variables change. You can use this feature to make sure that a program is storing the values you intend.

Figure 3.19   The assembly language version of a function

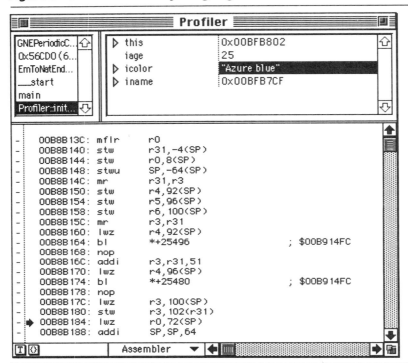

The CodeWarrior debugger makes a guess about the type of data you are storing in a variable and uses that guess to format that display of a variable's contents. The debugger's guess, however, isn't always what you want to see. To change the way a variable's value is displayed, click on the value of the variable whose format you want to change. Then choose the new display format from the bottom section of the Data menu. As you can see in Figure 3.20, only those formats that are appropriate for a given type of variable are available.

When the function you are viewing is a member function, the debugger's variable list shows you the contents of the object on which the member function is operating. The object first appears under the name this. The value for this that appears initially is the main memory address where storage for the object's data begins. If you look carefully at the top right of Figure 3.19, you'll notice that the value for this begins with 0x, indicating that it is a hexadecimal main memory address. In Figure 3.20 the object named you is also represented by its main memory address.

Figure 3.20   Changing a variable's display format

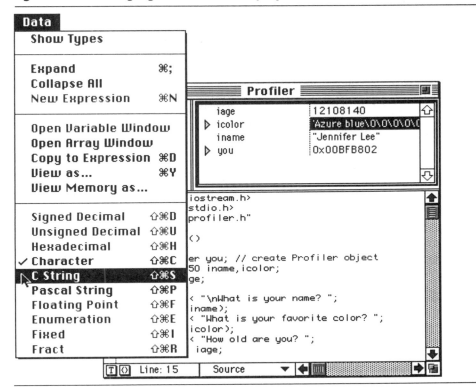

The right-facing arrows to the left of this and you indicate that there are variables within each object that you can view. To see the contents of an object, click on the arrow. (This works much like expanding a folder in a Finder window.) As you can see in Figure 3.21, the object expands to show you all the variables that are part of the object and those variables' current contents. Other variables that store multiple values can also be expanded in the same way.

A common error that occurs in a C++ program is not allocating enough space for the storage of strings of text. The computer doesn't warn you when you store too many characters in a string. Instead the extra characters spill over into the main memory allocated to other variables. Usually the only way to detect this type of error is to use the debugger and watch the contents of variables. If you happen to see the value in an unrelated variable change immediately after you have entered a string of text, you should suspect that you don't have enough room for the text. The solution,

Figure 3.21   Viewing the variables that make up an object in main memory

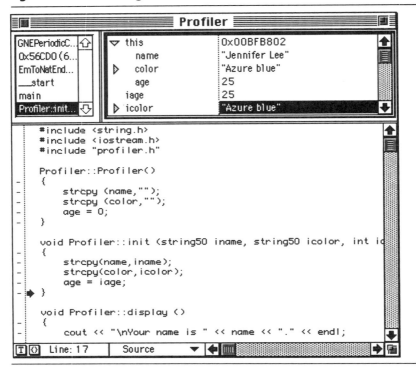

of course, is to allocate more space for the text, something you will learn how to do in Chapter 5.

EXITING THE DEBUGGER

Because the debugger is a separate application from the CodeWarrior compiler, you must exit by choosing Quit from the File menu or by pressing ⌘-Q. If a program is running when you quit, the debugger will ask whether you want to kill the program. At that point you can confirm the "kill" or cancel your exit from the debugger.

Writing Classes

4

Because classes provide the foundation for an object-oriented program, the first step in learning to write C++ programs is to learn to write class declarations. In this chapter you will therefore read about how classes are declared, including declarations for variables and member functions.

Variables

As you have read, variables are labels that are placed on storage locations so that it is easy to reference those places in main memory. You also know that the amount of storage set aside when you declare a variable depends on the type of data you will be storing.

Before you can use a variable, either in a class or in a nonmember function, you must declare it. The declaration includes a name for the variable and a data type, and may also include an initial value for the variable. The general format for a variable declaration ends with a semicolon:

```
data_type variable_name;
```

If you are declaring more than one variable of the same data type, you can place them in the same declaration, separated by commas, as in:

```
data_type variable_name1, variable_name2, variable_name3;
```

Variable names can include letters, numbers, underscores (_), and a few special characters, such as # or $. However, you cannot use characters that have meaning to C++, including those in Table 4.1. In addition, variable names must not duplicate C++ keywords. Identifying a variable name that matches a keyword is easy if you have syntax color turned on in your source code window: The keyword appears in its own color. (See Chapter 3 for details.)

Table 4.1   Characters that *cannot* be used in C++ variable names

:	;	~	!	@
%	&	*	(	)
+	=	|	\	?
/	{	}	[	]
<	>	'	"	

C++ is case sensitive; it recognizes the difference between upper- and lowercase letters. For example, C++ sees `sum` and `Sum` as different variables. If you want to be sure that you aren't duplicating a C++ keyword, put an uppercase character or an underscore in a variable name. (All keywords are lowercase words.)

There is one other very important issue concerning the naming of variables. The names you give variables should be meaningful. In other words, a variable's name should remind you of what you are storing in the variable. When you look at variable names such as `customer#`, `retail_price`, and `invoiceTotal`, you know exactly what the variables store. However, variable names such as `x5` or `cba` don't give you any information. If you come back to a program without meaningful variable names after even a few days, you are going to have a hard time figuring out the purpose of those variables.

Declaring Integer Variables

C++ supports two types of integer variables—int and long. On a microcomputer an int sets aside a 16-bit storage location; long sets aside a 32-bit location. For example, the following declaration declares three 16-bit integers:

```
int Counter, oldTotal, newTotal;
```

By the same token, the following declarations set aside storage space for four 32-bit integers:

```
long Population, Sum;
long howMany, account#;
```

Adding Comment Statements

As has been mentioned, using meaningful variable names helps document the logic of a program. The most useful self-documentation tool, however, is comment statements. A *comment* is text that is included in a header or source code file to describe how the code works or the purpose of parts of the code. Comment statements are ignored when a file is compiled. Adding comments is vital to making code easy to understand, even if a long time passes from when you originally wrote the program.

C++ supports two forms of comments, both of which appear in color (by default, red) in a text file if syntax coloring is active. Anything on a single line that is preceded by two slashes (//) is accepted as a comment. The // can appear at the beginning of a line (the entire line is a comment) or following executable code. For example, in the following statements the expression "// Counts items as entered" is a comment:

```
int Counter; // Counts items as entered
```

You can create multiline comments in two ways. First, you can precede each line in the comment with //, as in:

```
// This is an example of a multiline comment
// using the C++ style. It is a very "safe"
// type of comment because there's no risk of
// confusing the comment with executable code.
```

Alternatively, you can use the comment style that C++ has inherited from C. C-style comments begin with the characters /*. The compiler assumes that everything following those characters is a comment until it encounters the characters */, as in the following:

```
/* This is an example of a multiline comment using
the C style. It can be easier to use than C++ comments
for a long block of comments, but you run the risk
of not closing the comment block and accidentally
causing the compiler to skip some executable code. */
```

If syntax coloring is on, typing /* causes everything in the text file following the /* to turn red (or whatever color is assigned to comments). When you type the */, the remainder of the file turns back to its original color. This can be an enormous help in making sure that you always close C-style comments.

DECLARING FLOATING POINT VARIABLES

To set aside a standard-sized (single-precision) floating point storage area, use the variable type float, as in:

```
float average, balance;
```

If you need both a greater range of values and more places to the right of the decimal point, use the medium-sized (double-precision) floating point format, as in:

```
double quotient, dividend, divisor;
```

If even double-precision doesn't give you enough range or precision, use the Macintosh's largest floating point format:

```
long double quotient, dividend, divisor;
```

Keep in mind, however, that there is a trade-off between the amount of memory used and the size of the floating point storage locations you use. As your programs grow larger, you may need to be concerned about the space consumed by double and long double variables.

Declaring Character Variables

A `char` variable holds one ASCII code. Used by itself, a `char` variable is handy for things like holding the answer to a yes/no question or for storing data that can be coded, such as gender (*m* or *f*, perhaps). You can declare a character variable just like an integer or floating point variable:

```
char yes_no; // store response to yes/no questions
```

A First Look at Strings

A *string* is a sequence of characters, such as a word or a sentence, handled as a unit. Strings are used for names, addresses, phone numbers, descriptions of items, and so on. Although much of today's data manipulation involves strings, C++ does not have a string data type; string handling requires special techniques. Chapter 10 is devoted to an in-depth discussion of strings. However, until we reach that point, you should be able to at least handle simple string input and output so that you can include string data in your classes.

You can think of a C++ string as a linear sequence of characters terminated by a special character—a null, usually represented as '\0'. When you declare a string variable, you must tell the compiler how many bytes to set aside for the string, including the terminating null. The general syntax is as follows:

```
char variable_name [ length+1 ];
```

If you want to store an 80-character string, you could use a declaration like:

```
char inputText [81];
```

Keep in mind that you must always declare a string to be one character longer than the maximum number of characters you want to store to leave room for the terminating null.

There is one important thing to keep in mind about C++ strings. When you declare the string, the number you place in brackets after the variable name simply tells the compiler how much space to set aside for the string. However, there is no automatic mechanism for alerting the program if a user enters more characters than the string has been defined to hold. Storing too many characters in a string usually results in the destruction of the contents of other variables (those whose storage location immediately follows the string). Because string overflow if a common source of program errors, if you have variables whose contents mysteriously change, you should use the debugger to watch what happens when you enter data into strings.

INITIALIZING AND ASSIGNING VALUES TO VARIABLES

When you declare a variable, the compiler sets aside storage space for that variable. However, the compiler doesn't automatically assign a value to that storage space. In fact, when a program is loaded into main memory to begin its run, variable storage locations assume whatever value is currently in the location. This may be a value left over from a previous program, a value that is totally unrelated to your program. To ensure that your program doesn't accidentally pick up irrelevant data, you should give every variable an initial value before you attempt to use that variable's contents for output or in other data manipulation operations.

There are three ways to initialize variables:

- Initialize variables in the variable declaration statement. *This is available only for program variables; class variables cannot be initialized when they are declared.*
- Perform input to give the variable a value. This is available for both program and class variables.
- Assign an initial value to a variable as part of a function. This can be done anywhere in a program. Class variables are typically initialized in the class's constructor, the function that is run automatically whenever an object is created from the class.

For all types of variables except strings, you assign a value to a variable using the *assignment operator* (=). For example, the following expression declares an integer storage location and assigns an initial value of 0 to that location:

```
int sum = 0;
```

It is tempting to read the assignment operator as "equals." However, its action isn't precisely the same as evaluating an algebraic expression.

Keep in mind that a computer's main memory is nothing more than a collection of electronic circuits. Each circuit can hold one voltage (either high or low). When you give a group of circuits (for example, 16 circuits that have been set aside to store an integer) a value, each circuit takes on a voltage. When you change the value, any of the circuits may take on different values. Because a circuit can carry only one voltage level at a time, the previous value held by the storage location is lost.

Assignment is therefore a replacement operation. It really says "take the value on the right side of the assignment operator and place it in the storage location labeled with the variable name that appears on the left side of the assignment operator." (This will become extremely important when we look at arithmetic operations in Chapter 6.)

If you are initializing a numeric storage location, you can do so when the variable is declared, as in the previous example. You can also do it as part of a function:

```
total = 0.0;
```

This is an executable assignment statement. In other words, each time the computer encounters the statement, it places 0.0 in the storage location labeled `total`. (You will read about simple input, which also can be used to initialize a variable, in Chapter 5.)

> **NOTE**
> *C++ will not allow you to use a variable unless it has been declared. The statement total = 0.0; will be allowed only if the initialization float total; precedes the assignment statement somewhere in the program.*

How do you decide whether to initialize a variable when it is declared or to use an assignment statement in the body of the program? The answer lies in whether you need to return the variable to its initial value during the program run. Initialization that appears in a variable declaration occurs only once, when the program is first loaded into main memory. However, an assignment statement can be executed as many times as needed.

Assume, for example, that you have written a program that computes the total sales for each of 12 salespeople. Each time the program begins summing sales, the contents of the `total` variable should be reset to 0. Otherwise, you won't get a correct result for any of the salespeople after the first one; the total will continue to accumulate. In this case, you should place the assignment statement in the body of the program.

Initializing Characters

Although it's a good idea to avoid single-character variable names, there's nothing in the C++ language to prevent you from doing so. There must therefore be some way for a C++ compiler to differentiate between character data and single-character variables names. The answer is single quotes. Whenever the compiler sees a character surrounded by single quotes, it assumes that you want character data. To initialize a character storage location, you therefore surround the character with single quotes:

```
char yes_no = 'y';
```

As with numeric variables, character variables can be initialized when they are declared or with an assignment statement within a function. They can also be initialized by performing keyboard input.

If you don't want to place a character in a `char` variable but simply want to wipe out any contents the storage location may have, you can assign a null:

```
char yes_no = '';
```

The null is represented by two single quotes typed next to each other. (This is *not* a double quote.)

Initializing Strings

Strings can be initialized when they are declared using the assignment operator. However, once strings are declared, the assignment operator can't be used; you must use a special string function from the ANSI C libraries.

There are several ways to initialize strings as part of the variable declaration, two of which are commonly used. The first is to declare the string variable in the usual way (with the number of characters following the variable name):

```
char sampleString[26] = "This is a test";
```

This sets aside 26 bytes for the string and assigns the string This is a test to the first 15 positions. (Don't forget that although there are only 14 characters in the string, the 15th position is used by the terminating null.)

Alternatively, you can leave out the number of characters, using only the square brackets:

```
char sampleString[] = "This is a test";
```

In this case, the compiler sets aside only 15 bytes for the string, just enough to hold the value with which the variable was initialized.

Notice that in both of these examples, the string was surrounded by double quotes. This is the signal to the C++ compiler that you want a string, not a character. In fact, the following two statements request very different types of storage:

```
char oneChar = 'z';
char shortString[] = "z";
```

The variable named oneChar sets aside one byte of storage, which contains just a z. However, the variable named shortString sets aside two bytes of storage, one for the z and the other for the terminating null, \0.

As you will see in Chapter 5, you can also initialize a string variable by accepting input from the keyboard into that variable. However, what you can't do is assign a value to a string using an assignment statement. The reason is that storing a string isn't a simple replacement operation; it involves many bytes of storage and requires adjusting the position of the terminating null. You must therefore use a function from the standard C libraries: strcpy (string copy).

To use a library function, you must be sure to include the associated header file in your source code file anytime before you attempt to use the function for the first time:

```
#include <string.h>
```

The function itself has the following general syntax:

```
strcpy (string_variable, string);
```

The string_variable is the name of a string variable that has been previously declared. The string is either a string constant (a string surrounded by double quotes) or another string variable. For example, the following statements are needed to give a string variable a value inside the body of a program:

```
#include <string.h>
char sampleString[26];
strcpy (sampleString, "This is a test");
```

DEFINING YOUR OWN VARIABLE TYPES

In addition to C++'s built-in variable types, you can use the `typedef` statement to create your own data types. You can then use a custom data type to declare variables, either in a class or in a program.

The `typedef` statement has the following general syntax:

```
typedef data_type new_type_name
```

One of the most useful uses of `typedef` is to simplify creating and using string variables. For example, you might define a new type—`string80`—to hold an 80-character string:

```
typedef char string80[81];
```

Then you use the new data type like any of the built-in variable types:

```
string80 name, street, city;
```

THE SCOPE OF VARIABLES AND VARIABLE STORAGE CLASSES

C++ variables have a *scope*, the portion of the program in which the variables exist. Variables can be
global, in which case they are accessible to the entire program, or they can be *local*, in which case they are accessible only within the function in which they are defined.

Global variables are defined outside any function (even the `main` function). Although they are conceptually easy to use and therefore very attractive to beginning programmers, there are at least two good reasons to avoid them:

- Global variables exist the entire time the program is running. Thus they take up space in main memory even if they are used for only a short time.
- As a program grows large, it is difficult to keep track of where global variables have been declared. It therefore becomes difficult, for example, to make sure that you don't attempt to use a variable name a second time or to remember the name or data type of a variable.

By default, a local variable is created when you call the function in which it is declared. When the function finishes, the space allocated for the variable is released. In most cases, this provides for more efficient use of main memory during program execution. In addition, it keeps variable declarations with the functions that use them, making it easier to keep track of how variables are declared and how they are used. You also can use the same local variable name in more than one function.

In some circumstances, you may not want a variable destroyed when the function in which it was declared finishes. To make sure that a variable stays around, you can change its *storage class*. A storage class is an expression of how you want a variable's storage handled. There are three storage classes:

- `auto`: The storage space allocated to an automatic variable (the default) is released when the function in which the variable was declared terminates.
- `static`: The storage space allocated to a static variable is retained throughout the program run.
- `register`: A register variable is stored in the CPU whenever possible. This significantly speeds up access to the contents of the variable. However, the amount of storage space in the CPU is very limited. As a result, register variables may be swapped from the CPU to main memory if the program needs the storage space in the CPU so it can execute. Most C++ programs rarely use register variables.

To change a variable's storage class from `auto` to `static`, precede the variable declaration with the word `static`. For example, if you want a string to stay in main memory throughout a program run, you might use the following declaration:

```
static char immortalString[81];
```

Constants

A *constant* is a value that doesn't change during the run of a program. You have already seen three types of constants: numeric constants (for example, the zeros used to initialize integer and floating point variables), character constants (single characters surrounded by single quotes), and string constants (groups of characters surrounded by double quotes). The constants you have seen are included in variable declarations or as part of a source code file. However, there is a major drawback to using many constants in this way: If the same constant appears throughout a program's source code, a change in that constant means that you will have to find every occurrence of that constant and change it. You run a great risk of missing one or more places the constant has been used.

The solution is to provide constants with meaningful names that you can use in the same way you use variable names. Assuming that you place the definitions of constants in a header file, changing the constants means simply changing the definition in the header file and recompiling the program.

There are two ways to define a constant: one that is a holdover from C and another that is unique to C++. The C method of defining a constant uses an assembler directive, `define`. For example, to values for true and false, you might use:

```
#define TRUE 1
#define FALSE 0
```

The directive is preceded by the pound sign, followed by the name of the constant and the constant's value. When the program is compiled, the compiler substitutes the value of the constant into the program everywhere it sees the name of the constant. In effect, a C constant is a *macro*, a small snippet of code that is copied into source code during compilation.

NOTE

By convention, the names given to constants are in uppercase letters. This makes them easy to distinguish from variables and keywords.

The C++ constant style works more like a variable, setting aside a place in main memory that is labeled with the name of the constant. The advantage to this approach is that you can look at the value of the constant with a debugger. Defining a C++ constant uses the keyword `const` and looks very much like an assignment statement. To set up the true and false constants used in the previous example, a program would use the following:

```
const TRUE = 1;
const FALSE = 0;
```

Because these are C++ declarations and not compiler directives, they end with a semicolon.

By default, a constant declared with the `const` statement is an integer. If you want to declare a constant of a different data type, you must include that data type in the declaration. For example, the following declarations create floating point constants:

```
const float INTEREST_RATE = .0789;
const float ROYALTY_RATE = .15;
```

Some constant declarations, including the true and false constants used as examples here, can be found in the library header files. It is therefore useful to open the header files and look at the constants in them so that you don't inadvertently try to redefine an existing constant, something that the compiler will detect as an error.

Declaring Member Functions

When you write a class declaration, you include prototypes for the class's member functions. Before we can turn to writing classes, we first need to take an in-depth look at function prototypes, including return values and formal parameters.

RETURN VALUES

As you read previously, a C++ function prototype has the following general syntax:

```
return_value_type function_name (formal_parameters);
```

The *return_value_type* is the data type of the value sent back to the calling function when the function finishes execution. For example, the following function returns a floating point value:

```
float Add (float, float);
```

The return value is sent back with the `return` statement. For example, if a function is declared to return an `int` value, the function might contain the following statements:

```
int sum;
: some processing goes here
return sum;
```

The `return` statement also causes the function to stop execution. This means that there can be more than one `return` statement in a function. The first one the computer encounters will send a value back to the calling function and terminate the function.

FORMAL PARAMETERS

A function's formal parameter list includes the data types of the values that are sent from the calling function into the function. For example, the following `Subtract` function requires two floating point values:

```
float Subtract (float, float);
```

The preceding parameters are *value parameters*, values that are used only for input into the function. If the values of the parameters are changed within the function, the changes stay within the function. When the function terminates, the changes disappear. In other words, any changes made to value parameters are not sent back to the calling function. This is also known as a *pass by value*.

The alternative to a value parameter is a *reference parameter* (a *pass by reference*). To perform a pass by reference, you send a function the main memory address of a parameter. The function then makes changes directly to main memory so that any changes to the parameter are available to the calling function when the function terminates. This is the only way you can get a C++ function to "return" more than one value. However, because reference parameters require the use of pointers, we will defer discussion of them until Chapter 11.

Class Declaration Syntax

When you declare a class, you are defining a combination of variables for data storage and member functions for data manipulation that the C++ compiler will view as a unit. The declaration uses the general syntax in Figure 4.1.

As you look at this syntax, notice that the contents of the class are surrounded by braces. Throughout C++, braces serve to group items. For a class, the closing brace is followed by a semicolon. In fact, this is the only situation in which you will place a semicolon *outside* a closing brace.

Figure 4.1 General syntax for a class declaration

```
class class_name
{
    private:
        private members
    public:
        public members
};
```

A class's private members are variables and functions that are accessible only to functions within the class. In most cases, all variables are private. Because private functions can be called only by other functions in the same class, private functions are usually utility functions that are shared by other class functions.

A class's public members represent the class's interface to the outside world. Public members usually include the prototypes of functions that can be called by other functions.

As an example, consider the class in Listing 4.1. The class is stored in a file named *Calculator.h*. This class, which forms the basis of a program you will see in Chapter 6, has one private variable: the result of an arithmetic operation. The class also has five public member functions that perform the arithmetic operation suggested by each function's name.

Listing 4.1   The Calculator class

```
class Calculator
{
    private:
        float result;
    public:
        Calculator ();
        float Add (float, float);
        float Subtract (float, float);
        float Multiply (float, float);
        float Divide (float, float);
        float Exponentiate (float, float);
};
```

In addition to the member functions that perform the arithmetic, there is a member function that has the same name as the class (Calculator). This member function also has no return data type. This is a *constructor*, a function that is run automatically whenever an object is created from the class. In most cases, constructors are used to initialize an object's private variables. This particular example has no formal parameters, but many constructors do.

Writing Simple Constructors

As an introduction to writing member functions, let's look at the constructor for the `Calculator` class, which appears in Listing 4.2. First, the file containing the constructor must include the header file in which the class declaration is stored. This makes the class variables and function prototypes available to the constructor.

Listing 4.2   The constructor for the Calculator class

```
#include "Calculator.h"

Calculator::Calculator () // :: tells the compiler which class
{
     result = 0;
}
```

The function header contains the name of the function and its formal parameter list. The function header also must let the compiler know the class to which the function belongs. That is handled by placing the name of the class and the *scope resolution operator* (::) before the name of the function.

NOTE

In member functions other than constructors, the return value data type precedes the name of the class.

The body of the function is surrounded by braces. (Because this isn't a class declaration, no semicolon follows the closing brace.) The function's executable statements appear within those braces. In this example there is only one executable statement, which assigns an initial value to an object's variable.

NOTE

Don't forget that you can't initialize class variables when they are declared as part of the class. Initialization must take place elsewhere using an assignment operation. This usually occurs in a constructor.

Writing Other Member Functions

The structure of member functions that aren't constructors is slightly different from that of constructors. As an example of a nonconstructor member function, look at Listing 4.3. (For the purposes of this discussion, you can ignore the body of the function.)

Listing 4.3   A member function that isn't a constructor

```
float Calculator::Add (float value1, float value2)
{
    result = value1 + value2;
    return result;
}
```

Notice first that the return value's data type appears first in the function header, just as it did in the prototype you saw earlier in this chapter. The return value data type is followed by the name of the class to which the function belongs, the scope resolution operator, and the name of the function.

The formal parameter list, however, looks a bit different than it did in the prototype: It contains variable names to which the formal parameters will be assigned. In other words, the first floating point value sent into the function will be stored under the variable name value1; the second floating point value will be stored under value2. The parameter list in a function declaration header therefore does double duty: It matches the prototype to ensure that the function is being used properly and also declares variables for incoming values. The variable names assigned to formal parameters in the function declaration header can be used in the body of the function without further declaration.

Program functions (functions that aren't member functions) are declared just like nonconstructor member functions. The only difference is the absence of a class name and a scope resolution operator.

Simple Input and Output

One of the most important things a computer program needs to do is accept input from the outside world (usually from the keyboard, mouse, or disk drive) and transmit output from within the program back to the outside world (usually to a monitor's screen or a printer). In this chapter you will learn how ANSI C++ supports simple I/O. You will learn to accept input from the keyboard, display text on the screen, and work with text files.

NOTE
Macintosh applications handle most of their I/O through the Macintosh's graphical user interface. Support for that interface is contained the ROM-based ToolBox. Although in Chapter 17 you will see an overview of how a program can call ToolBox routines, you do need to know some simple I/O procedures so that you can learn other programming concepts without getting bogged down by trying to deal with the complexities of the ToolBox.

Introducing Stream I/O

C++ views I/O as a stream of characters, flowing from one location to another. Each input or output stream is an object into which you can insert characters for output or from which you can extract characters for input.

Whenever you run an ANSI C++ program, the computer creates three stream objects for the program. These streams are directed toward the keyboard and a default computer "terminal" known as the *console*. In the CodeWarrior environment, the console is a window that appears whenever you run a program that uses CodeWarrior's SIOUX library.

The console input stream, `cin`, accepts data from the keyboard. The characters you type are echoed to the console window; in other words, you can see what you type. The console output stream, `cout`, displays characters in the console window. The third console stream, console error (`cerr`), is used for dealing with errors that occur when a program is running. Throughout this book we will be dealing primarily with `cin` and `cout`.

File I/O is handled very much like console I/O. When you want to write to or read from a file, you tell the program to create a stream object for the file. Then you use that file stream object just as you would a console stream object, inserting characters for output and extracting characters for input.

Because I/O streams are objects, they have member functions. As you will see in Chapter 10, you will need to use some of these member functions when dealing with character strings, which present special challenges for stream I/O.

The classes that support stream I/O and the prototypes for stream I/O member functions are found in the header file *iostream.h*. You must include that header file in any program that uses stream I/O. In addition, programs that use file streams must also include *fstream.h*.

Console Output

To send characters to a console output stream, you insert data into the stream using the *stream insertion operator*—<<. The values you insert can be the contents of variables (either program variables or object variables) or constants (numbers, characters, or strings). In general, you insert a value by using the name of the stream, followed by the stream insertion operator, followed by the value. For example, the following statement displays a string constant in the console window:

```
cout << "This is a string constant";
```

There are two things to keep in mind when working with the console output stream. First, cout starts its display where the window's insertion point happens to be. In other words, the display begins right after the last output, regardless of whether that happens to be at the left edge of the console window. Later in this section you will see how to make sure that output starts on a new line.

Second, you can insert more than one value into the console output stream with at a time. Just be sure to precede each value with the stream insertion operator. For example, the following statement displays two string constants, one right after the other:

```
cout << "This is string 1. " << "This is string 2.";
```

INSERTING CONSTANTS INTO A STREAM

The cout stream can display numeric, character, or string constants. To display a numeric constant, you follow a stream insertion operator by the digits you want to output. For example, the following statement displays the number 16 on the screen:

```
cout << 16;
```

Character or string constants are inserted in a similar way, by placing the constant after a stream insertion operator. There are two things to remember, however. First, a character constant is surrounded by single quotes; it can include only one character. Second, a string constant is surrounded by double quotes; it can include many characters. The following statement displays the characters Your grade was A:

```
cout << "Your grade was " << 'A';
```

Notice that there is a space after the s in was (before the closing double quote). This space is necessary to produce normal English spacing. As you read earlier, the cout display begins right where the previous display finished, regardless of whether there is a space after the last value.

INSERTING VARIABLE CONTENTS INTO A STREAM

To insert the contents of a variable into a stream, you put the name of the variable in the output statement following the stream insertion operator. For example, assume that you have the following lines of C++ code:

```
int Value1 = 16;
float Value2 = 22.5;
cout << Value1 << " " << Value2;
```

The console window displays 16 22.5.

Notice in particular that the preceding cout statement includes a blank (" ") between the two values. This is because cout doesn't automatically follow a value with a space. Therefore if you want to see spaces between values, you must be sure to insert them explicitly.

ADDING NEW LINES

Because cout always begins where it left off, it is often necessary to explicitly tell cout to begin a new line at the left edge of the console window. This helps you control exactly where output appears.

There are two ways to request a new line. The first is something C++ inherited from C—an *escape character*. Escape characters, single letters preceded by a backslash (\), provide formatting information to an output stream. When the compiler sees the \, it knows that what follows is a formatting character, not an output character. The escape character for a new line is n. To use it, you precede it with a backslash and include both characters in a string constant, as in the following:

```
cout << "\nThis appears starting on a new line";
```

NOTE

The use of \ to signal an escape character presents a bit of a problem: You can't simply include a single \ in a character string; C++ will think that whatever follows is for formatting, not for display. Therefore if you need to include \ in a string constant, you must use two backslashes—\\. Only one \ will appear, however.

The second way to get a new line is to request it at the end of a cout statement using endl (end of line), which is inserted into the output stream like any other value. For example, the following statement displays a string constant followed by a blank line:

```
cout << "Sample string" << endl << endl;
```

Why only one blank line? There are two `endl`s. The reason is that the first `endl` moves the console window's insertion point to the left edge of the window on the line below the string constant. At this point there's no blank line. It's the second `endl` that moves the insertion point down another line, leaving the line above without any visible characters. When output starts again, there will therefore be one blank line between `Sample string` and the following output.

Console Input

To accept data from the keyboard into variables, use the *stream extraction operator* (>>) to extract values from a `cin` stream. Assume, for example, that a program includes the following statements:

```
int firstValue, secondValue;
cin >> firstValue >> secondValue;
```

The user types 156 232 and presses the Return key. The program places 156 in `firstValue` and 232 in `secondValue`.

The preceding example illustrates two important characteristics of `cin`. First, a single `cin` statement can handle more than one variable. In that case, the computer recognizes the end of a value by a space. Second, the end of all input is indicated by the Return key.

The `cin` stream has one very annoying characteristic: If you press Return without entering all the values that `cin` expects, the program simply waits. It won't proceed any further until you give it a value for each of the variables in the `cin` statement.

String Input

Strings present a problem for cin. As you know, cin detects the end of an input value by looking for a space. However, strings are full of spaces that mark the end of words. If you attempt to read a string using cin, all you'll get is the first word. The solution to the problem is to use a library function that accepts all input up to pressing the Return key as one string. There are two library functions that perform string input. The first (gets) is part of the C libraries; the second (getline) is a cin member function.

To use gets, include the header file *stdio.h* at the beginning of your program. The function itself takes one parameter: the name of a string variable. For example, the following statement accepts one string into the string variable Text:

```
gets (Text);
```

When used to accept data from the keyboard, the getline member function requires two parameters: the string variable's name and the maximum number of characters that can be accepted. If the Text variable is declared to hold 50 characters (a length of 51 to include the terminating null), the getline function is used in the following manner:

```
cin.getline (Text, 50);
```

The preceding syntax is one of two ways to call a member function. Using this method, you use the name of the object (cin), followed by a period, followed by the name of the member function and the parameters you are sending to the function. You will learn more about the details of calling member functions in the next section.

The Ticket Printer Program

As an example of using console input and output, we'll be taking a look at a very simple program for printing tickets to an event. The Ticket Printer program conducts a dialog with the user, asking for the name and date of the event. It then asks the user how many tickets should be printed. Figure 5.1 contains a transcript of a sample run of the program. Notice that the program pauses after each ticket so you can look at it.

Figure 5.1   Output of the Ticket Printer program

```
════════════════ Ticket printer.out ════════════════
SIOUX state: application has terminated.

What is the name of the event? Macworld Expo

What is the date of the event? 01/04/96

How many tickets do you want to print? 2

****************************************************************
                    Event: Macworld Expo
                    Date: 01/04/96

        Ticket number: 1

****************************************************************
Next? y
****************************************************************
                    Event: Macworld Expo
                    Date: 01/04/96

        Ticket number: 2

****************************************************************
Next? y
```

DECLARING THE CLASS

The Ticket Printer program uses one class—Ticket—that stores the data for the ticket that is being printed. The complete header file (*ticket.h*) can be found in Listing 5.1. Notice that this class has two class variables: event_date for the date of the event and event_title for the name of the event. Both variables are character strings.

Listing 5.1   Header file for the Ticket Printer program

```
class Ticket
{
    private:
        char event_date[9]; // date of event
        char event_title[51]; // title of event
    public:
        Ticket(); // constructor
        void init (char [], char []); // places data in class variables
        void print (int); // displays one ticket
};
```

The class has three member functions. The constructor (Ticket) assigns a null to each of the two strings. The init function takes data collected by the program that works with a `Ticket` object and stores that data in the class variables. The third function (`print`) displays one ticket on the console.

NOTE

There are other ways to handle dates instead of simply storing them as text. However, at this point, when a date is simply for display, it is easiest to work with it as a string of text. You'll be introduced to a more sophisticated and accurate way to deal with dates in Chapter 13.

THE MEMBER FUNCTIONS

In Listing 5.2 you will find the member functions for the Ticket Printer program. (This code is stored in the file *ticket.cpp*.) The constructor, which you first saw in Chapter 4, initializes the class variables by loading them with a null (two double quotes types right next to each other).

The `init` function takes data gathered by the `main` function and stores it in an object's variables. Look carefully at the `init` function's header line and compare that line to the function's prototype in Listing 5.1. In the prototype each parameter appears as `char []`, indicating that the function should expect a string of characters of an unknown length. In the function header the string of characters is given a variable name but still no length (for example, `ievent[]`). This is different from declaring a string variable within a function, where the name of the variable is followed by the maximum number of characters you intend to store in that string. When the program is running, the computer will set aside storage for an incoming string parameter based on the size the string is given when it is declared, in this case, in the `main` function.

The final member function—`print`—displays a ticket. In this simple program the ticket is created by using a sequence of `cout` statements. Because the SIOUX console window displays its output in a monospaced font (the Monaco font chosen in the Font preferences panel), the characters line up in a reasonable fashion.

THE MAIN FUNCTION

Because the Ticket Printer program is very short and simple, the program that manipulates the `Ticket` object requires no more than a `main` function (Listing 5.3). Nonetheless, it contains many of the elements typical of C++ programs.

Listing 5.2   Member functions for the Ticket Printer program

```
#include <iostream.h>
#include <string.h>
#include "ticket.h"

Ticket::Ticket ()
{
    strcpy (event_date,""); // put null in the string variable.
    strcpy (event_title,""); // put null in the string variable
}

void Ticket::init (char ievent[], char idate[])
{
    strcpy (event_title, ievent);
    strcpy (event_date, idate);
}

void Ticket::print (int ticket_numb)
{
    cout << endl;
    cout << "************************************************************"
         << endl << endl;
    cout << "                    Event: " << event_title << endl;
    cout << "                     Date: " << event_date << endl << endl;
    cout << "            Ticket number: " << ticket_numb << endl << endl;
    cout << "************************************************************"
         << endl << endl;
```

Creating Objects and Function Binding

Although the Ticket Printer program's header file contains a declaration of the Ticket class, the presence of the class doesn't set aside memory for objects. Objects must be declared in a function (either a member function or a program function). There are two ways to create objects. The differences between them relate to when the computer sets aside memory for the object and when the computer links, or *binds*, member functions to objects.

Binding creates linkages between an object and the member functions of its class. When the program is running, the computer uses the binding information to locate the correct functions for the object. Binding can be performed when the program is compiled (*static binding*) or while the program is running (*dynamic binding*).

Objects created for static binding are declared like variables, using the following general syntax:

```
class_name variable_name
```

Listing 5.3   The main function for the Ticket Printer program

```
#include <iostream.h>
#include <stdio.h>
#include "ticket.h"

void main ()
{
    Ticket Tix; // object of class Ticket
    int i; // index for "for" loop
    int howMany; // number of tickets to print
    char go_on;
    char event[51]; // name of the event
    char date[9]; // date of the event

    cout << "\nWhat is the name of the event? ";
    gets (event);
    cout << "\nWhat is the date of the event? ";
    gets (date);
    Tix.init (event, date);

    cout << "\nHow many tickets do you want to print? ";
    cin >> howMany;
    for (i = 1; i <= howMany; i++ ) // print more than one ticket
    {
        Tix.print (i);
        cout << "Next? ";
        cin >> go_on;
    }
}
```

In the Ticket Printer program's main function, for example, an object to handle the ticket is declared with:

```
Ticket Tix;
```

When the program is compiled, memory is set aside for an object declared for static binding. Like any other variable, the object remains in memory as long as the function in which it is declared is running.

NOTE

Creating objects for dynamic binding requires the use of pointers. We will therefore defer a discussion of dynamic binding until Chapter 11.

Calling Member Functions

The way in which you call a member function depends on whether the object has been declared for use with static or dynamic binding. When you are using static binding, a member function call looks like this:

```
object_name.function_name (parameter_list);
```

The Ticket Printer program's main function calls two functions directly: init and print:

```
Tix.init (event, date);
Tix.print (i);
```

However, main never calls the class's constructor. This is because constructors are called automatically whenever an object is created. In this case, the constructor is called when the program is loaded into main memory at the beginning of the program run, as the program is allocating data storage space.

Performing the I/O

The I/O performed by the Ticket Printer program appears in two places: the print function for the ticket itself and the main function for gathering data needed by the Ticket object's member functions.

The reason for separating the I/O in this way is to make the program more flexible. You can modify the layout of the printed ticket without making any changes to the main program; you can modify the main program's user interface without making any change to the class's member function that prints the ticket.

The program can create any number of tickets, up to the maximum value that can be stored in an integer storage location. To repeat the call to the print function, the program uses a for statement, one of several C++ statements that repeat a group of actions. (You will be introduced to the details of this type of statement in Chapter 8.)

> **NOTE**
>
> *If you look carefully at the for statement, you'll see a variable named "i." This single-letter variables appears to be a violation of the rule that you should always use meaningful variable names. However, most programmers recognize the single letters i, j, and k for use in statements that repeat actions. This is the one case where it is therefore acceptable to use single-letter variables.*

PROGRAMMING CHALLENGE NUMBER 1

At this point, the ticket shows only the name of the event, the date of the event, and the ticket number. Your job is to modify the program so that it also includes the ticket price. To add the ticket price, you will need to do the following:

- Add a float variable to the class definition in the header file for the ticket price.
- Modify main so that it asks the user for the ticket price. (Hint: Don't forget to add a float variable to main to hold the user's input.)
- Modify the init function's prototype so that it expects a float parameter as well as the two string parameters.
- Modify the init function's header so that it includes the float parameter and gives the parameter a name.
- Modify the body of the init function so that it includes a line that assigns the value in the input parameter to the class variable.
- Modify the print function so that it includes printing a line for the ticket price.
- Modify main so that the function call to print includes the new parameter.

Run the program to test your modifications. If you aren't satisfied with the appearance of the modified ticket, fix the cout statements and try again. Keep fiddling with the program until the ticket meets your criteria.

> **NOTE**
> *If you are tired of responding to the "Next?" question after each ticket prints, remove the cout statement that prints the prompt and the cin statement that follows. The tickets will then print without pausing.*

File Operations

ANSI C++ can create two types of files: text files and binary files. A *text file* contains readable characters. You can examine its contents with any text editor or word processor, including the CodeWarrior editor. A *binary file* contains an unformatted stream of bits. Although you can open the file with a text editor, its contents will be unintelligible. For the purposes of learning throughout this book, we will be using only text files so that it's easy to check the files for accuracy.

Text file input and output is very similar to console stream I/O. To write to or read from a file, you create an object for a file stream and then use the stream insertion or extraction operator (as appropriate) to send values to the stream. The file is closed when the function in which its object was created terminates; you can also close a file explicitly.

Support for file I/O is part of a large C++ class hierarchy. All the classes in this hierarchy are ultimately derived from the class ios. Throughout this section you will therefore see references to parts of the ios class that are used by file stream I/O. Prototypes for the file I/O functions are found in *fstream.h*, which must be included in any source file that uses file stream objects.

For your first experience with file I/O, you will be looking at a program that stores precious metals prices. As you can see in Figure 5.2, the program displays yesterday's prices (read from a text file) and asks you for today's prices. The current prices are written back to the file just before the program terminates.

Figure 5.2   Output of the Metals Prices program

```
╔══════════ Metals prices.out ═══════════╗
║ SIOUX state: application has terminated.    ▲
║                                             ▓
║ Yesterday's precious metals prices were:    ▓
║    Gold: 475.75                             ▓
║    Silver: 18.88                            ▓
║    Copper: 47                               ▓
║ Today's gold price: 460.21                  ▓
║ Today's silver price: 17.75                 ▼
║ Today's copper price: 48.80                
╚═════════════════════════════════════════╝
```

The Metals Prices program uses one class—Metals_prices—that stores the prices for gold, silver, and copper. Notice in Listing 5.4 that the class has three variables, one for each price. The member functions include a constructor, a function to read data from the file (read), a function to write data to the file (write), and a function to change the data stored in an object created from the class (modify).

The remaining three functions—those whose names start with get—return the value in one private class variable to a calling function. This is a frequently used mechanism to give functions outside the class access to private class variable values. If you look at the bottom of Listing 5.5 (the member functions for the Metals Prices program, you will see that the body of each of the get functions includes nothing more than a return statement.

The constructor (the function with the same name as the class) assigns 0 to each of the class variables. The modify function accepts three values from a calling function and copies those values into the class's variables.

Listing 5.4   The header file for the Metals Prices program

```
class Metals_prices
{
    private:
        float gold, silver, copper;
    public:
        Metals_prices();
        void read ();
        void write ();
        void modify (float, float, float);
        float getGold();
        float getSilver();
        float getCopper();
};
```

The actions of the program are, of course, controlled by the program's main function (Listing 5.6). The program first calls the read function to load the object's data from the file. It displays yesterday's prices, using the get functions to retrieve the values the read function stored in the object.

Notice that the cout statements that display yesterday's prices include the get function calls. The value returned by these functions (in each case, a floating point value) is inserted directly into the output stream.

NOTE

A common error when placing a function call in an output stream is to forget to include the parentheses for the parameter list after the name of a member function that has no input parameters. If you leave the parentheses off, the compiler will think you are trying to access a class variable and will produce an error message that indicates that the variable either doesn't exist or is inaccessible.

After displaying yesterday's prices, the program asks for today's prices, which are collected in local variables. The program then modifies the prices stored in the object with the modify function and completes its work by writing the new prices to the file with the object's write function.

FILE OUTPUT

Writing to a file is very similar to using cout to display characters in a SIOUX console window. However, the values must be formatted in such a way that they can be read correctly the next time the file is used. In this section you will learn to create a

Listing 5.5 Member functions for the metals_prices class

```cpp
#include <fstream.h>
#include "metals_prices.h"

Metals_prices::Metals_prices ()
{
    gold = 0;
    silver = 0;
    copper = 0;
}

void Metals_prices::read ()
{
    // create the input stream
    ifstream pricesIn ("prices");

    // Actually should check to see if file exists
    // before attempting to read from it. See
    // Chapter 7 for details.

    // read the data
    pricesIn >> gold >> silver >> copper;
    // file is closed automatically when function terminates
}

void Metals_prices::write ()
{
    // create the output stream
    ofstream pricesOut ("prices");
    // write to the output file
    pricesOut << gold << " " << silver << " " << copper;
}

void Metals_prices::modify (float igold, float isilver, float icopper)
{
    gold = igold;
    silver = isilver;
    copper = icopper;
}

float Metals_prices::getGold()
    { return gold; }

float Metals_prices::getSilver()
    { return silver; }

float Metals_prices::getCopper()
    { return copper; }
```

Listing 5.6   The main function for the Metals Prices program

```
#include <iostream.h>
#include "metals_prices.h"

void main ()
{
    float igold, isilver, icopper;
    Metals_prices prices; // create an object

    prices.read();

    cout << "Yesterday's precious metals prices were:" << endl;
    cout << "  Gold: " << prices.getGold() << endl;
    cout << "  Silver: " << prices.getSilver() << endl;
    cout << "  Copper: " << prices.getCopper() << endl;

    cout << "Today's gold price: ";
    cin >> igold;
    cout << "Today's silver price: ";
    cin >> isilver;
    cout << "Today's copper price: ";
    cin >> icopper;

    prices.modify(igold, isilver, icopper);
    prices.write();
}
```

file output stream object and to use that object to send data to that file so that it can be read.

Opening a File for Output

To open a file for output, you create a file output stream object, using the following general syntax:

```
ofstream stream_name ("file_name");
```

The file name can be a string constant, surrounded by double quotes as it is in the preceding syntax, or it can be a string variable name, in which the quotes aren't necessary.

For example, the Metals Prices program stores its data in a file named `prices`. The program therefore opens the file for output with:

```
ofstream pricesOut ("prices");
```

When you create an `ofstream` object, the computer first looks to see if a file already exists. If it does, the computer opens the file. Writing to the file begins at the beginning of the file, wiping out any contents the file might already have. If the file doesn't exist, the computer creates an empty file.

Writing Simple Values to the File

When you write to a file, you must explicitly separate the values so that when the file is read, the computer knows where one value stops and another begins. You do this by placing a space after each numeric or character value. (Strings add considerable complications to managing text files. Adding strings to files is therefore covered in Chapter 10.)

For example, to write the three floating point values, the Metals Prices program uses:

```
pricesOut << gold << " " << silver << " " << copper;
```

It isn't necessary to place a space after the last value.

If the gold price is 467.50, the silver price 12.00, and the copper price 46.86, the file contains:

```
467.5 12 46.86
```

Notice that trailing zeros, even if you enter them from the keyboard, are not included in the file.

NOTE

Most ANSI-compatible compilers automatically place a space after each numeric or character value that is written to a file. The explicit spaces usually aren't needed unless you are also storing strings in the file. CodeWarrior acts consistently when it requires you to explicitly insert the spaces regardless of the type of data you are writing. However, if you switch to another compiler, watch your text files carefully to determine whether explicitly adding a space after each value results in two spaces between values. If that is the case, you will need to remove the explicit spaces to get a file that can be read correctly.

FILE INPUT

Reading numeric and character values from a text file is very similar to using `cin` to read values from the keyboard. First, you create an input file object. Then you use the stream extraction operator to retrieve the values from the stream.

Opening a File for Input

To open a file for input, you create an object from the class `ifstream`, using the general syntax:

```
ifstream stream_name ("file_name");
```

The Metals Prices program, for example, creates its input file with:

```
ifstream pricesIn ("prices");
```

NOTE

There is a very real possibility that an attempt to open a file for reading will fail (for example, if the file doesn't exist). A good program always checks to see whether a file has been opened successfully and takes appropriate action if a problem has occurred. You will learn how to do this in Chapter 7.

Reading Simple Values from a File

To read numeric and character values from a file, you extract the values from the input stream, placing them into variables just as you would with the `cin` stream. For example, the Metals Prices program reads its three values with:

```
pricesIn >> gold >> silver >> copper;
```

When you are reading numeric and character values, the computer automatically skips over the spaces that have been inserted to separate the values.

Formatting Stream Output

If you look back at Figure 5.2, you'll notice that the output isn't particularly well formatted. The values don't look much like currency because some of the values don't have two places to the right of the decimal point. What decimal points do appear don't line up. The output should probably look more like Figure 5.3. Notice that the values are now formatted to appear as currency and that the decimal points are in a line.

Figure 5.3   The Metal Prices program, including formatted output

There are two elements to creating the formatted output. The first is careful preparation of the string constants that appear in the `cout` statements. The second is the use of *manipulators*, `ios` class member functions that set stream formatting characteristics.

In Listing 5.7 you will find the modified `main` function for the Metals Prices program that produced the output in Figure 5.3. Notice first that the labels for the prices and the dollar signs that precede the numbers are part of the string constant that begins the `cout` statements. The colons that follow the name of the metals line up simply because the strings have been created so that they contain the right number of spaces for the desired effect. This works, by the way, only with a monospaced font.

The formatting of the numbers themselves is handled by the `ios` manipulators. Before using them, be sure to include *iomanip.h* in your program.

SETTING PRECISION, WIDTH, AND FILL

Three of the most commonly used stream manipulators set the precision of a number (the number of digits to the right of the decimal point), the width of the field in

Listing 5.7   The main function for the Metals Prices program, including stream output formatting

```
#include <iostream.h>
#include <iomanip.h>
#include "metals_prices.h"

void main ()
{
    float igold, isilver, icopper;
    Metals_prices prices; // create an object

    prices.read();
    cout << setiosflags (ios::fixed | ios::right) << setprecision(2)
         << setfill('*');
    cout << "Yesterday's precious metals prices were:" << endl;
    cout << "    Gold: $" << setw(7) << prices.getGold() << endl;
    cout << "  Silver: $" << setw(7) << prices.getSilver() << endl;
    cout << "  Copper: $" << setw(7) << prices.getCopper() << endl;

    cout << "Today's gold price: ";
    cin >> igold;
    cout << "Today's silver price: ";
    cin >> isilver;
    cout << "Today's copper price: ";
    cin >> icopper;

    prices.modify(igold, isilver, icopper);
    prices.write();
}
```

which a number appears, and the character used to fill the width of the field if the value is smaller than the field. Each of these is a function call that can be inserted directly into an output stream.

Setting Precision

To set the precision of numeric values, insert the `setprecision` function into an output stream. The function takes one parameter: the number of character that are to appear to the right of the decimal point. For example, to format numbers for currency, the Metals Prices program uses:

```
cout << setprecision(2);
```

The precision you set affects only the stream into which it is inserted. It stays in effect until you insert a different value for precision into that stream.

Setting Width

To set the width of the field in which a value is displayed, insert the `setw` function into an output stream. Like `setprecision`, `setw` takes only one parameter. In this case, it is the width of the field. The output fields in the Metals Prices program are set to seven spaces with:

```
cout << setw(7);
```

The `setw` function returns to the default (just enough space to display the entire value) immediately after a value is displayed. You must therefore repeat it before every value whose display field is to be set. In Listing 5.7, for example, it appears three times, once for each metal price.

Setting Fill

By default, the computer fills the empty spaces in an output field with spaces. However, you change that character with the `setfill` function. For example, the Metals Prices program fills the empty spaces with asterisks using:

```
cout << setfill('*');
```

Notice that the function's single parameter is the new fill character, surrounded by single quotes.

Like `setprecision`, a fill character affects only the stream into which `setfill` is inserted. It stays in effect until you specify another fill character for that stream.

SETTING THE IOS FLAGS

The `ios` flags set a variety of formatting characteristics. Some of the most commonly used can be found in Table 5.1. If you want to use the formatting provided by an `ios` flag, you *set* the flag, giving the bit that represents the flag a value of 1.

To set the `ios` flags, use the `setiosflags` functions. The flags you want to set become the function's parameter. If you want to set more than one flag, you must combine them with an operation known as a *logical OR*, which is represented by a

Table 5.1   Some commonly used ios flags

Flag	Use
left	Left align the contents of the field
right	Right align the contents of the field
showpoint	Display a decimal point even if the value is an integer
uppercase	Display characters in all uppercase
showpos	Precede positive numbers with a + sign
scientific	Use scientific (floating point) notation for numbers
fixed	Use fixed-point notation for numbers

single bar (|). The logical OR operates on the bits in two values, one bit at a time. If either bit is a 1, the bit in the result value is a 1; if both bits are 0, the result is 0.

The Metals Prices program sets the showpoint flag and the fixed flag. The former ensures that the decimal point always appears; the latter requests the fixed point notation. To set the flags, the program includes the following:

```
cout << setiosflags (ios::fixed | ios::right);
```

Notice that the name of each flag is preceded with ios::. This tells the compiler that the flags are defined in the ios class, not in the file stream class.

As with the other manipulators, the ios flags affect only the stream into which they are inserted. They remain in effect until you reset them with the resetiosflags function. For example,

```
cout << resetiosflags (ios::fixed | ios::right);
```

Each flag is *cleared*, or reset to 0.

PROGRAMMING CHALLENGE NUMBER 2

The ticket price that you added to the Ticket Printer program earlier hasn't been formatted to appear like currency. To get some experience using ios flags, do the following to format the ticket price:

1. Set the precision to two places to the right of the decimal point.

2. Set the `fixed` and `showpoint` flags.
3. Add a dollar sign as a string constant.

   In addition, set the `uppercase` flag so that only the name of the event appears in all uppercase characters. As you do this, experiment to find out whether the `uppercase` flag affects string constants or only strings that are stored in variables.

Arithmetic Operations

6

Just after World War II, when computers were first being viewed as practical machines, most people thought that the only thing computers could do well was handle high volumes of arithmetic computations. In fact, the first commercially sold computer went to the U.S. Bureau of the Census.

We've come a long way from those vacuum tube-based early computers. However, computers are still very good at performing arithmetic. They can rapidly and accurately perform computations that would be tedious to do by hand. In this chapter you will learn how to instruct a C++ program to perform arithmetic. The operations you learn here can be included in a class's member functions or in program functions.

The Arithmetic Operators

The C++ arithmetic operators are summarized in Table 6.1. The add, subtract, and divide operators may look familiar; however, the actions or symbols used for the other operators are probably new to you. In this section you will therefore learn the function of each of the arithmetic operators.

Table 6.1   The C++ arithmetic operators

Symbol	Action
+	Unary plus
-	Unary negation
*	Multiply (the asterisk; type Shift-8)
/	Divide
%	Modulo
+	Add
-	Subtract
++	Increment (post- or pre-)
- -	Decrement (post- or pre-)

Arithmetic operations can be performed on the right side of an assignment operator. In that case, the result of the operation is assigned to the variable on the left side of the assignment operator. For example, the following statement takes the contents of `Value1`, adds 5 to that value, and places the result of the addition back into `Value1`, replacing the variable's original contents:

```
Value1 = Value1 + 5;
```

Alternatively, an arithmetic operation can be placed in a stream output statement. In that case, the result of the arithmetic is inserted into the stream. If, for example, `Value1` contains 5 and `Value2` contains 2, the following statement would display a 7.

```
cout << Value1 + Value2;
```

ADDITION, SUBTRACTION, AND MULTIPLICATION

The addition, subtraction, and multiplication operators work in the same way as they do in algebra. However, instead of an *x*, the multiplication operator is an asterisk ($*$, generated by pressing Shift-8). An x would appear to the compiler as a variable name and therefore isn't very practical as an operator.

As with any other operators, you can combine more than one addition, subtraction, or multiplication operator in a single expression. An expression can contain any combination of variable names, constants, and operators. Any of the following are therefore legal arithmetic expressions:

```
const CONSTANT = 63;

Value1 + Value2 + Value3
Value1 + 63
Value1 + CONSTANT
Value1 - 63 - Value2
Value1 - CONSTANT * Value2
Value1 - Value2 + Value3
Value1 * Value2 * Value3
Value + Value2 * Value3 - Value4
```

Notice that the preceding examples aren't followed by semicolons. This is because they aren't complete C++ statements. To make up a complete statement, the result of an arithmetic expression must be assigned to a variable across an assignment operator, used as a parameter in a function call, or placed in an output stream, as in the following:

```
Cost = Price * Quantity;
Object.store_info (Price * Quantity);
cout << Price * Quantity;
```

When an arithmetic expression is used as a parameter in a function call or is placed in an output stream, the result of the expression is used by the program but isn't retained in main memory after that use. A program could, for example, first compute the cost of a purchase, saving the cost in a variable, and then use that variable in a function call or output stream.

```
Cost = Price * Quantity;
Object.store_info (Cost);
cout << Cost;
```

Which should you do? Store a computation in a variable first and then use the contents of the variable in other statements? Or should you put the computation directly into a function call or output stream? There is a trade-off between the two strategies. Storing the result in a variable requires main memory space for the variable and time to store the result. However, if the result of the computation needs to be used more than once, the program will execute more quickly if the computation is performed only once; it takes less time to retrieve a single value stored in main memory than to retrieve all the values needed in a computation and perform the computation. Therefore, if you need the result of a computation only once, go ahead and put it directly into a function call or output stream. However, if space in main memory isn't an overriding concern and you need to use the result of a computation many times, store the result in a variable that you can then reference.

DIVISION

C++ provides two operators that perform division: / and %. The divide operator (/) performs either an integer or floating point division and returns the quotient. The modulo operator (%) performs an integer division and returns the remainder.

Integer versus Floating Point Division

The result of a division varies depending on whether the numbers being divided are integers or floating point values. Consider, for example, the following declarations:

```
int Integer1 = 5, Integer2 = 2;
float Float1 = 5.0, Float2 = 2.0;
```

The expression Integer1 / Integer2 produces a result of 2. Although internally the computer has a result of 2.5, because the two values being divided are integers, the result is *truncated* to an integer. (Truncating means that the fraction part of the number—the digits to the right of the decimal point—is dropped.)

As you might expect, the expression Float1 / Float2 produces 2.5. Because both values being divided are floating point values, the result is returned as a floating point value. However, what happens if you write an expression like Integer1 / Float2 or Float1 / Integer2? The computer performs a floating point division. When values of different precisions (different number of digits to the right of the decimal point) appear in the same arithmetic statement, the computer by default converts them all to match the value of the highest precision before performing the arithmetic.

If you place an expression like `Float1 / Integer2` in a `cout` statement, you will see a floating point value. However, if the result of the division is placed in a variable across an assignment operator, what you get in the variable depends on the data type of the variable. For example, the following performs a floating point division, but truncates the result to 2 when assigning it to the integer variable `Integer1`:

```
Integer1 = Float1 / Integer2;
```

By the same token, the following statement performs the integer division and then assigns 2.0 to the floating point variable:

```
Float1 = Integer1 / Integer2;
```

The data type changing that C++ performs when operations include more than one type of data is known as *typecasting* and is discussed in more depth later in this chapter.

Modulo Division

Modulo division performs an integer division and returns as its result the remainder of the division; the quotient is thrown away. For example:

```
5 % 2 returns 1
25 % 7 returns 4
18 % 5 returns 3
```

Modulo division will work only with integer values. For example, if you use the following in a program, the compiler will report an error:

```
float Value1, Value2;
Value1 = Value1 % Value2;
```

THE UNARY SIGN OPERATORS

Some of the C++ arithmetic operators are *unary* operators. This means that they operate on only one value at a time. Two of those operators—unary plus and negation—are also used for addition and subtraction. The way in which the C++ compiler interprets the operator depends on how it appears in an arithmetic statement.

The unary plus operator (+) preserves the sign of a value during an arithmetic operation. For example, if `Value1` contains 1 and `Value2` contains -2, the following statements are true:

```
+Value2 + Value1 returns -1
Value1 - +Value2 returns 3
+Value2 - Value1 returns -3
```

How does the compiler know which of the plus signs represents a unary plus operation and which represents an addition operation? The answer lies in where the plus signs appear in the expression. When a plus sign begins an expression and is followed by only one value (a constant or a variable), it is interpreted as a unary plus; when a plus sign is surrounded by two values, it is interpreted as an addition.

In the case of the subtraction example, the compiler knows that ` - +` must be a minus operator and a unary plus because ` - +` doesn't represent any other possibility. However, what might the compiler make of the following?

```
Value1 + +Value2
```

Even if you intend a unary plus and an addition, the compiler can't distinguish the two plus signs from the increment operator. (Keep in mind that with the exception of string constants, spaces in source code are ignored.) The solution is to clarify the expression by using parentheses:

```
Value1 + (+Value2)
```

The parentheses make it clear that you want the unary plus performed first, followed by the addition. Parentheses are an important tool in determining the *precedence of operations*, which will be discussed in depth shortly.

The unary negation operator changes the sign of a value. For example, assuming once again that `Value1` contains 1 and that `Value2` contains -2, the following statements are true:

```
-Value2 + Value1 returns 3
-Value1 + Value2 returns -3
 Value1 + -Value2 returns 3
-Value2 - Value1 returns 1
 Value1 - (-Value2) returns 4
```

Notice that the last example required parentheses to distinguish the subtraction and a unary negation from the decrement operator.

THE INCREMENT AND DECREMENT OPERATORS

The increment and decrement operators (++ and --) are shorthand for expressions that add or subtract 1 from an integer or floating point variable. They are particularly handy for counting things or for keeping track of where you are when you are processing a list of things. Although unary operators, they can be placed either before or after a variable name. Their action depends on their position.

Preincrement and Predecrement

When the increment and decrement operators are placed in front of a variable name, they are known as *preincrement* and *predecrement*. This means that the computer increments or decrements the value in the variable before doing anything else in the expression. As an example, consider the following expression:

```
Value1 = Value1 + (++Value2);
```

The computer first adds 1 to Value2 and then performs the addition. If Value1 contains 1 and Value2 contains 3, after the expression is evaluated Value1 contains 5 and Value2 contains 4. Notice that Value2 is modified by the increment operator and retains the modified result. By the same token, the following expression first subtracts 1 from Value2 and then performs the addition:

```
Value 1 = Value1 + (--Value2);
```

Given Value1 beginning with 1 and Value2 beginning with 3, Value1 ends up with 3 and Value2 with 2.

Postincrement and Postdecrement

When the increment and decrement operators are placed after a variable name, they are known as *postincrement* and *postdecrement*. As you might expect, this means that the computer increments or decrements the value in the variable after completing the evaluation of the rest of the expression. The following expression performs the addition and then increments the contents of `Value2` by 1:

```
Value1 = Value1 + Value2++;
```

It is important to realize that the postincrement applies to `Value2` only, not to the result of the entire expression. In other words, the preceding example is equivalent to the following statements:

```
Value1 = Value1 + Value2;
Value2 = Value2 + 1;
```

A postdecrement works in the same way. The following expression performs the addition and then subtracts 1 from `Value2`:

```
Value1 = Value1 + (--Value2);
```

It is equivalent to the following two statements:

```
Value1 = Value1 + Value2;
Value2 = Value2 = 1;
```

Assignment Shorthand

C++ provides a shorthand for assignment operations, such as

```
Value1 = Value1 + arithmetic_expression;
Value1 = Value1 = arithmetic_expression;
Value1 = Value1 * arithmetic_expression;
Value1 = Value1 / arithmetic_expression;
Value1 = Value1 % arithmetic_expression;
```

The shorthand combines the assignment and arithmetic operator into one new operator. The preceding statements can be rewritten in the following way:

```
Value1 += arithmetic_expression;
Value1 -= arithmetic_expression;
Value1 *= arithmetic_expression;
Value1 /= arithmetic_expression;
Value1 %= arithmetic_expression;
```

You can use one of these combined, shorthand operators whenever an assignment statement takes the current value in a variable, uses that value in an arithmetic expression, and places the result back in the variable's storage location.

Notice that these shorthand operators reverse the order of the operators from the longer assignment statements you saw on the preceding page. A common error is therefore to reverse the combined operator. For example, if you reverse +=, the compiler sees the following statement:

```
Value1 =+ arithmetic_expression;
```

It thinks you want to perform a unary plus followed by an assignment. Although the compiler will flag =*, =/, and =% as errors, =+ and =- will slip by because + and - are valid unary operators.

Precedence

When an arithmetic expression contains more than one operator, the computer must decide which operation to perform first. As an example, consider the following expression:

```
15 + 2 / 10
```

There are two possible answers: 1.7 (15 + 2 = 17; 17 / 10 = 1.7) and 15.2 (2 / 10 = 0.2; 0.2 + 15 = 15.2), depending on whether the addition or division is performed first. Unless the programmer tells the computer otherwise, computers use rules of *precedence* to decide the order of operations in an expression.

C++'s default rules of precedence for arithmetic operators can be found in Table 6.2. When more than one operator of the same precedence occurs in the same expression, the computer performs the operations from left to right. In the example on the preceding page, the computer would return a result of 15.2, because the division operation takes precedence over the addition.

Table 6.2   Default rules of precedence for arithmetic operators

Evaluated first	`++`	`- -`	`unary + unary -`
Evaluated second	`*`	`/`	`%`
Evaluated third	`+`	`-`	

Often the default rules of precedence don't produce the result you want. For example, what if you really do want the addition of 15 and 2 to occur before the division by 10? The solution is to use parentheses to defeat the default precedence. The computer evaluates what is within parentheses first. In other words, parentheses have even higher precedence than any of the arithmetic operators. To get the addition and division to occur in the correct order, you could use:

```
(15 + 2) / 10
```

More than one set of parentheses can occur in an expression. In that case, the expression is evaluated from left to right. For example, to evaluate the following expression the computer first adds 15 + 2, then subtracts 4 - 1, and finally multiplies 17 times 3, producing the final result of 51:

```
(15 + 2) * (4 - 1)
```

Parentheses can be nested. When that occurs, the inner set of parentheses is evaluated first. For example, in the following expression the computer first adds 12 plus 6 and then multiplies by 2, resulting in 36:

```
((12 + 6) * 2)
```

There is theoretically no limit to how deep parentheses can be nested. However, every time you use an opening parenthesis, there must be a closing parenthesis to match. The compiler will generate an error message if the parentheses in a statement aren't balanced. As you may remember from Chapter 3, however, the CodeWarrior editor helps you match opening and closing parentheses by showing you the opening parenthesis that is associated with each closing parenthesis as you type.

Typecasting

In its most general sense the term *typecasting* refers to temporarily changing the data type of a value during processing of the data. As you read earlier in the discussion of division, some typecasting is done automatically by C++. In addition, you can explicitly typecast a value.

DEFAULT TYPECASTING

Default typecasting occurs when C++ temporarily changes the data type of a value for use in an expression. When you combine numeric values of differing precisions in the same expression, the values will be typecast to match the value with the highest precision. As examples, consider the following:

```
2.5 * 3 returns 7.5
5 / 2 returns 2
5 / 2.0 return 2.5
```

Note that if the values involved in the expression are stored in variables, the default typecasting doesn't affect the stored values. It is performed temporarily, for use only in the specific expression.

Default typecasting also occurs when you assign a value to a variable across an assignment operator. If an expression produces an integer result, assigning that result to a floating point variable typecasts the result into a floating point value. By the same token, if an expression produces a floating point result, assigning that result to an integer variable truncates the result to an integer.

Characters can also be involved in default typecasting. If you use a character variable in an expression that ordinarily requires an integer, the computer uses the character's ASCII code as if it were an integer value. You will see an example of this in Chapter 7.

EXPLICIT TYPECASTING

In some cases, you may explicitly want to tell the computer to typecast a value. This is used primarily when you want to force an arithmetic expression to be evaluated with a specific precision. Explicit typecasting is also used occasionally when expressions include pointers.

To explicitly typecast a value, place the data type to which you want to cast the value in parentheses in front of the value. For example,

```
FloatVariable = (float) 5 / (float) 2;
```

typecasts the integer values 5 and 2 to floating point before the division is performed. Although the values involved are integer, the typecasting instructs the computer to perform a floating point division, assigning 2.5 to the floating point variable rather than the 2.0 that would have been generated by an integer division.

Math Library Functions

It may seem to you that C++ arithmetic operators are fairly basic. In fact, they don't even cover the range of operations found on a $10 calculator. Does this mean that C++ is relatively weak in terms of arithmetic power? Not at all. The missing operations are provided through library functions.

Functions for traditional math operations (for example, exponentiation, square root, and trigonometric functions) are part of the ANSI C math library. Prototypes can be found in *math.h*.

Documentation for C library functions is contained in the *C Library Reference* file on the CodeWarrior CD-ROM. There you will find the prototypes for the functions and, in some cases, short program examples of how to use the functions. To get you started, however, the rest of this section looks at a few of the more commonly used math library functions.

NOTE

The C libraries are quite extensive. To find out the extent of what is available, take some time to browse through the documentation. That's really the only way you'll discover all the things that a compiler has provided for you. The time spent scanning the library documentation is well made up in savings of programming time.

EXPONENTIATION

Unlike many other programming languages, C++ has no operator for exponentiation (raising a number to a power). You must therefore use pow, a library function, for that purpose. In the C library documentation you will find that the pow entry begins with Listing 6.1. Notice that the Synopsis section tells you that the prototype is in *math.h* and also shows you the function's prototype.

Listing 6.1   Documentation of the pow function

```
Purpose         Calculate x^y.
Synopsis        #include <math.h>
                double pow(double x, double y);
Return value    pow() returns x^y.  The pow() function assigns EDOM to errno if
                x is 0.0 and y is less than or equal to zero or if x is less
                than zero and y is not an integer.
```

This function is written to operate on double-precision floating point values. By default, it also returns a double-precision floating point value. However, because C++ performs automatic typecasting, the function will also accept integer and standard format floating point values. In other words, when you see documentation of a math library function, the data types indicate the maximum precision at which the function will operate. You can always also give the function values of lower precision.

For example, to cube a number, you could use the following statements:

```
int cube = 3;
float myValue, answer;
answer = pow (myValue, cube);
```

SQUARE ROOT

The square root function—sqrt—has the following prototype:

```
double sqrt (double x);
```

To get an accurate result from the function, make sure that your result variable is either a float or a double, although the number of which you are taking the square root could be an int, float, or double. For example, you could use the function and assign its result to a variable:

```
double root;
int value = 279;
root = sqrt (value);
```

Or, as with any other function that returns a value, you could place it directly in an output stream:

```
cout << sqrt (value);
```

ABSOLUTE VALUE

The absolute value of a number is the positive value of a number. In other words, positive values remain positive, and negative numbers are made positive. This operation is used frequently in both financial and statistical calculations. The absolute value function has the following prototype:

```
double fabs (double x);
```

If you include the following source code, the abs_value variable will contain 12.53:

```
float abs_value, float_value = -12.53;
abs_value = fabs (float_value);
```

FLOATING POINT MODULO DIVISION

Although there is no operator for floating point modulo division, you can perform the operation with the fmod function:

```
double fmod (double x, double y);
```

The computer divides x by y and returns the remainder. For example, the following statements produce a result of 1.:

```
double value1 = 11.0, value2 = 2.5, result;
result = fmod (value1, value2);
```

The Calculator Program

To see arithmetic operations in action, we will be looking at a simple program that simulates the action of a calculator. A sample run of the program appears in Figure 6.1. The calculator processes a simple expression that consists of a value, an operator, and a second value. Because the program uses `cin` to accept the three parts of the expression into individual variables, each value must be separated by a space.

Figure 6.1   Output of the Calculator program

```
═══════════════ Calculator.out ═══════════════
SIOUX state: application has terminated.

Arithmetic expression: 5.5 + 2

Answer: 7.5

Another? y

Arithmetic expression: 5.5 - 2

Answer: 3.5

Another? y

Arithmetic expression: 5.5 * 2

Answer: 11

Another? y

Arithmetic expression: 5.5 / 2

Answer: 2.75

Another? y

Arithmetic expression: 5.5 ^ 2

Answer: 30.25

Another? n
```

The program is based on the Calculator class (Listing 6.2). The class stores one value: the result of an arithmetic operation on two numbers. The member functions perform the computations. Notice that all of the functions are defined to handle floating point numbers and can therefore be used with either integers or floating point values.

Listing 6.2   The header file for the Calculator program

```
class Calculator
{
    private:
        float result;
    public:
        Calculator ();
        float Add (float, float);
        float Subtract (float, float);
        float Multiply (float, float);
        float Divide (float, float);
        float Exponentiate (float, float);
};
```

The member functions can be found in Listing 6.3. The constructor simply initializes the result variable to 0. Each of the remaining functions performs one calculation, assigns a value to result, and then returns the contents of result to the calling function. As mentioned earlier, these functions are limited to expressions that contain only two values. (It's a *very* simple calculator.)

NOTE

This program could get away without having any private variables; the way the program is currently written, the contents of the result variable aren't used. The member functions could therefore simply place the computation in their return statements, sending the result value directly back to the main function.

The main function, which controls the program's actions, appears in Listing 6.4. As you saw from the sample run of the program, the user is asked whether he or she want to perform another calculation each time the program completes one calculation. This action is controlled by the statement grouping that begins with while. The boundaries of the grouping are indicated by the braces that are opened immediately below the line containing while. Using while is one way to get a computer to repeat actions. You will learn the details of how this works in Chapter 8.

Listing 6.3   Member functions for the Calculator program

```
#include <math.h> // location of prototype for "pow" function
#include "Calculator.h"

Calculator::Calculator ()
{
    result = 0;
}

float Calculator::Add (float value1, float value2)
{
    result = value1 + value2;
    return result;
}

float Calculator::Subtract (float value1, float value2)
{
    result = value1 - value2;
    return result;
}

float Calculator::Multiply (float value1, float value2)
{
    result = value1 * value2;
    return result;
}

float Calculator::Divide (float value1, float value2)
{
    result = value1 / value2;
    return result;
}

float Calculator::Exponentiate (float value1, float value2)
{
    result = pow (value1, value2); // computes value1 to the value2 power
    return result;
}
```

Notice in Listing 6.4 that the arithmetic expression is read from the keyboard into three separate variables. The operator, stored in the variable Operator, is a character that is then used in a switch statement to choose the correct member function to call. A switch is one way to get a computer to make a choice among several alternative actions and is discussed in detail in Chapter 8.

A call to a member function places the result of the expression into a variable named answer. The program finishes by displaying the result and then asking the user whether he or she wants to perform another computation.

Listing 6.4   The main function for the Calculator program

```
#include <iostream.h>
#include "Calculator.h"

void main ()
{
    Calculator Calc; // declare a Calculator object named "Calc;

    // local variables
    char Operator; // arithmetic operator used in an expression
    char yes_no = 'Y';
    float first_value, second_value; // values used in computation
    float answer;

    while (yes_no == 'Y' || yes_no == 'y') // a way to repeat actions
    {
        cout << "\nArithmetic expression: ";
        cin >> first_value >> Operator >> second_value;

        switch (Operator) // a way to make choices
        {
            case '+':
                answer = Calc.Add (first_value, second_value);
                break;
            case '-':
                answer = Calc.Subtract (first_value, second_value);
                break;
            case '*':
                answer = Calc.Multiply (first_value, second_value);
                break;
            case '/':
                answer = Calc.Divide (first_value, second_value);
                break;
            case '^':
                answer = Calc.Exponentiate (first_value, second_value);
                break;

// Note: for the programming challenge, add code right here!

            default:
                cout << "\nUnidentified operator";
        }
        cout << "\nAnswer: " << answer << endl;
        cout << "\nAnother? ";
        cin >> yes_no;
    }
}
```

PROGRAMMING CHALLENGE NUMBER 3

Given what you now know about math library functions, you can add another capability to the Calculator program: support for modulo division, using the percent sign (%) as the operator. To add the modulo division, make the following changes:

- Modify *main.cpp* at the location noted in Listing 6.4, inserting the following statements:

```
case '%':
    answer = Calc.Mod (first_value, second_value);
    break;
```

- Add a function to the `Calculator` class in the *Calculator.h* file with the prototype:

```
float Mod (float, float);
```

- Add the member function to the *Calculator.cpp* file, which contains the other member function declarations.

Test your program to make sure it works. If the program compiles but doesn't execute properly, don't be afraid to use the debugger to help you see where problems are occurring.

Making Choices

7

One of the most common things a program does is to choose between alternative groups of actions, based on logical criteria. For example, if an employee has no overtime hours, a program could compute gross pay by multiplying the number of hours worked by the employee's hourly wage. However, if the employee did work overtime, the gross-pay computation would also need to include time-and-a-half computations for the overtime hours. This type of choice is typical of those programs make all the time.

In this chapter you will learn how to create logical expressions that a computer can evaluate. You will also learn how to place those expressions in statements that control the actions performed by a program.

Formulating Logical Expressions

A *logical expression* is an expression that produces a result of true or false. As far as C++ is concerned, the result of evaluating a false expression is 0; a true expression is represented by some integer value greater than 0, usually 1.

FORMULATING SIMPLE LOGICAL EXPRESSIONS

Logical expressions are constructed using *logical operators*. Those in Table 7.1 are used to make comparisons between two numeric values or characters. If the expression is true, the result of the expression is 1; if the expression is false, the result is 0. Notice in particular that the operator that checks to see whether two values are equal is made up of two equal signs right next to each other. This distinguishes it from the assignment operator, which is a single equal sign.

Table 7.1   Logical operators used to make comparisons

Operator	Example	Action
==	a == b	Returns 1 if a is equal to b; returns 0 if they are not equal
>	a > b	Returns 1 if a is greater than b; returns 0 if a is less than or equal to b
>=	a >= b	Returns 1 if a is greater than or equal to b; returns 0 if a is less than b
<	a < b	Returns 1 if a is less than b; returns 0 if a is greater than or equal to b
<=	a <= b	Returns 1 if a is less than or equal to b; returns 0 if a is greater than b
!=	a != b	Returns 1 if a is not equal to b; returns 0 if a is equal to b

NOTE

Because strings vary in length, you can't use the logical operators to compare them; you must use a string function. Comparing strings is discussed in Chapter 10.

As an example, assume that `value1` is initialized to 5 and that `value2` is initialized to -10. In Table 7.2 you will find the result of evaluating a variety of expressions using all of C++'s logical operators. Because `value1` and `value2` are numeric, the evaluation of the expressions are made using numerical order.

Table 7.2   Sample simple logical expressions (value1 = 5; value2 = -10)

Expression	Result
`value1 == value2`	false
`value2 == value1`	false
`value1 > value2`	true
`value2 > value1`	false
`value1 >= value2`	true
`value2 >= value1`	false
`value1 < value2`	false
`value2 < value1`	true
`value1 <= value2`	false
`value2 <= value1`	true
`value1 != value2`	true
`value2 != value1`	true

Character Considerations

If the values used in a simple logical expression are characters, evaluation appears to be based on alphabetical order. However, the computer is in fact basing its evaluation of the ASCII code values of the characters. In other words, the computer is treating the ASCII codes as if they were integers. The problem this presents is that *A* isn't equal to *a*.

Assume, for example, that you've asked a program's user to respond to a question with *y* for *yes* and *n* for *no*. If the user enters *y* but you test the response with an expression such as `yes_no == 'Y'`, the result will be false, even though the user responded *yes*.

There are two solutions to the problem. First, you could use two expressions:

```
yes_no == 'Y'
yes_no == 'y'
```

In fact, you will see how to do that in the next section. However, you can avoid the need for two expressions by converting the user's input to uppercase before you evaluate it in the logical expression. To do so, use the `toupper` function. (Its prototype appears in *ctype.h*.) For example, the following expression evaluates to true, regardless of whether the user entered *y* or *Y*:

```
toupper(yes_no) == 'Y'
```

THE UNARY NOT OPERATOR

C++'s logical operators include one unary operator: !, read *not*. When placed in front of an expression, ! inverts the result of the expression. In other words, it makes a true expression false and a false expression true. For example, if `value1` contains **0**, `!value1` is true. By the same token, if `value1` contains something greater than **0**, `!value1` is false.

FORMULATING COMPLEX LOGICAL EXPRESSIONS

A complex logical expression is formed by combining simple logical expressions using the logical operators && (AND) and || (OR). If you are combining two simple logical expressions with &&, the result will be true only if both simple expressions are true. (You will find this summarized in Table 7.3.)

Table 7.3   Logical AND truth table

&&		Expression 2	
		true	false
Expression 1	true	true	false
	false	false	false

As a first example, consider the following expression:

```
5 > 6 && 1 > 2
```

The entire expression evaluates is false because although $5 > 6$ is true, $1 > 2$ is false. By the same token, the following expression is true:

```
3 == 2+1 && 10 > 8
```

In this case, the computer performs the addition before evaluating the logical portion of the expression.

If you are combining two simple expressions with ||, the result will be true if either of the two simple expressions is true. The expression is false only if both simple expressions are false. (For a summary of ||, see Table 7.3).

Table 7.4   Logical OR truth table

||		Expression 2	
		true	false
Expression 1	true	true	true
	false	true	false

For example, the following expression is false:

```
1 > 2 || 5 > 5+1
```

But the next two expressions are true:

```
1 > 2 || 5 > 1+1
2 > 1 || 5 > 6
```

NOTE

The bit-wise AND operator (&) is easily confused with the logical AND (&&). By the same token, the bit-wise OR operator (|) is easily confused with the logical OR (||). The bit-wise operators work on one bit at a time; the logical operators combine simple logical expressions. For an example of the way in which the bit-wise operators can be used, see Formatting Stream Output at the end of Chapter 5.

PRECEDENCE

As it does with arithmetic operators, the computer applies rules of precedence to logical operators. By default, arithmetic operators have precedence over logical operators. Within the logical operators, the unary not operator has the highest precedence, followed by the inequality comparison operators (>, >=, <, <=), the equality comparison operators (== and !=), &&, and finally ||. When two operators of the same precedence appear in the same expression, evaluation proceeds from left to right.

In the following expression, for example, the computer first evaluates each of the three simple logical expressions:

```
1 > 2 && 1 > 6 || 2 < 5
```

These evaluations produce the intermediate result:

```
false && false || true
```

The next step is to evaluate the &&, which reduces the expression to:

```
false || true
```

The final part of the process is to evaluate the ||. Because one of values being joined by the || is true, the entire expression is true.

As you would expect, you can change the precedence of logical expressions by using parentheses. To see how this works, first consider the evaluation of the following expression without parentheses:

```
2 > 1 && 1 > 6 && 1 > 5 || 5 < 6
true && false && false || true
false && false || true
false || true
true
```

To evaluate this expression, the computer first evaluates the simple logical expressions and then performs the && operations from left to right. The final step is to perform the ||. As you saw, the result is true. However, look what happens if you use parentheses to change the order of evaluations:

```
(2 > 1 && 1 > 6) && (1 > 5 || 5 < 6)
(true && false) && (false || true)
(true) && (true)
false
```

In this case, the first && and the || are evaluated first, followed by the second &&. The final result is false, the opposite of what it was when the expression was evaluated using the default precedence.

Handling Not

When you include the unary not in a logical expression and mix it up with a few parentheses, the results are often not what you'd expect. Consider, for example, the following two expressions:

```
!(1 > 2 && 3 > 2)
!(false && true)
!false
true
```

```
!(1 > 2) && !(2 > 3)
!false && !true
true && false
false
```

As you can see, the placement of the ! operator produces two different results. If it is placed outside parentheses that contain the entire expression, its effect is to invert the result of the expression, after the expression has been evaluated. However, when applied to the individual components of the expression, the ! operator inverts the result of the individual expressions, before the final logical operation is performed.

Making Choices: if/else

You use logical expressions in a program to instruct the computer to choose between two or more sets of alternative actions. The most commonly used statement for making choices is if/else. In its simplest form this statement has the following general syntax:

```
if (logical expression)
    statement to execute if expression is true
```

If the logical expression is true, the program executes the statement that follows. If the logical expression is false, the program skips the statement that follows.

The statement that is to be executed if the logical expression following if is true may be a simple statement, such as:

```
if (1 < 2)
    cout << "The expression was true";
```

It may also be a complex statement, in which case the statement must be grouped by braces:

```
if (1 < 2)
{
    cout << "Even though it's a silly expression";
    cout << "it is still true and all these";
    cout << "statements will be executed.";
}
```

You can provide an alternative set of actions to an if by adding an else, using the following general syntax:

```
if (logical expression)
    statement to execute if true
else
    statement to execute if false
```

As with the simpler form of the statement, the statements that follow if and else can be either single statements or compound statements grouped by braces.

Because the statements that follow if and else can be any C++ statement, if/else statements can be nested within each other. To see how this works, we will be looking at a simple program that accepts input data from the user and then decides which of four people (if any) the data entered describes. A sample run of this program (called *Who am I?*) can be found in Figure 7.1. Notice that the program asks the person's age; whether the person likes broccoli, cats, and dogs; and whether the person owns a computer.

Figure 7.1 Output of the Who am I? program

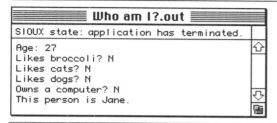

The class on which this program is based—Who—appears in Listing 7.1. There is one variable for each personal characteristic and two member functions, a constructor and a function to check a person's identity. Notice that in this class, the constructor has input parameters and that there is no separate member function to initialize an object. Although you may often not know the contents of objects created for use with static binding before a program begins, there is no reason that such objects can't load data when they are created. You will see how this is handled by both the constructor and the main function shortly.

Listing 7.1   The header file for the Who am I? program

```
class Who
{
    private:
        int id_numb, age;
        char like_broccoli, like_cats, like_dogs, own_computer;
    public:
        Who (int, int, char, char, char, char);
        int checkIdentity (int, char, char, char, char);
};
```

The member functions for the Who class can be found in Listing 7.2. The constructor accepts input data just like any other function. It takes the values that are supplied through its parameters and uses them to initialize an object's variables.

The checkIdentity function is little more than a lengthy if statement. The function compares the input data (all class variables except the ID number) and compares them to the object's stored data. If every piece of data matches, the function returns the object's ID number. (Keep in mind that because the simple logical expressions are joined with &&, every one of them must be true for the entire expression to be true.) Otherwise, the function returns a 0.

Listing 7.2   Member functions for the Who am I? program

```
#include "who.h"

Who::Who (int id, int iage, char ibroc, char icats, char idogs, char icompute)
{
     id_numb = id;
     age = iage;
     like_broccoli = ibroc;
     like_cats = icats;
     like_dogs = idogs;
     own_computer = icompute;
}

int Who::checkIdentity (int iage, char ibroc, char icats, char idogs,
                        char icompute)
{
     if (age == iage && like_broccoli == ibroc && like_cats == icats &&
         like_dogs == idogs && own_computer == icompute)
             return id_numb;
     return 0;
}
```

When looking at checkIdentity, keep in mind that a return statement not only sends data back to the calling function, but also terminates execution of the function. Therefore, there is no need for an else following the if. If the logical expression following if is true, the program returns the ID number and terminates, never reaching the second return statement. However, if the expression following if is false, the program skips the first return statement and executes the second, which sends a 0 back to the calling function. It is then up to the calling function to interpret the result as either a valid object ID or a 0.

The main function for the Who class can be found in Listing 7.3. To make the program easier to read, the object IDs are first created as constants. Then the IDs are used along with answers to the program's questions as input data in the statements that create the objects. These data are passed directly into the constructor by placing them in each object's parameter list.

After creating and initializing the objects, the program asks the user to enter data describing a person. Then it enters an if/else statement that checks the data the user entered against each object. In this statement each if after the first is the statement that follows the else of the preceding if. The order in which this nested if/else statement is processed is as follows:

Listing 7.3   The main function for the Who am I? program

```cpp
#include <iostream.h>
#include "who.h"

const JOHN = 1;
const JANE = 2;
const MIKE = 3;
const MARY = 4;

void main ()
{
    // Declare and initialize objects
    Who John (JOHN,21,'Y','Y','Y','Y');
    Who Jane (JANE,27,'N','N','N','N');
    Who Mike (MIKE,32,'Y','Y','N','N');
    Who Mary (MARY,42,'N','N','Y','Y');

    // Local variables
    int iage;
    char ibroc, icats, idogs, icompute;

    cout << "Age: ";
    cin >> iage;
    cout << "Likes broccoli? ";
    cin >> ibroc;
    cout << "Likes cats? ";
    cin >> icats;
    cout << "Likes dogs? ";
    cin >> idogs;
    cout << "Owns a computer? ";
    cin >> icompute;

    if (John.checkIdentity (iage,ibroc,icats,idogs,icompute) == JOHN)
        cout << "This person is John.";
    else if (Jane.checkIdentity (iage,ibroc,icats,idogs,icompute) == JANE)
        cout << "This person is Jane.";
    else if (Mike.checkIdentity (iage,ibroc,icats,idogs,icompute) == MIKE)
        cout << "This person is Mike.";
    else if (Mary.checkIdentity (iage,ibroc,icats,idogs,icompute) == MARY)
        cout << "This person is Mary.";
    else
        cout << "I don't know this person.";
}
```

- If the person is John, display the phrase *This person is John.* Then skip to below the last `else` (the end of the program).

- Otherwise, if the person is Jane, display the phrase *This person is Jane.* Then skip to below the last `else` (the end of the program).

- Otherwise, if the person is Mike, display the phrase *This person is Mike*. Then skip to below the last else (the end of the program).
- Otherwise, if the person is Mary, display the phrase *This person is Mary*. Then skip to below the last else (the end of the program).
- Otherwise, display the phrase *I don't know this person*. End the program.

The most important thing to notice about this order of execution is that once the computer finds a logical expression that is true, it skips the rest of the statement, dropping to the next executable statement. In this particular example there are no more executable statements, so the program simply terminates.

Making Choices: switch

There is theoretically no limit to how deep you can nest if/else statements. However, the deeper you nest them, the more difficult to understand and debug they become. If you are testing for more than two or three possible values of the same variable, you can use a switch statement to simplify the logic of the program.

A switch statement makes its choice based on the value in an integer variable. It has the following general syntax:

```
switch (integer value or expression)
{
    case value1:
        statement(s) to execute
        break;
    case value2:
    case value3:
        statement(s) to execute
        break;
    :
    :       additional cases as needed
    :
    default:
        statement(s) to execute
}
```

There are several important things to notice about this construct:

- The parentheses following the keyword `switch` must contain an integer variable or an expression that generates an integer result. If you use a character variable, it will work as well, because C++ can interpret the ASCII character code as an integer. However, floating point values and strings can't be used.
- The entire contents of the `switch` construct are surrounded by braces.
- Each value you want the `switch` to check is a constant that is preceded by `case` and followed by a colon.
- The statements that are to be executed when the computer encounters the value following `case` appear immediately after `case`. Any C++ statements are allowed.
- The last statement in a group of statements after a `case` is usually `break`, which instructs the computer to skip the rest of the `switch` and continue processing with the statement following the closing brace.
- The statements following `default` are executed only if none of the `case` values have been matched.

The computer processes a `switch` by scanning the `case` values from the top down. Processing stops when the computer finds a match. If you have more than one value that should trigger the same set of statements, you can place more than one `case` in the `switch`. In the general syntax example on the previous page, for example, *value2* and *value3* will trigger the execution of the same set of statements.

As a first example of a `switch`, let's take another look at the `switch` construct from the Calculator program you saw in Chapter 6. In Listing 7.4 you can see that the `switch` is based on the value in `Operator`, a character variable. Notice that the character constants have been placed in single quotes. Each `case` is followed by a call to the member function indicated by the character following `case`. This logic is therefore simpler to understand than a series of nested `if/else`s would be.

As a second example, in Listing 7.5 you will find the nested `if/else` statement from the Who am I? program rewritten as a `switch`. Because `switch` operates on a single integer value, there must first be some way to determine the ID number of the correct person. In this case, the program resorts to a bit of a trick. A variable for the ID number is set equal to the sum of the result of the `checkIdentity` functions for all four objects. Because the four objects are unique, no more than one of the function calls will return a value other than 0. If the data match one of the objects, the result of the addition will be that object's ID number; otherwise, the sum will be 0. This works only because an unsuccessful check of an object has been programmed to return a 0!

In this example, the constants following `case` are named constants rather than literals, as they were in the Calculator program. The computer selects the correct `case` based on the value in `id_numb` and then displays the associated message. Although

Listing 7.4   The switch statement from the Calculator program

```
switch (Operator)
        {
        case '+':
                answer = Calc.Add (first_value, second_value);
                break;
        case '-':
                answer = Calc.Subtract (first_value, second_value);
                break;
        case '*':
                answer = Calc.Multiply (first_value, second_value);
                break;
        case '/':
                answer = Calc.Divide (first_value, second_value);
                break;
        case '^':
                answer = Calc.Exponentiate (first_value, second_value);
                break;
        default:
                cout << "\nUnidentified operator";
        }
```

this is certainly easier to understand than the nested if/else statement, the ability to use a switch in this instance does rely on a programming trick.

PROGRAMMING CHALLENGE NUMBER 4

In this programming challenge you will get a chance to work with both if/else and switch statements and be able to compare their use. You will be adding characteristics and objects to the Who am I? program and using both methods to test for those characteristics .

First, add four objects to the main function and modify the program to handle them:

- Give each object a four-character name.
- Assign each object an ID number (5, 6, 7, 8) and create a constant for the number.
- Create the objects, including data for the objects that are different from the other existing objects. (Keep in mind that all you need is one unique value in each object to keep them distinct; the age will do nicely.)
- Modify the existing main function so that it tests all eight objects, expanding the if/else statements as needed.
- Run the program several times to be sure it works.

Listing 7.5   The if/else statement from the Who am I? program rewritten as a switch

```
int id_numb;

// Only one of these can be > 0. Therefore, sum either is the ID number
// of the correct person or 0, if none match.

id_numb = John.checkIdentity (iage,ibroc,icats,idogs,icompute) +
          Jane.checkIdentity (iage,ibroc,icats,idogs,icompute) +
          Mike.checkIdentity (iage,ibroc,icats,idogs,icompute) +
          Mary.checkIdentity (iage,ibroc,icats,idogs,icompute);

switch (id_numb)
{
    case JOHN:
        cout << "This person is John.";
        break;
    case JANE:
        cout << "This person is Jane.";
        break;
    case MIKE:
        cout << "This person is Mike.";
        break;
    case MARY:
        cout << "This person is Mary.";
        break;
    default:
        "I don't know this person.";
}
```

Now open the copy of the Who am I? program that is on your disk. Modify this program so that it uses a `switch` rather than the nested `if/else` statements:

- Add the four new objects as you did to the first version of the program. (Cut and paste will work well here.)

- Add the `id_numb` variable and compute its value.

- Replace the `if/else` statements with a `switch`. Use Listing 7.5 as your guide, if you like.

- Run the program several times to be sure it works.

At this point, which program is easier to understand? Which one seems to have the simpler logic? Just to be sure, try adding four more objects to each version of the program. *Now* which one is easier to understand?

Making Choices: The ?: Operator

C++ has a hybrid operator (?:, the *conditional operator*), which can be used to return one of two values based on a logical condition, in some cases eliminating the need for an if/else statement. The conditional operator is used in the following way:

```
logical expression ? true value : false value
```

The logical expression can be any logical expression. If the expression is true, the conditional operator returns the value following the question mark; if the expression is false, it returns the value following the colon.

For example, assume that you want to use the larger of two values in an arithmetic operation. You could include the following:

```
sum += (value1 > value2) ? value1 : value2;
```

The computer first evaluates the logical expression and returns either value1 or value2. That result is the value that is added to the existing value in sum to complete the arithmetic operation.

Without the conditional operator, the preceding would have required code something like this:

```
if (value1 > value2)
    sum += value1;
else
    sum += value2;
```

The use of the conditional operator has shortened the code considerably. However, because the conditional operator buries the logical expression inside an arithmetic statement, it may make the program more difficult to understand. You should therefore use this operator judiciously.

NOTE

The conditional operator is one of those features that gives rise to contests in which C and C++ programmers see who can write the most obfuscated code possible, using only one executable statement. Because you can place function calls and logical operations inside other statements, C++ logic can become very convoluted if you aren't careful.

Verifying File Operations

File operations don't always succeed. A program might, for example, attempt to open a file that doesn't exist. If it then tries to read from the nonexistent file, the program will generate a run-time error and stop running. (In other words, it will "bomb.") To avoid such problems, a program should check file operations to make sure they occur successfully.

The key to checking file operations is knowing that if a file is opened successfully, the name of the file stream contains the address in main memory where storage for that stream begins. If the file can't be opened successfully, the name of the stream contains 0. You can therefore check for a successful file opening by determining whether the stream name is zero or nonzero.

As an example, consider Listing 7.6, in which you will find a modified version of the `read` function from the Metals Prices program you saw in Chapter 5. The expression `!pricesIn` evaluates as true when the contents of `pricesIn` is 0, triggering the error message telling the user that the file doesn't exist and giving the user the choice whether to continue with the program.

Because the function gives the user the choice to end the program, the function must return something to the calling function to indicate whether the program should continue. This function therefore has been modified to return an integer, either the constant TRUE (1) or FALSE (0). The calling program must then be modified to accept a return value from the function and to act on that value:

```
file_result = prices.read();
if (!file_result)
    return;
```

When `file_result` is 0 (the `read` function returns the constant FALSE), the logical expression following `if` is true, and the `main` function terminates, ending the program.

Any time you open a file for reading or for writing, make it a habit to check for the success of the file operation. This will prevent your program from crashing in unexpected ways and annoying a user no end!

Listing 7.6   Checking for the success of file operations

```
int Metals_prices::read ()
{
    char yes_no;
    // create the input stream
    ifstream pricesIn ("prices");

    if (!pricesIn)
    {
        cout << "The prices file can't be found. Continue?"
        cin >> yes_no;
        if (toupper(yes_no) = 'N')
            return FALSE;
    }
    else
    {
        // read the data
        pricesIn >> gold >> silver >> copper;
        return TRUE;
    }
    // file is closed automatically when function terminates
}
```

Repeating Actions

8

The third thing that computers can do very well is repeat actions as many times as needed. This is commonly known as *iteration*. It is also often called *looping,* and the block of code that is a repeated, a *loop.*

Iteration makes it possible for a computer to do things such as adding a series of values or displaying a menu many times so that the user can perform many actions without quitting the program. In this chapter, you will learn how to tell a C++ program how to repeat a group of statements and how to control when the repetition ends.

The Number Fun Program

As an example of the ways in which C++ programs can perform iteration, we'll be looking at a program called Number Fun, which performs some interesting transformations on integers. You can find a sample run of the program in Figure 8.1. At this point, the program can generate a factorial, convert a number to what appears to be binary (it's really a base 10 representation of the number's binary equivalent), and compute a number's square root. (You'll get a chance to add more to this program in a programming challenge later in the chapter.)

Figure 8.1   Output from the Number Fun program

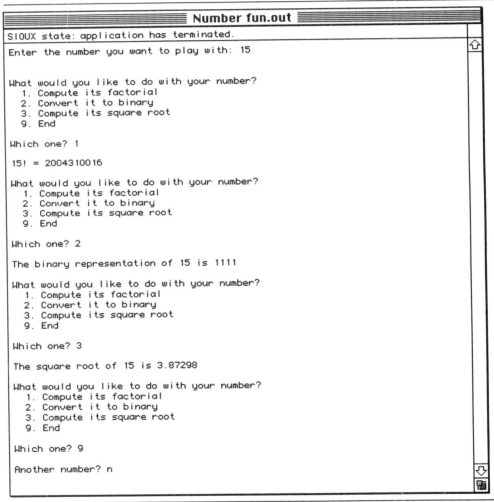

The Number Fun program is based on a class named number. As you can see in Listing 8.1, an object created from the class stores the number that the object will be manipulating. The class includes a constructor, an initialization function to store a value in the object's variable, and three functions that perform the number manipulations. As we look further into this program, you'll see that iteration plays a major role in both the member functions and the main function that drives the program.

Listing 8.1   The header file for the Number Fun program

```
class number
{
    private:
        int theNumber;
    public:
        number();
        void init (int);
        long factorial();
        long binary ();
        float root ();
};
```

Repeating Actions: while

The most general way to perform iteration is to use a while statement. Although there are other ways to repeat actions, you can write an entire program using no other type of iteration. A while has the following general syntax:

```
while (control condition)
{
    statement(s) to execute
}
```

A while instructs the computer to repeat actions as long as the condition inside the parentheses (the *control condition*) following while are true. If more than one action is to be repeated, the actions are grouped inside braces. The computer executes the statements in the body, jumping from the bottom of the loop to the top with each repeat.

When the control condition becomes false, the program skips the body of the while and continues execution with the statement below the closing brace. The control condition can be any legal logical expression, including all the operators you read about in Chapter 7.

There are three very important things to keep in mind about a while: the state of the control condition when execution begins, nesting, and avoiding infinite loops.

INITIALIZING THE CONTROL CONDITION

The test of the control condition that controls a while occurs at the top of the loop. If the condition is false the first time the computer encounters the while, the body of the loop is never executed. Consider, for example, the following:

```
while (1 > 2)
{
    cout << "This is a loop";
    cout << " that will never execute.";
    cout << " No one will see these lines.";
}
```

Because the control condition (1 > 2) is false, the three cout statements never appear on the computer screen.

In most cases, the condition that controls a while includes a variable whose value changes inside the body of the loop. This *control variable* must be initialized to produce a true statement to ensure that the loop executes at least once. This is another reason why you should always get into the practice of initializing variables.

NESTING LOOPS

The second important fact about while statements is that they can be nested, one within the other. As an example, take a look at the main function for the Number Fun program in Listing 8.2. The outer while is controlled by a character variable (yes_no). Notice that this variable is initialized to Y when it is declared, ensuring that the outer loop will execute at least once. The inner while is controlled by the choice variable. This variable gets its value from the simpleMenu function (Listing 8.3).

Notice that the inner loop is completely contained within the outer loop. When a program is compiled, the compiler matches closing braces with opening braces from the inside out. In other words, as the compiler encounters opening braces, it keeps track of them. When it encounters a closing brace, the compiler always pairs it with

Listing 8.2   The main function for the Number Fun program

```cpp
#include <iostream.h>
#include <ctype.h>
#include "numbers.h"

int simpleMenu(); // function prototype

void main ()
{
    number aNumber;
    char yes_no = 'Y';
    int funNumber, choice;

    while (toupper(yes_no) == 'Y')
    {
        cout << "Enter the number you want to play with: ";
        cin >> funNumber;

        aNumber.init (funNumber);

        // initialize the choice variable
        choice = simpleMenu();
        // use can exit without ever entering loop
        while (choice != 9)
        {
            switch (choice)
            {
                case 1:
                    cout << "\n" << funNumber << "! = " <<
                        aNumber.factorial();
                    break;
                case 2:
                    cout << "\nThe binary representation of " <<
                        funNumber << " is " << aNumber.binary();
                    break;
                case 3:
                    cout << "\nThe square root of " << funNumber <<
                        " is " << aNumber.root();
                    break;
                default:
                    cout << "Unknown option.";
            }
            // grab another value for choice to evaluate at top of loop
            choice = simpleMenu();
        }
        cout << "\nAnother number? ";
        cin >> yes_no;
    }
}
```

Listing 8.3 The menu function for the Number Fun program

```
int simpleMenu()
{
    int option;

    cout <<"\n\nWhat would you like to do with your number?" << endl;
    cout << "  1. Compute its factorial" << endl;
    cout << "  2. Convert it to binary" << endl;
    cout << "  3. Compute its square root" << endl;
    cout << "  9. End" << endl << endl;
    cout << "Which one? ";
    cin >> option;
    return option;
}
```

the last encountered opening brace. You must therefore be certain that your loops don't cross one another.

As an example of correct and incorrect nesting, take a look at Figure 8.2. The braces represent the bodies of loops. On the left side of the illustration, you'll see incorrect nesting. The writer of the program intended that the loops cross one another. However, the compiler doesn't cross the loops but instead closes them, based on the "last opened, first closed" rule. On the right side of the illustration, however, you'll see correct nesting. Each loop is completely contained within another. CodeWarrior's editor will help you with correct nesting by showing you the opening brace that is associated with a closing brace as you type each closing brace. (For details, see Chapter 3.)

The inner `while` in this program illustrates a common dilemma that occurs when control loops: When should the program call `simpleMenu` to get a value for `choice`? It is certainly possible to initialize `choice` when it is declared and to place one call to `simpleMenu` right after the inner `while`.

However, what happens when the user chooses the `End` option? If you look at the `switch` that forms the body of the inner `while`, you'll notice that there is no `case` for the `End` option. Nonetheless, if the call to `simpleMenu` is the statement immediately following `while`, the `switch` will attempt to process the `End` option and will up display the `Unrecognized command` error message. This isn't a good interface for the user; the loop should end cleanly.

The solution is a structure that is commonly used for `while` loops. The first element is to obtain a value for the control variable before the loop begins. In Listing 8.2, for example, this means that there is a call to `simpleMenu` just before the `while`. If the user doesn't pick the `End` option, the program enters the `while` with a meaningful value in `choice`. The body of the loop then contains the `switch` logic

Figure 8.2   Nesting loops

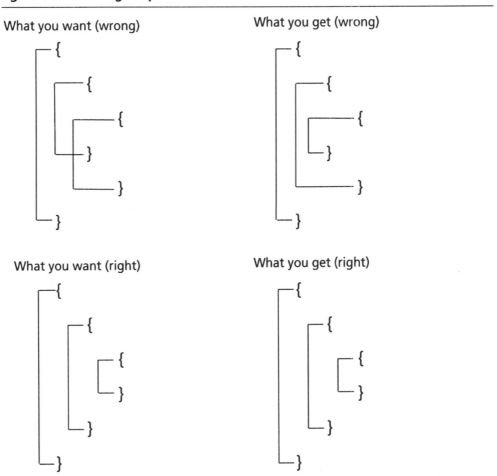

What you want (wrong)

What you get (wrong)

What you want (right)

What you get (right)

to process the user's choice and to execute the correct member function. Finally, the last action within the body of the loop is to call `simpleMenu` again, giving the `while` a new value to check at the top. Although this may appear to be an unnecessary repetition of a function call, it nonetheless provides a clean, easily understood logic and is therefore commonly used.

AVOIDING INFINITE LOOPS

An *infinite loop* is a loop that never stops. It is one of the most common reasons a program hangs (runs continually without appearing to do anything). Although, as you will discover in the next section, there are a few situations in which you purposely write an infinite loop, in most cases, infinite loops are errors.

The most common cause of an infinite loop is forgetting to change the control variable's value within the loop. For example, if there was no call to `simpleMenu` within the inner loop of the Number Fun program's inner `while`, the loop would never ask the user to choose another option. It would simply keep repeating whatever choice the user entered as a response to the call to `simpleMenu` that was made before the loop began. You must therefore be especially careful to make sure that the body of a loop contains statements that ultimately will cause the control condition to become false, stopping the loop.

There are two signs that a program has entered an infinite loop. The first is that it just sits there and does nothing. The second is that it repeats the same output, over and over again, without stopping. If you are testing the program inside the CodeWarrior environment, you can stop the program by typing ⌘-Option-Esc. This is known as a *force quit*. It will stop almost any program, including the Finder.

When you press the force quit key combination, the Macintosh operating system displays a dialog box asking you to confirm the force quit. Click the Force Quit button. You will then be able to quit the application and return to the CodeWarrior development environment.

Once you suspect that your program contains an infinite loop, the best solution is to turn to the debugger. Step through the program at the point where the problem appeared. You should then be able to see what code is being repeated. Watch the value in your control variable; also evaluate the control condition in your head each time the loop repeats. As you step through the loop, the reason the loop isn't stopping properly will become clear.

QUICK EXITS: BREAK

In the preceding section you read that there are occasionally circumstances under which you need to purposefully write an infinite loop. This arises when there are so many different conditions that should stop a loop that it isn't feasible to build them all into one control condition. In that case, you set up an infinite loop and then use the `break` statement to exit the loop. The `break` statement exits any statements that happen to be grouped with braces, including the `switch`, statement blocks following if or else, and the body of for loops, to which you will be introduced in the next section.

As an example, consider the while loop in Listing 8.4. The control value is a constant that has been declared to be 1; because it never changes, the loop is infinite. However, there are three places where the loop can exit, each depending on a different condition. Although in this relatively simple example it is possible to write the control condition as a single logical expression, such an expression would be relatively complex.

Listing 8.4   Using break to exit a while

```
while (TRUE)
{
    if (i > 0)
        break;
    else
        i--;
    if (i > MAX)
        i--;
    else
        break;
    sum += i;
    if (sum >= SUPER_MAX)
        break;
    else
        cout << "We're still going."
}
```

The drawback to using break to exit a loop is that it buries the conditions for exiting the loop inside the loop. This means that the program is more difficult to understand and debug, because the control condition isn't readily apparent. You therefore are faced with a trade-off: create a complex control condition and make it part of the while where it is easy to find, or use break to simplify the control condition but make it more difficult to find. In general, you should opt to make your control condition part of the while unless it is virtually impossible to do so.

USING A WHILE LOOP

There are many ways in which a program can use a while loop. In Listing 8.5, for example, you will find the member functions for the Number Fun program. A while loop forms the basis of the binary function, which converts a base 10 number to

Listing 8.5   Member functions for the Number Fun program

```
#include <math.h>
#include "numbers.h"

number::number()
     { theNumber = 0; }

void number::init (int iNumber)
     { theNumber = iNumber; }

long number::factorial()
{
     long result = theNumber;

     for (int i = theNumber-1; i > 1; i--)
          result *= i;
     return result;
}

long number::binary()
{
     int bit, placeValue = 1, numberTemp;
     long binaryTemp = 0;

     numberTemp = theNumber;

     while (numberTemp)
     {
          bit = numberTemp % 2; // get the remainder (a binary digit)
          numberTemp /= 2; // divide by 2
          // shove digits over and add the new digit
          binaryTemp += bit * placeValue;
          placeValue *= 10;
     }
     return binaryTemp;
}

float number::root()
     { return sqrt(theNumber); }
```

what appears to be its binary equivalent. As you study this function, keep in mind that what it is really doing is showing the user a base 10 number that *looks* like a binary number.

To convert from base 10 to base 2, you can repeatedly divide the base 10 number by 2. The remainder of each division becomes a digit in the result, working from right to left. For example, if the number you are trying to convert is 13, the math is performed as in Table 8.1. Each time a division is performed, the new binary digit is

Table 8.1   Converting from decimal to binary

Division	Quotient	Remainder	Binary number
13/2	6	1	1
6/2	3	0	01
3/2	1	1	101
1/2	0	1	1101

multiplied by a power of 10 and added to the existing number, inserting it at the left of the existing number.

If you look at the `while` loop in the `binary` function, you'll see that it uses exactly the method described in the preceding paragraph. The loop continues as long as the number being divided (`numberTemp`) is greater than 0. Each repetition performs a modulo division by 2 to obtain the binary digit, divides the number by 2, adds the binary digit to the binary number, and increases the value by which a binary digit will be multiplied during the next repetition of the loop.

NOTE

The binary function returns a long integer. However, it doesn't take a very large input number to cause even a long integer to overflow when you are converting to "binary." How do you know if you've overflowed? The result will be negative and will probably include digits other than 0 or 1.

Repeating Actions: for

In the examples of iteration you have seen to this point, the program hasn't needed to keep track of the number of times that the loop was repeated. However, in some circumstances you may want to count the iterations and use that count in the body of the loop. One way to do that is with a `while`:

```
i = 0;
while (i < MAX)
{
      process data in some way
      i++;
}
```

Alternatively, you can use a `for` statement, a type of loop that, when used appropriately, can simplify writing a loop. The `for` statement has the following general syntax:

```
for (initial index value; control condition; index change)
{
    body of loop
}
```

The parentheses following `for` contain three expressions. The first initializes an index value. For example, if you are counting the number of times the loop repeats, you might initialize the index variable to 0, using something like `i = 0`. The second expression is a control condition; the loop continues as long as the condition is true. If you want the loop to repeat five times and the index variable is initialized to 0, the control condition would be `i < 5`.

The third expression tells the computer how to change the value of the index variable. In the example we've been using, the change is an increment and is written `i++`. The complete `for` statement is therefore written as:

```
for (i = 0; i < 5; i++)
{
    body of loop
}
```

NOTE

Index variables are just about the only variables to which programmers commonly give single-letter names. By convention, index variables are named alphabetically, beginning with i, j, and k.

Although you can't use a `for` for every loop, it can sometimes come in very handy. As an example, consider again the member functions for the Number Fun program in Listing 8.5. In particular, look at the `factorial` function. The formula for the factorial of a number `n` is:

```
n * n-1 * n-2 ... n * 2
```

Five factorial (written 5!), for example, is:

```
5 * 4 * 3 * 2 = 80
```

Because the formula requires a sequence of multiplications, starting at some known value, and multiplying by values that decrease at a known interval, the factorial is an ideal use for a `for` statement:

```
long result = theNumber;
for (int i = theNumber-1; i > 1; i--)
      result *= i;
```

In this case, the `result` variable is initialized to the value in the object' only variable. The `for` loop can then begin the multiplication with one less than the value in that variable. The loop's index variable is therefore initialized to `theNumber - 1`.

Notice in this example that the index variable is declared within the `for` statement by placing `int` as the variable's data type within the parentheses, just before the index variable is used for the first time. Should you choose to do this, be sure to declare the index variable only once in the program. If you need the same variable for a loop later in the program, don't declare it again.

This loop continues as long as the index variable is greater than 1. To be completely accurate, the formula for computing a factorial includes multiplying by 1. However, since multiplying by 1 has no impact on the result of the computation, there is no reason to perform the multiplication. The loop can therefore be written to stop when `i` is equal to 1.

Each time the loop repeats, it should decrease the value of the index variable by 1. The change to the index variable is therefore a decrement, written `i--`.

The loop to compute the factorial could also have been written to compute from low values to high:

```
long result = 2;
for (int i = 3; i <= theNumber; i++)
      result *= i;
```

In this case, the first multiplication is 2 * 3. If the user is requesting 2!, then the loop never executes, because the index value's initial value is greater than the contents of `theNumber`. The result is nonetheless correct, because 2! is 2.

Programming Challenge Number 5

For this programming challenge you will modify the Number Fun program so that it can display successive powers of the number being manipulated. For example, if the user wanted to play with the number 3 and asked for six powers, the output might appear as in Figure 8.3.

Figure 8.3   Sample output for powers of a number

```
3 to the 0 power = 1
3 to the 1 power = 3
3 to the 2 power = 9
3 to the 3 power = 27
3 to the 4 power = 81
3 to the 5 power = 243
```

To add the ability to raise a number to a power, do the following:

- Add a member function to the `number` class to raise `theNumber` to a power. Send the power into the function as an input parameter. Return the `theNumber` raised to the power. (Hint: You'll be able to handle larger numbers if the return value is a `long` rather than an `int`.)
- Add a menu option for raising a number to a power to the `simpleMenu` function.
- Create a program function (not a member function) named `Exponents` that will handle raising the number to a power. This function is necessary because the member function returns only one value at a time; you will need to call the member function several times (once for each power the user requests). The `Exponents` function should have the following prototype:

```
void Exponents (number);
```

The single input parameter is an object of class `number`. The function header should therefore appear as:

```
void Exponents (number someNumber)
```

Use someNumber as the name of the object inside the Exponents function.
- Write the body of the Exponents function. Ask the user how many powers he or she wants to see. Then write a for loop that calls the new member function and prints out the result returned by the member function call. Use the for loop's index variable as the input parameter to the member function. (Hint: If you want to start producing powers at 0, as was done in Figure 8.3, don't forget to stop the for loop at one less than the number of powers entered by the user.)
- Add a case to the switch in main.cpp to call Exponents.

Be sure to test your modified program to be certain that it works. As you test the program, keep a sharp eye out for overflow of storage locations. Remember that when an integer storage location overflows, its value becomes negative.

Arrays

9

One of the biggest programming limitations you have encountered so far is that when you create more than one object from the same class, each needs to have a different name. If you think back to the Who am I? program, you'll realize that this created at least two problems. First, when the program needed to call the same member function for each object, it required four different expressions to do so, one for each object name. Second, adding more objects to the program was clumsy. Each would have to have its own name, requiring even more distinct expressions for calling member functions.

The solution is to find some way to handle multiple objects from the same class as parts of a group. Groups of objects or data values stored under the same name are known as *arrays*. All objects or data values in an array are of the same type.

You have already been introduced to one type of array: a string, which is an array of characters. In this chapter you will be introduced to arrays of data values and arrays of objects. Because strings are handled somewhat differently from other arrays, we will leave them until Chapter 10.

Declaring Arrays

An array is a special type of variable that is declared much like a simple variable. However, you must tell the compiler how many values you want the array to hold. In general, an array is declared in the following manner:

data_type array_name [*number of values*];

Notice that the number of values the array is to hold is placed in brackets following the name of the array. As examples, consider these arrays:

```
int integerArray[10];
long longArray[25];
float floatArray[15];
```

The `integerArray` sets aside space for 10 integers. By the same token, `longArray` can hold 25 long integers, and `floatArray` can hold 15 floating point values. Each of the values in an array is known as an *array element,* or an *element of an array.*

Arrays can also hold objects. For example, when modifying the Who am I? program to handle many objects of class `Who`, the program could use the following declaration:

```
Who people[25];
```

The program can now handle up to 25 people.

When you declare an array variable, the compiler sets aside enough storage in main memory to hold the entire contents of the array. This brings up two important points. First, space is allocated for an entire array, regardless of whether you fill that space with data. Arrays that are too large waste main memory. However, if an array is too small, the only solution is to modify the array declaration and recompile the program.

The second major issue in declaring arrays is that the computer doesn't check to make sure that you aren't trying to store more values in the array than the array was declared to hold. If, for example, you've declared an array to hold 25 values and use a program to store a 26th, the computer won't stop you from doing so. In fact, the computer will store the value without a murmur. The effect, however, can be disastrous.

To see what can happen, take a look at Figure 9.1. The top portion of the illustration represents a section of a computer's memory that has been set aside to hold two arrays. The first array has space for nine integers, the second for six characters. Everything is fine until the program places a 10th value into the integer array. As you can see, the extra value overwrites the first value in the character array, in effect changing the value in that array. You must therefore write your programs so that they check to be sure that you don't overflow arrays.

Figure 9.1   The effect of overflowing array storage

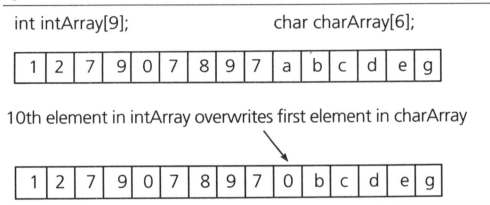

NOTE

Because overflowing an array usually means that the value in some other variable changes, the primary indication that you've overflowed is mysterious changes in the contents of unrelated variables. The best way to catch this sort of problem is to use the debugger to watch the changes in variable contents as you step through the program. If a statement that modifies an array causes a change in another variable, then you've probably identified an array overflow situation.

Referencing Array Values

Each value in an array is referenced by its position in the array, which is often called an *array index*. For example, suppose that an array is declared as follows:

```
int numbers[10];
```

In that case, the individual values in the array are as follows:

```
numbers[0]
numbers[1]
numbers[2]
numbers[3]
numbers[4]
numbers[5]
numbers[6]
numbers[7]
numbers[8]
numbers[9]
```

Each of these represents an individual variable. As you can see, although the array has been declared to hold 10 values, the values are numbered from 0 to 9. All C++ arrays begin counting places in the array with 0.

Assigning Values to Arrays

The name of an array represents the beginning address in main memory of a group of storage locations, not the addresses of the individual storage locations that are part of the group. For that reason, you can't simply assign values to the name of an array; you must assign them to the individual variables that are part of the array.

Assume, for example, that you want to initialize each member of the numbers array that you saw in the preceding section of this chapter. You could do so with the following code:

```
for (int i = 0; i < 10; i++)
    numbers[i] = 0;
```

The index variable of the for loop also serves as an index to the array. As the for loop's index is incremented, the assignment statement affects a different member of the array.

Be very careful *not* to assign a value to the name of an array. As mentioned earlier, the name of an array contains the address in main memory of the beginning of the array's storage location. Suppose that you do something like

```
numbers = 0;
```

You'd be telling the compiler to look for the contents of the array at main memory address 0. This can be very dangerous. If you later attempt to store something in the array, you run a significant risk of overwriting parts of the operating system or other programs that happen to be running at the same time. The result will be a system crash from which you can't recover without restarting the computer.

Using One-Dimensional Arrays

The arrays that you have seen to this point are *one-dimensional*, in that they are a single list of values. The easiest way to visualize such an array is to think of it as a list whose contents are numbered beginning with 0. When you want to access a member of the list, you reference it by its position in the list. Such lists can be made up of numbers or characters. In this section you will therefore see examples of how both types of arrays are used. In addition, you will see how you can manipulate multiple objects of the same class using an array of objects.

PASSING DATA FOR AN ARRAY INTO A FUNCTION

As a first example of using an array, let's look at a program that collects the high temperatures on seven successive days and then returns the average weekly temperature (see Figure 9.2). The program is based on the class `temps`, whose header file you can find in Listing 9.1. In this case, the array to hold the seven temperatures is a class variable. The class also keeps track of the last used array position in the `lastUsed` variable.

Notice that this header file defines a constant to use for the size of the array. This is a good habit to get into. If you need to change the size of the array, all you need to do is look at the top of the header file for the constant's definition. You won't need to search through program files to look for every place the program references the maximum size of the array.

Figure 9.2   Output of the Temperatures program

```
========== Temperatures.out ==========
SIOUX state: application has terminated.

High temperature #1: 45                        ⬆
High temperature #2: 52
High temperature #3: 31
High temperature #4: 47
High temperature #5: 45
High temperature #6: 35
High temperature #7: 39

The average weekly high temperature was 42     ⬇
                                               ▣
```

Listing 9.1   The header file for the Temperatures program

```
const NUM_TEMPS = 7;

class temps
{
    private:
        int dailyTemps[NUM_TEMPS];
        int lastUsed;
    public:
        temps ();
        void init (int);
        int average (); // average the weekly temps
};
```

The `temps` class has three member functions. As you can see in Listing 9.2, the constructor uses a `for` loop to initialize each position in the array to 0. It also initializes the `lastUsed` variable, which keeps track of the last used array index, to -1.

Why -1 instead of 0? To answer that, take a look at the `init` member function. This function accepts one temperature from the calling function and inserts it into the array. However, before the assignment is performed, `lastUsed` is incremented. For example, when the first temperature is stored in the array, `lastUsed` is incremented from -1 to 0, which correctly places the first value in the first position in the array. The `lastUsed` variable also correctly contains the index of the last used array position. You could certainly start `lastUsed` at 0 and increment it *after* a value is stored, but in that case the variable's value would be the next position to be filled rather than the last position used.

Listing 9.2   Member functions for the Temperatures program

```
#include "temps.h"

temps::temps()
{
    for (int i = 0; i < NUM_TEMPS; i++)
        dailyTemps[i] = 0;
    lastUsed = -1; // begins at -1 because of preincrement in init function
}

void temps::init (int temp)
{
    dailyTemps[++lastUsed] = temp;
}

int temps::average ()
{
    int sum = 0;

    for (int i = 0; i < NUM_TEMPS; i++)
        sum += dailyTemps[i];
    return sum / NUM_TEMPS;
}
```

NOTE

Does the preceding seem like a silly exercise in semantics? It's not. You always want to make a program as clear as possible. If you come back to a program after having let it sit for even a few days, you will find it difficult to follow your own logic. This happens to even the most experienced programmers. Anything you can do to make the program self-documenting, including using clear, meaningful variable names and writing useful comment statements, will help make the task of understanding what you've done much easier.

The `average` member function sums each of the values in the array and then returns the average by dividing the sum by the total number of temperatures. Notice that the program uses a `for` loop to compute the sum, adding each element in the array individually. (It helps to remember that although all the elements in an array have the same name, they are really a group of individual variables into which values must be stored one at a time and from which values must be retrieved one at a time.)

The `main` function, which controls the Temperatures program, can be found in Listing 9.3. The function first collects seven temperatures from the user with a `for` loop. Each time the user enters a temperature, the program calls the `init` member function to store the new temperature in the next position in the array. Because the

Listing 9.3   The main function for the Temperatures program

```
#include <iostream.h>
#include "temps.h"

void main ()
{
    temps Weekly; // declare an object
    int temp, stop;

    for (int i = 0; i < NUM_TEMPS; i++)
    {
        cout << "High temperature #" << i+1 << ": ";
        cin >> temp;
        Weekly.init(temp);
    }

    cout << "\nThe average weekly high temperature was " << Weekly.average();
}
```

Weekly **object is keeping track of how many temperatures have been entered at any given time, the** main **function doesn't have to. By the same token, the** main **function avoids overflowing the object's array by using a** for **loop that is stopped by the** NUM_TEMPS **constants.**

Once the array is filled, the main function can call the average function. In this case, because the average is only for display purposes, there's no reason not to embed the function call right in the cout statement. Storing the average would only take extra time and main memory.

PASSING ARRAYS TO FUNCTIONS

In the preceding example the main function collected data for an object's array one value at a time. However, doing so isn't always feasible. Occasionally you may need to fill an array in one function and pass the entire array to another function for processing. The program we'll be using as an example in this section—a program that scores responses to a series of questions to determine how much a person likes chocolate (see Figure 9.3)—works in exactly that manner. It collects an entire array of data and then sends the entire array to an object's member function.

The array in this case is an array of characters because the answers to the questions posed by the program are either *y* for "yes" or *n* for "no." As you can see in Listing 9.4, the class—quiz—contains just one variable, the character array (answers).

Figure 9.3   Output of the Chocoholics program

```
┌══════════════════ Chocoholics.out ══════════════════┐
│ SIOUX state: application has terminated.            │⇧│
│                                                     │ │
│ Do you spend more than 10% of your grocery money on chocolate? y │
│ When you go to the grocery store, do you head for the candy aisle first? y │
│ Do you eat more than 7 chocolate bars a week? y    │ │
│ Do you eat more than 14 chocolate bars a week? y   │ │
│ Do you eat more than 21 chocolate bars a week? n   │ │
│ Do you eat more than 28 chocolate bars a week? n   │ │
│ Do you think that white chocolate isn't really chocolate? n │
│ Do thing that cherry filling pollutes chocolate? y │ │
│ Do you think that peanut butter pollutes chocolate? y │
│ Do you think that the only good nuts in a chocolate bar are no nuts? y │
│                                                     │⇩│
│ You're definitely a chocolate lover.                │▣│
│                                                     │ │
└─────────────────────────────────────────────────────┘
```

Listing 9.4   Header file for the Chocoholics program

```
const NUM_QUEST = 10;

class quiz
{
    private:
        char answers[NUM_QUEST];
    public:
        quiz();
        void init (char []); // pass in entire array
        int score (); // score the quiz
};
```

The quiz class has three member functions. The constructor (see Listing 9.5) uses a for loop to place a blank (two single quotes with a space between them) in each array element. This is the same process used by the constructor for the Temperatures program. However, the init function for the Chocoholics program is different from the Temperatures program because it expects an entire array of values rather than a single value as an input parameter.

When you are specifying an array as a function parameter in a function prototype, you need to tell the compiler that the parameter is indeed an array. To do so, use the following general syntax:

array_data_type []

Listing 9.5   Member functions for the Chocoholics program

```
#include <ctype.h>
#include "chocoholics.h"

quiz::quiz()
{
    for (int i = 0; i < NUM_QUEST; i++)
        answers[i] = ' '; // blank for each character
}

void quiz::init (char newAnswers[])
{
    for (int i = 0; i < NUM_QUEST; i++)
        answers[i] = toupper(newAnswers[i]);
}

int quiz::score ()
{
    int total_yes = 0;

    for (int i = 0; i < NUM_QUEST; i++)
        if (answers[i] == 'Y')
            total_yes++;
    return total_yes;
}
```

Notice that all you need to do is include the type of data that will be included in the array, along with opening and closing brackets ([ ]).

When you write the function declaration, you include the name by which the array will be called within the function, as in:

```
char newAnswers[]
```

It isn't necessary to include the number of elements in the array. This is because the computer automatically determines the number of elements in the parameter from the size of the array that is passed into the function when the function is called.

To pass an array into a function, you simply place the name of the array in the function call. For example, in Listing 9.6, the main function for the Chocoholics program, one call to the init member function is placed with:

```
oneQuiz.init (newAnswers);
```

Listing 9.6   The main function for the Chocoholics program

```
#include <iostream.h>
#include "chocoholics.h"

void main ()
{
    quiz oneQuiz; // declare an object
    char newAnswers[NUM_QUEST];
    int index = 0, result;

    cout << "Do you spend more than 10% of your grocery money on chocolate? ";
    cin >> newAnswers[index++];
    cout << "When you go to the grocery store, do you head for the candy aisle first? ";
    cin >> newAnswers[index++];
    cout << "Do you eat more than 7 chocolate bars a week? ";
    cin >> newAnswers[index++];
    cout << "Do you eat more than 14 chocolate bars a week? ";
    cin >> newAnswers[index++];
    cout << "Do you eat more than 21 chocolate bars a week? ";
    cin >> newAnswers[index++];
    cout << "Do you eat more than 28 chocolate bars a week? ";
    cin >> newAnswers[index++];
    cout << "Do you think that white chocolate isn't really chocolate? ";
    cin >> newAnswers[index++];
    cout << "Do thing that cherry filling pollutes chocolate? ";
    cin >> newAnswers[index++];
    cout << "Do you think that peanut butter pollutes chocolate? ";
    cin >> newAnswers[index++];
    cout << "Do you think that the only good nuts in a chocolate bar are no nuts? ";
    cin >> newAnswers[index];

    oneQuiz.init (newAnswers);
    result = oneQuiz.score();
    switch (result)
    {
        case 0: case 1:
            cout << "\nYou couldn't care less about chocolate.";
            break;
        case 2: case 3: case 4:
            cout << "\nYou like chocolate, but you're not a fanatic.";
            break;
        case 5: case 6: case 7:
            cout << "\nYou're definitely a chocolate lover.";
            break;
        case 8: case 9: case 10:
            cout << "\nYou're a certified chocoholic!";
            break;
        default:
            cout << "\nError in scoring routine.";
    }
}
```

Notice that no array indexes are included in the call; only the name of the array appears. What you are doing when you pass an array in this way is passing the address of the array's starting location in main memory. Arrays are therefore always passed by reference. This way of passing parameters to functions is very different from all the other parameter passing you have seen to this point.

When you use the name of a simple variable, such as an `int` or `char`, to send a parameter to a function, the computer makes a copy of the contents of the variable and gives that copy to the function to manipulate. Because the function is working on a copy, any modifications made to that copy don't affect the original variable in main memory. This is the pass by value that you have been using to this point.

However, when you send a function the address of a variable rather than the variable's contents, you allow the function to modify main memory directly and thus make it possible for the function to modify the original copy of the parameter. This is a pass by reference. Because the name of an array is the address of the array's storage location, the only way to send an array to a function is by reference.

To make this a bit clearer, assume that you are working with a 10-element integer array named `values`. If you pass `values` to a function as a parameter, you are passing the starting address of the array in main memory, making the entire array available for direct modification by the function into which it is passed.

If you pass `values[0]` or `values[4]`, however, you are passing individual variables that are part of the array. Passing a specific array element, therefore, is a pass by value, just like passing any other type of simple variable.

NOTE

When you pass work with the names of arrays, you are working with pointers. The term "pointer" is simply another word for a main memory address. The idea is that a pointer "points to" some location in memory. You will learn a great deal more about using pointers in Chapter 11.

The Chocoholics program's third member function—`score`—evaluates the contents of a `quiz` object's array. Like the Temperatures program, it checks each element in the array individually, incrementing the counter each time it finds a Y. The number of positive results is returned to the `main` function, which then uses a `switch` to determine how the results are to be reported back to the user.

NOTE

If the switch statement in Listing 9.6 looks a bit odd, keep in mind that the case statements can check only for equality with some value. If you want to match more than one value with a given set of actions, you must have one case for each value; you can't use such operators as < or >. A C++ compiler doesn't care how you position source code in *a text file. The case statements don't need to be on separate lines. In Listing 9.6 several were put on the same line simply to save space, just so the entire listing would fit on one page!*

ARRAYS OF OBJECTS

One of the problems that faces any object-oriented program is the need to find a method for organizing multiple objects declared from the same class. There are many techniques for doing so, including using an array of objects. In this section you will be introduced to one way of handling arrays of objects. As an example, we will be looking at a version of the Chocoholics program (Chocoholics 2 on the disk that came with this book) that has been modified to process more than one survey at a time.

All the modifications to the Chocoholics program have been made in the `main` function (Listing 9.7). Notice first that the declaration for an object now looks like an array declaration:

```
quiz oneQuiz[NUM_SURVEYS];
```

The `oneQuiz` array has `NUM_SURVEYS` elements, each of which is an object created from class `quiz`, each of which has an array as a variable.

Like elements in any other array, the elements in an array of objects are referenced using their position in the array. Therefore, `oneQuiz[0]` is the first object of class `quiz`, and `oneQuiz[NUM_SURVEYS-1]` is the last object. (Remember that the constant `NUM_SURVEYS` refers to the total number of elements in the array, but because we start numbering the elements with 0, the index of the last element is always one less than the total number of elements.)

When you reference an object in an array of objects, you must always use the object's array index. For example, when the revised Chocoholics program is ready to send an array full of answers to an object, it uses:

```
oneQuiz[count++].init (newAnswers);
```

where `count` is the array index. Keep in mind that the `++` following `count` is performed *after* the function call is complete (because it's a postincrement).

There is an important programming logic issue of which you should be aware when looking at Listing 9.7: the difference in the use of the index variables for the two arrays managed by this function. One array is the array of objects (`oneQuiz`);

Listing 9.7   The Chocoholics main function handling an array of objects

```
const NUM_SURVEYS = 10;

void main ()
{
     quiz oneQuiz[NUM_SURVEYS]; // declare an array of objects
     char newAnswers[NUM_QUEST];
     char yes_no = 'Y'; // variable to stop while loop
     int index, result;
     int count = 0; // keeps track of the number of surveys entered

     while (toupper(yes_no) == 'Y')
     {
     index = 0; // must reset answer array index for each new survey
     cout << "\nSurvey #" << count+1 << ":" << endl << endl;
     cout << "Do you spend more than 10% of your grocery money on chocolate? ";
     cin >> newAnswers[index++];
     cout << "When you go to the grocery store, do you head for the candy aisle first? ";
     cin >> newAnswers[index++];
     cout << "Do you eat more than 7 chocolate bars a week? ";
     cin >> newAnswers[index++];
     cout << "Do you eat more than 14 chocolate bars a week? ";
     cin >> newAnswers[index++];
     cout << "Do you eat more than 21 chocolate bars a week? ";
     cin >> newAnswers[index++];
     cout << "Do you eat more than 28 chocolate bars a week? ";
     cin >> newAnswers[index++];
     cout << "Do you think that white chocolate isn't really chocolate? ";
     cin >> newAnswers[index++];
     cout << "Do thing that cherry filling pollutes chocolate? ";
     cin >> newAnswers[index++];
     cout << "Do you think that peanut butter pollutes chocolate? ";
     cin >> newAnswers[index++];
     cout << "Do you think that the only good nuts in a chocolate bar are no nuts? ";
     cin >> newAnswers[index];

         oneQuiz[count++].init (newAnswers); // identify object using array index

         if (count < NUM_SURVEYS)
         {
             cout << "\nAnother survey? ";
             cin >> yes_no;
         }
         else
         {
             cout << "\nThe survey array is full. All surveys will be scored." << endl;
             yes_no = 'N'; // do this to stop the while loop
         }
     }
```

Continued next page

Listing 9.7 (Continued)   The Chocoholics main function handling an array of objects

```
for (int i = 0; i < count; i++)
    {
         result = oneQuiz[i].score(); // reference individual object by array index

         cout << "\nPerson #" << i+1 << " ";
         switch (result)
         {
             case 0:
             case 1:
                 cout << "couldn't care less about chocolate.";
                 break;
             case 2:
             case 3:
             case 4:
                 cout << "likes chocolate, but isn't a fanatic.";
                 break;
             case 5:
             case 6:
             case 7:
                 cout << "is definitely a chocolate lover.";
                 break;
             case 8:
             case 9:
             case 10:
                 cout << "is a certified chocoholic!";
                 break;
             default:
                 cout << "\nError in scoring routine.";
         }
    }
}
```

the other is the array used to collect the answers for a single survey (newAnswers). The variable count keeps track of how many surveys the user enters. It is initialized to 0 at the beginning of the program and is never reinitialized. This is correct because the for loop that scores the survey data needs to know exactly how many were entered so that it doesn't attempt to process objects for which there are no data.

However, the variable index keeps track of the answers for a single survey and must be reset to 0 for each new survey. If it isn't, the second survey will attempt to fill the newAnswers array beginning in position 10, one beyond the maximum size of the array; the third survey would begin at position 20, and so on. The result would be mangled memory and inaccessible data!

In this program, the newAnswers array is reloaded with data, from the beginning, for each object that is part of the oneQuiz array. You must therefore reset its index for each reuse. The `oneQuiz` array is also used twice. However, it is loaded with data only once. The second use scores existing data; it doesn't replace that data (as do the repeated uses of `newAnswers`). Therefore, the `count` variable must remain intact so that the remainder of the program knows how many objects in `oneQuiz` have been loaded with data. When the program needs to process the contents of `oneQuiz`, it uses a different index variable (the `i` in the `for` loop) that can be initialized to 0 and run until it reaches `count`.

Using Two-Dimensional Arrays

Arrays are not limited to a single dimension. Programs occasionally use arrays that can be thought of as a grid. These *two-dimensional* arrays are made up of columns and rows. When you declare such an array, you must specify both the number of columns and the number of rows:

```
data_type array_name [# rows][# columns];
```

For example, the following declares an array with five rows and four columns:

```
int integerGrid[5][4];
```

The array will hold 20 integers, each of which is referenced by giving the two numbers that identify its cell in the grid. As far as the programmer is concerned, the array indexes do define a grid (see Figure 9.4). However, when the array is stored in main memory, the array elements are stored linearly, row by row.

NOTE
There is theoretically no limit to the number of dimensions you can give an array. For example, a three-dimensional array might be visualized as a cube. However, when you get beyond two dimensions, arrays are very difficult to conceptualize. In practice, arrays of more than two dimensions are rarely used.

As an example of some of the special issues that arise when you are working with two-dimensional arrays, let's look at a program that can be used to score a multiple-

Figure 9.4   Viewing and storing a two-dimensional array

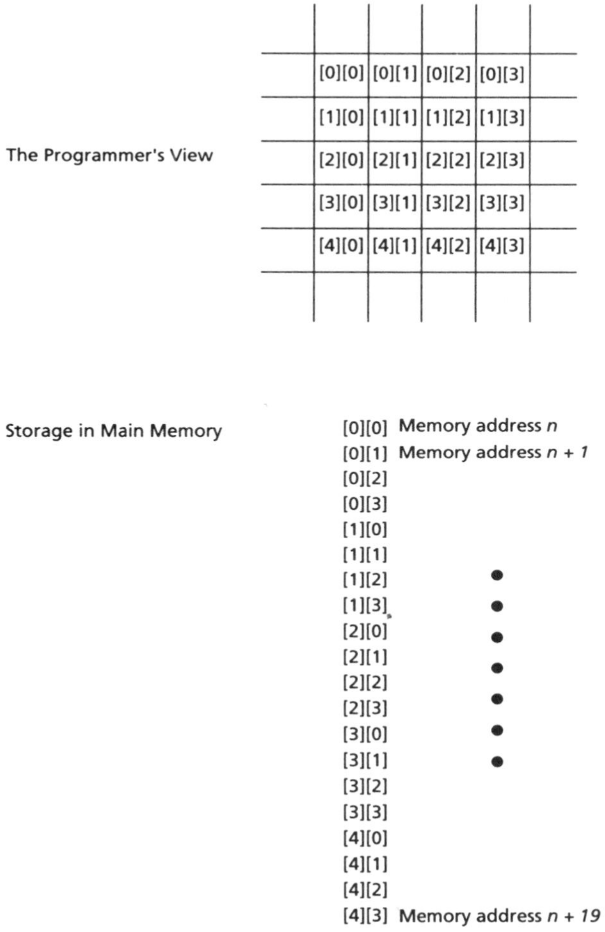

The Programmer's View

[0][0]	[0][1]	[0][2]	[0][3]
[1][0]	[1][1]	[1][2]	[1][3]
[2][0]	[2][1]	[2][2]	[2][3]
[3][0]	[3][1]	[3][2]	[3][3]
[4][0]	[4][1]	[4][2]	[4][3]

Storage in Main Memory

[0][0] Memory address n
[0][1] Memory address $n + 1$
[0][2]
[0][3]
[1][0]
[1][1]
[1][2]   •
[1][3]   •
[2][0]   •
[2][1]   •
[2][2]   •
[2][3]   •
[3][0]   •
[3][1]   •
[3][2]
[3][3]
[4][0]
[4][1]
[4][2]
[4][3] Memory address $n + 19$

choice exam that permits the student to choose more than one answer for each question. The Exam class, which forms the foundation for the program, can be found in Listing 9.8. Notice first that the class has just one variable, an array to hold a student's answers to an exam. Each row in the array represents a separate question; a student's answers to a question are stored in the columns across each row. The number of questions in the exam and the maximum number of possible answers for a

Listing 9.8   Header file for the Exam Scoring program

```
const MAX_ANS = 3;
const MAX_QUEST = 10;

class Exam
{
    private:
        char answers[MAX_QUEST][MAX_ANS];
    public:
        Exam();
        void init (char [][MAX_ANS]); // pass in student's asnwers
        int score (char [][MAX_ANS]); // pass in the key
};
```

question have been declared as named constants. This makes it easy to change the program by simply changing the constants. This is particularly important for this program, in which, as you will see, the dimensions of the array are used repeatedly.

The Exam Scoring program has three member functions, which can all be found in Listing 9.9. The constructor uses nested for loops to initialize each element in the answers array to an *x*. Although it may make more sense to initialize an array to blanks, keep in mind that cin won't accept a blank as a legal input character. Therefore, the program won't be able to use a blank as a placeholder for an answer a student left empty. The program arbitrarily uses *x* as that placeholder because it represents a character that won't be used as a legal answer; no multiple-choice exam that a teacher would write would ever have that many possible answers for one question.

The remaining two member functions both have two-dimensional arrays as input parameters. As you can see in Listing 9.8 and Listing 9.9, the way in which the prototype is written and the way in which the function header is written are different from when you use a one-dimensional array as a parameter.

FUNCTIONS AND TWO-DIMENSIONAL ARRAYS

When you pass a one-dimensional array to a function, the computer needs to know only the data type of the array to figure out where one element ends and another begins. For example, if the array is of type int, the computer knows that each element takes up 16 bits. However, when you are dealing with a two-dimensional array, the computer needs to know not only where one element ends and another begins, but also where each row ends and another begins. For this reason, you must specify

Listing 9.9   Member functions for the Exam Scoring program

```
#include "exam.h"

Exam::Exam()
{
    for (int i = 0; i < MAX_QUEST; i++)
        for (int j = 0; j < MAX_ANS; j++)
            answers[i][j] = 'x'; // initialize each cell to the placeholder
x
}

void Exam::init (char student[][MAX_ANS])
{
    for (int i = 0; i < MAX_QUEST; i++)
        for (int j = 0; j < MAX_ANS; j++)
            answers[i][j] = student[i][j]; // copy from input array
}

int Exam::score (char key[][MAX_ANS])
{
    int numb_right = 0;

// The logic here is a bit tricky, because we can't be sure that
// the student's three answers are in the same order as the
// key's three answers. Therefore, we have to check each student
// answer against all three answers in the key for each question.

    for (int i = 0; i < MAX_QUEST; i++)
        for (int j = 0; j < MAX_ANS; j++)
            for (int k = 0; k < MAX_ANS; k++)
                if (answers[i][j] != 'x' && answers[i][j] == key[i][k])
                    numb_right++;
    return numb_right;
}
```

the number of columns in a two-dimensional array when it is used as a function parameter; you can continue to let the computer figure out the number of rows.

A two-dimensional array that is used as a function prototype is therefore written in the following way:

```
data_type [][number of columns]
```

For the Exam Scoring program, the arrays used for input to member functions appear in the function prototypes as follows:

```
char [][MAX_ANS]
```

By the same token, the function headers must also include the number of columns in the array, although the number of rows can continue to be left out:

```
init (char student[][MAX_ANS])
score (char key[][MAX_ANS])
```

PROCESSING TWO-DIMENSIONAL ARRAYS

Processing every element in a two-dimensional array requires nested loops (usually for loops). As a first example, look at the Exam class's constructor in Listing 9.9. The outer for loop (index variable i) controls movement from one row to the next; the inner for loop (index variable j) controls movement from one column to the next. As you study this function, keep in mind that the inner for loop is completed first. It is repeated once for each repetition of the outer for loop. This means that in this particular program the inner loop is executed 10 times and that the outer loop is executed only once.

The same logic appears in the init function. The major difference is that instead of assigning a constant to each element in the answers array, a value is copied from the student array (the function's input parameter).

The logic in the score function, however, is a bit tricky. The function's input parameter is an array that holds the correct answers to the exam. However, there is no way to be certain that the student recorded his or her answers for a given question in the same order that the answers for that question appear in the key. For example, assume that *a*, *d*, and *e* are correct responses for question 2 (stored in row 1 in the array, because array elements are numbered beginning with 0). The key array contains key[1][0] = 'a', key[1][1] = 'd', and key[1][2] = 'f'. The student, however, recorded the answers in a different order, and therefore the answer array contains answer[1][0] = 'd', answer[1][1] = 'f', answer[1][2] = 'a'.

If the score function attempted to score the exam by looking only at matching array elements between the two arrays, this student would score a 0 for question 2— even though the student has identified all three responses correctly—because no two of the array elements are equivalent. The score function therefore compares each possible answer to a given question to each response the student made for that question. In the example we have been considering, this means that key[1][0], key[1][1], and key[1][2] are all compared to answer[1][0]; key[1][0], key[1][1], and key[1][2] are compared to answer[1][1]; and key[1][0], `key[1][1]`, and `key[1][2]` are compared to `answer[1][2]`. To do this the `score` function uses a third `for` loop (index variable k) that cycles through the columns of a given row of the `key` array for each element in the `answers` array.

The `main` function, which uses the an object created from the `Exam` class, can be found in Listing 9.10. As you can see, the program first gathers data for the exam key, using nested `for` loops to fill the array elements in order. All student exams evaluated during the program run will be evaluated against this key.

The program then enters a `while` loop that lets the user key in the responses made by one student, again using nested `for` loops to access every element in the array. Once all responses have been entered, the program calls the `init` member function to transfer those responses to the `Exam` object. Then the `main` function scores the exam and produces its output. The `while` loop finishes by giving the user the chance to process another student's exam.

Programming Challenge Number 6

One of the problems with the Exam Scoring program is that it handles only one student at a time. Once a student's exam score is displayed on the screen, the student's answers are essentially lost. For this challenge, you will be modifying the program so that it can handle and store many students' scores.

To make these changes, you should first modify the program so that it can handle an array of `Exam` objects:

- Add to the `Exam` class an integer variable that stores a student's ID number.
- Change the declaration of the `Exam` object into an array declaration. For the purposes of this exercise, 10 exams should be enough.
- Modify the `main` function so that it collects data for all the students and initializes all the `Exam` objects *before* scoring any exams. (Hint: Use a `while` loop that asks the user whether there are any more students after entering data for each exam.) Don't forget to enter the student ID number.
- Modify the `main` function so that it scores all the exams at once. (Hint: Use a `for` loop for this.)
- Format your output so that it appears as a report showing the student's ID number, the student's raw score, and the percentage of correct responses.

Listing 9.10 Main function for the Exam Scoring program

```
#include <iostream.h>
#include <ctype.h>
#include <iomanip.h>
#include "exam.h"

void main ()
{
    Exam oneExam; // declare an exam object
    char key[MAX_QUEST][MAX_ANS]; // array for the key
    char student[MAX_QUEST][MAX_ANS]; // array for student answers
    char yes_no = 'Y';
    int max_possible = 0, result;

    // get data for the key
    cout << "Enter the answer key ('x' if no answer):" << endl << endl;
    for (int i = 0; i < MAX_QUEST; i++)
        for (int j = 0; j < MAX_ANS; j++)
        {
            cout << "Question " << i+1 << ", answer " << j+1 << ": ";
            cin >> key[i][j];
            if (key[i][j] != 'x')
                max_possible++;
        }

    while (toupper(yes_no) == 'Y')
    {
        cout << "\n\nEnter student answers: " << endl << endl;
        for (i = 0; i < MAX_QUEST; i++)
            for (int j = 0; j < MAX_ANS; j++)
            {
                cout << "Question " << i+1 << ", answer " << j+1 << ": ";
                cin >> student[i][j];
            }
        // initialize the object with student answers
        oneExam.init (student);
        // score the exam
        result = oneExam.score(key);
        // display raw results
        cout << "\n\nThe student had " << result <<
            " correct responses out of " << max_possible << ".";
        // set formatting for percentage display
        cout << setprecision(2) << setiosflags(ios::fixed);
        // compute and display percent correct answers
        cout << "\nThe students grade is " <<
            ((float) result/max_possible) * 100 << "%.";
        cout << "\n\nAnother student? ";
        cin >> yes_no;
    }
}
```

Strings

10

Strings—collections of characters that usually represent meaningful words—are stored as arrays of characters, terminated by the ASCII code for *null* (usually written '\0'). Because strings are in fsct arrays, they can't be handled by a program in the same way as simple variable types, such as integers or floating point numbers. As you will see in this chapter, a number of functions in the ANSI C string library make it possible to perform operations on entire strings, to a large extent eliminating the need to treat the characters in the string as individual array elements.

Declaring Strings: A Review

As you will remember, to declare a variable to hold a string, you declare an array of characters. The maximum length of the array should be one character longer than the maximum number of characters the string will hold so that there is a place for the terminating null. For example, an 80-character string might be declared using:

```
char aString[81];
```

To simplify declaring strings, programmers often use the `typedef` statement to create a data type for a string. Assume, for example, that your program will be using 80- and 50-character strings. You could then use:

```
typedef char string80[81];
typedef char string50[51];
```

Once the new data types have been created, you declare variables from them wherever needed:

```
string80 title, publisher;
string50 city, author;
```

Referencing Strings

Just like any other array, the name of a string represents a pointer to where the string begins in main memory. This means that you can reference the characters in a string like the individual elements in an array. For example, assume that you are working with the string `title` that was declared previously. The variable `title[0]` stores a single character, the first character in the string. By the same token, `title[1]` represents the second character in the string and `title[2]` the third.

In contrast, the notation `&title[0]` is the same as `title`: It represents the address of the starting position of the array. C++ interprets an ampersand (&) in front of a variable name as a request for the variable's starting address in main memory rather than for the contents of the variable. Although you will be learning much more about the & operator in Chapter 11, it is important to introduce it now because it does give you access to parts of strings and will help you learn to manipulate strings easily.

Assume, for example, that you are working with the string "My dog has fleas," which is stored in the string variable `sillyString`. The contents of the string can be seen in Figure 10.1. If you want to work with the address of the entire string, you can use either `sillyString` or `&sillyString[0]`. However, if you want to work with just the characters "has fleas," you can use `&sillyString[7]`, because `sillyString[7]` contains the first character in the part of the string in which you are interested. When you indicate the beginning of a string using the ampersand operator to generate an address, the computer views the string as everything beginning with that address and continuing until it encounters a null. For example, using `&sillyString[11]` references the string "fleas" and `&sillyString[6]` references " has fleas," including the leading space that is in `sillyString[6]`.

Figure 10.1   The contents of the sillyString variable

```
sillyString[0]     M
sillyString[1]     y
sillyString[2]         (a blank)
sillyString[3]     d
sillyString[4]     o
sillyString[5]     g
sillyString[6]         (a blank)
sillyString[7]     h
sillyString[8]     a
sillyString[9]     s
sillyString[10]        (a blank)
sillyString[11]    f
sillyString[12]    l
sillyString[13]    e
sillyString[14]    a
sillyString[15]    s
sillyString[16]    \0  (terminating null; stored as a single ASCII code)
```

String Manipulation

With the exception of I/O using `cin` and `cout`, most string manipulation requires the use of C library functions. The C library functions that support string manipulation support copying strings, comparing strings to determine their relative alphabetical order, and combining strings *(concatenation)*. Prototypes for all ANSI C string functions are found in *string.h*.

COPYING STRINGS

As you saw earlier in this book, you assign a value to a string using the `strcpy` function. The action of `strcpy` is to transfer an entire string from one location to another, including the terminating null. The source string can be a string constant (characters inside double quotes) or another string variable. The destination must be a string variable. For example, the following are all valid uses of `strcpy`:

```
string25 string1, string2;
strcpy (string1, "This is a test.");
strcpy (string2, "This is another string.");
strcpy (string1, string2);
```

If the preceding three `strcpy` functions were executed, both `string1` and `string2` would contain "This is another string."

CONCATENATING STRINGS

Concatenation lets you combine two strings by pasting one string on the end of the other. It is performed with the `strcat` function. To see how it works, consider the following:

```
string50 string1, string2;
strcpy (string1,"My dog");
strcpy (string2,"has fleas");
strcat (string1,string2);
```

The `strcat` function call modifies the contents of `string1` so that it contains "My doghas fleas." The lack of a space between "dog" and "fleas" isn't an error. Because the `strcat` operation doesn't know anything about the meaning of words and that normal English usage requires spaces between words, it simply pastes the two strings together. To get normal spacing, you must explicitly add the space:

```
strcat (string1, " ");
strcat (string1,string2);
```

To help you see how string concatenation can be used in a program, let's look at a very simple program that plays tricks with a person's first name and last name. As you can see in Figure 10.2, the program asks for the first name and last name separately. It then combines them in Last, First order and finishes by reversing the order.

Figure 10.2   The output of the Name Reverse program

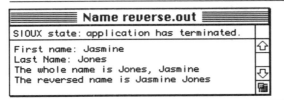

```
SIOUX state: application has terminated.

First name: Jasmine
Last Name: Jones
The whole name is Jones, Jasmine
The reversed name is Jasmine Jones
```

The program is based on the class Name in Listing 10.1. Notice that the class stores the first name, the last name, and the concatenated name (in Last, First order.) There are four member functions: the constructor, an initialization routine to store the first name and last name in the object, a function that returns the contents of the whole-Name variable, and a function that reverses the contents of the wholeName variable.

Listing 10.1   The header file for the Name Reverse program

```
typedef char string25[26];
typedef char string50[51];

class Name
{
    private:
        string25 First, Last;
        string50 wholeName; // stored Last, First
    public:
        Name ();
        void init (char [], char []);
        char * getWhole();
        char * reverse();
};
```

As you can see, the return value data type for the getWhole and reverse functions is char *, a notation to which you have not been introduced. The way in which strings are passed into and out of functions is slightly different from passing and returning simple variable types such as integers and single characters. We will therefore discuss this process in depth a bit later in this chapter.

The member functions themselves can be found in Listing 10.2. The constructor uses `strcpy` to place a null (two double quotes right next to each other) in each string variable. The `init` function is very similar. However, instead of placing a null in each string, it copies the contents of input variables into `First` and `Last`. Then it assembles the contents of `wholeName`. To do so, it first copies `Last` into `whole-Name`. The next step is to append (concatenate with `strcat`) a comma and a space. Notice that like any other string constant, these are surrounded by double quotes. The final step is to concatenate the contents of `First`.

Listing 10.2   Member functions for the Name Reverse program

```
#include <string.h>
#include "reverse.h"

Name::Name()
{
     strcpy (First,"");
     strcpy (Last,"");
     strcpy (wholeName,"");
}

void Name::init (char iFirst[], char iLast[])
{
     strcpy (First, iFirst);
     strcpy (Last, iLast);
     strcpy (wholeName, Last);
     strcat (wholeName, ", ");
     strcat (wholeName, First);
}

char * Name::getWhole()
     { return wholeName; }

char * Name::reverse ()
{
     static char reversed[51]; // must be static or it won't return
     int pos = 0;

     while (wholeName[pos] != ' ')
          pos++;

     strcpy (reversed, &wholeName[pos+1]);
     strcat (reversed, " ");
     strncat (reversed, wholeName, pos-1); // copy first name
     return reversed;
}
```

The logic of the reverse function is a bit more complicated. Remember that its purpose is to take the contents of the wholeName variable and to reformat them so that they appear as First Last. (Yes, of course you could use the First and Last variables to do this, but then there wouldn't be an opportunity to show you how to pull strings apart before you put them back together again!) The strategy is to look at each character in the string in turn until you find the space that precedes the first name. Then you can use the characters from one beyond the space to the end of the string as the first name.

The scan for the space is managed by the while loop in the reverse function. This loop begins with the array index (pos) initialized to 0. If the array element isn't a blank, the computer enters the body of the while, a single statement that increments pos. The loop stops when it encounters the blank. The value in pos is equal to the position of the blank because the while stops before entering the body of the loop.

Once the function has found the blank, it can copy the first name into a new string variable (reversed). Notice that the function indicates the address of the beginning of the source string (the first name) with &wholeName[pos+1]. The pos+1 is one array element—one character in the string—beyond where the blank was found. In other words, it's the first character of the first name.

After copying the first name, the reverse function concatenates a blank onto reversed. Then it uses a slightly different version of strcat—the strncat function—to copy the last name. The strncat function works exactly like strcat except that it copies up to a maximum number of characters. This function has the following general syntax:

```
strncat (destination, source, max_characters)
```

It concatenates the specified number of characters unless it reaches the end of the source string first. In the reverse function, concatenation should start with the beginning of the last name (the beginning of the string) and stop at the character before the comma.

Since the last character of the last name is two characters before the blank whose array index is stored in pos, why is the maximum number of characters in reverse pos-1 rather than pos-2? The answer lies in the difference between counting characters and counting array positions. You count array positions beginning with 0; however, you count characters beginning with 1. Therefore, the number of characters you want copied is really pos-2+1, or pos-1.

There is one more vitally important thing to notice about the reverse function. The reversed variable has been declared as static. As you may remember from much earlier in this book, variables declared in functions are by default removed from main memory when the function terminates. However, because arrays are always passed by reference (changes are made to the original, not a copy), the reverse function needs the reversed variable to remain in memory. If it doesn't, there is no way to return the modified string to the calling function, because the original will disappear when the function ends. The solution is to declare the variable as static. Once declared, static variables are left in memory as long as the program is running; they aren't destroyed when the function that created them terminates.

The main function for the Name Reverse program (Listing 10.3) is relatively simple. It collects the first name and last name data, uses them to initialize an object of class Name, and then displays both the contents of the wholeName variable and the result of the reverse function.

Listing 10.3   The main function for the Name Reverse program

```
#include <iostream.h>
#include <stdio.h> // for gets
#include <string.h>
#include "reverse.h"

void main ()
{
    Name person; // delcare an object
    string25 iFirst, iLast;

    cout << "First name: ";
    gets (iFirst);
    cout << "Last Name: ";
    gets (iLast);

    person.init (iFirst, iLast);
    cout << "The whole name is " << person.getWhole() << endl;
    cout << "The reversed name is " << person.reverse();
}
```

NOTE

Don't worry that we haven't discussed passing strings into and returning strings from functions. We'll return to this program a bit later in the chapter to take care of that.

COMPARING STRINGS

You can't compare strings by simply placing their variable names on the opposite sides of comparison operators. As you might guess, doing so asks the computer to base its decision on main memory addresses rather than on the contents of the strings. The solution is a function known as strcmp:

```
strcmp (first_string, second_string)
```

The strcmp function returns one of three values, based on the result of its evaluation of the relative alphabetical order of two strings. If the two strings are identical in every respect, including case, strcmp returns a 0. If the first string alphabetically precedes the second, it returns a -1; if the first string follows the second alphabetically, it returns a 1.

To experiment a bit with string comparisons, we'll be looking at a program that stores a person's name in a class variable and then compares that name to a name entered from the keyboard to see which of the two names comes first alphabetically. A sample program run appears in Figure 10.3. The first name entered is stored in the class; the second is the name that is compared to it.

Figure 10.3   Output of the Which is first? program

```
╔═══════════════ Which is first?.out ═══════════════╗
║ SIOUX state: application has terminated.          ║
║ ───────────────────────────────────────────    ⬆ ║
║ Enter the name to test: Barnes, Billy             ║
║ Enter a name to compare: Anderson, Sam            ║
║ The name in the class comes alphabetically first. ⬇ ║
║                                                  ▣ ║
╚═══════════════════════════════════════════════════╝
```

The Which is first? program is based on the class in Listing 10.4. The testName class has only one class variable—name—which stores the name to be tested. The three member functions are the constructor, an initialization function, and a function to perform the comparison between two names. The constants declared at the beginning of the header file are used by the main function to interpret the results of the testOne function

As you can see in Listing 10.5, the constructor and the init function both use strcpy to place a value in the name variable. The constructor copies a null, and the init function copies the contents of an input variable. The testOne function

Listing 10.4   Header file for the Which is first? program

```
const EQU = 0;
const CLASS_FIRST = 1;
const INPUT_FIRST = -1;

typedef char string50[51];

class testName
{
    private:
        string50 name;
    public:
        testName(); // constructor
        void init (string50); // initialization routine
        int testOne (string50); // function to compare the strimgs
};
```

Listing 10.5   Member functions for the Which is first? program

```
#include <string.h>
#include "first.h"

testName::testName()
    { strcpy (name,""); }

void testName::init(string50 iName)
    { strcpy (name, iName); }

int testName::testOne (string50 iName)
{
    return (strcmp (name, iName));
}
```

contains the call to strcmp. Because the strcmp function call is placed in the return statement, testOne sends the result of strcmp back to the calling function.

In this case, the calling function is in the Which is first? program's main function (Listing 10.6). The main function's first task is to ask the user for the name that will be stored in an object declared from the testName class. It then uses that data to initialize the object. The next step is to ask the user for a second name and to perform the comparison between the name stored in the class and the name just entered. Once the comparison has been made, the main function uses a nested if statement to evaluate the result and to display the appropriate message for the user.

Listing 10.6   The main function for the Which is first? program

```
#include <iostream.h>
#include <stdio.h>
#include <ctype.h>
#include "first.h"

void main ()
{
    testName person;
    string50 iName;
    int result;

    cout << "Enter the name to test: ";
    gets (iName);
    person.init (iName);


    cout << "Enter a name to compare: ";
    gets (iName);
    result = person.testOne (iName);
    if (result == EQU)
        cout << "The two names are the same.";
    else if (result == CLASS_FIRST)
        cout << "The name in the class comes alphabetically first.";
    else if (result == INPUT_FIRST)
        cout << "The name you just input comes alphabetically first.";
    else
        cout << "Something has gone wrong with the string comparison.";
}
```

NOTE

The nested if statement in the Which is first? program's main function could have been replaced with a switch—all decisions are based on the same integer variable. When you have only two, three, or four alternatives, it's always a toss-up whether to use nested if statements or a switch.

Strings as Function Parameters

Much of today's data processing involves passing strings into and out of functions, simply because so much of what we do with computers involves text. Unfortunately, because C++ strings are arrays, using them as function parameters means that they must be handled like other arrays. In this section we will review how arrays are passed into functions and look at how arrays of characters (in other words, strings) can be returned.

DECLARING STRING PARAMETERS

Before you can pass a string into a function, you must declare the string as a function parameter. In the function prototype the string can appear simply as an array of characters. For example, if you were to rewrite the reverse function so that the result string was passed into the function, the prototype might appear as:

```
void reverse (char []);
```

Notice that the function no longer has a return value. As you will see, this is because modifications made to an array passed into a function are made to the original in main memory, not to a copy. (Remember that all arrays are passed by reference.) There is therefore no need to have a return value.

Similarly, the function header includes the array as a parameter, this time giving it a variable name that will be used inside the function:

```
void Name::reverse (char result[]);
```

PASSING STRINGS INTO FUNCTIONS

You pass a string into a function just like you pass any other array: by using its name. If you were calling the modified version of the reverse function used earlier, you would do the following in the function placing the call:

```
char result[51]; // make sure you delcare the string
Name oneName; // make sure you have an object
oneName.reverse (result); // call the function
```

Don't forget that because you are passing an address in main memory rather than a copy of the contents of the variable, any changes you make to the variable in the called function will in fact be made to the original variable.

RETURNING STRINGS FROM FUNCTIONS

There are two ways to modify strings inside a function and make the result of that modification available to the calling function. One is to use the `return` statement to send a string's address back; the other is to use pass by reference, as you have just seen in the previous section.

When you want to return a string from a function using the `return` statement, the return data type is the address of (a pointer to) the beginning of the string. To do this, you use pointer notation. For example, `char *` tells the computer to expect a pointer to a character storage location. The asterisk means that the value is a main memory address rather than a piece of data.

If you look at Listing 10.1, you'll see that the return type of the original `reverse` function is `char *`. The original version of the function itself, found in Listing 10.2, declares the `reversed` string inside the function and then uses the following statement:

```
return reversed;
```

Because the `return` statement contains the name of the string, it sends the starting address of the string back to the calling function rather than the contents of the string. As you will remember, this string was declared as `static` so that its contents would remain intact in main memory after the `reverse` function ended.

> **NOTE**
>
> *There's a bit of a chicken-and-the-egg problem when it comes to deciding whether to present arrays and strings first or to present pointers first. You can't really talk about arrays and strings without introducing some pointer concepts. By the same token, you can't really explain the uses of pointers without array and string concepts. This book gives you arrays and strings first, but it could just have easily been done the other way around!*

In Listing 10.3 the call to the `reverse` function has been placed in a `cout` stream. This means that the address returned by the function doesn't need to be stored anywhere. It is passed directly to the output stream, which in turn displays the entire string. (As you will see in Chapter 11, however, it is often necessary to save such return addresses in variables.)

Should you choose to use pass by reference, as in the revised version of the `reverse` function (Listing 10.7), you can operate on the input parameter string as if it had been declared inside the function. However, you don't have to bother to return

Listing 10.7   A revised reverse function using pass by reference

```
void Name::reverse (char result[])
{
    int pos = 0;

    while (wholeName[pos] != ' ')
        pos++;

    strcpy (result, &wholeName[pos+1]); // copy last name
    strcat (result, " ");
    strncat (result, wholeName, pos-1); // append first name
}
```

the address of the string using the `return` statement, because you were operating on the original storage location all the time.

Arrays of Strings

Arrays of strings are really two-dimensional arrays. However, with a little help from a `typedef` statement, they can be almost as easy to handle as one-dimensional arrays. To explore how you can handle an array of strings, we'll be looking at a program that tracks parents and their kids. (Such a program might form the basis of a genealogy program. We'll be modifying it considerably throughout the rest of the book to make it more efficient.)

The program also contains examples of reading strings from and writing strings to a text file. For this reason, the program is considerably longer than any of those you've seen so far. Don't let its length throw you; other than the interaction of arrays, strings, and text files, there's nothing in it that we haven't discussed in depth.

> **NOTE**
> *There's really no such thing as a short C++ program, at least not one that does anything meaningful.*

The action of the Families program at this point (for example, Figure 10.4). is relatively simple. It reads family data from a file and then, assuming that the array that holds family objects isn't full, asks the user whether he or she wants to enter another family. Then the program displays all the family data it has in its array of objects and writes all the data back to its file.

Figure 10.4 Output of the Families program

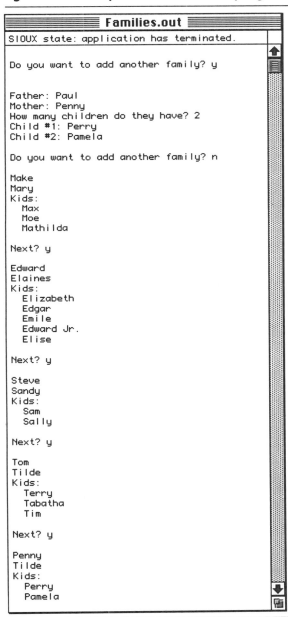

DECLARING AN ARRAY OF STRINGS

There are two ways to declare an array of strings: as a two-dimensional array and as a one-dimensional array using a string data type created with the typedef statement. The latter is by far the easier method and is the one used by the Families program.

The header file for the Families program can be found in Listing 10.8. The names of a father and mother are declared as strings, using a string25 data type that was created with the typedef statement. The children of those parents are stored in an array of strings. Notice that each element in this array has been declared as a string25. This means that the array has MAX_KIDS number of elements, each of which is an array of 25 characters. When you declare an array of strings in this way, you can deal with each string in the array as a unit, letting you work with a one-dimensional array rather than with a more complex two-dimensional array.

Listing 10.8   The header file for the Families program

```
typedef char string25[26];
const MAX_KIDS = 10;

class Families
{
    private:
        string25 father, mother;
        int numb_kids;
        string25 children[MAX_KIDS]; // array of strings
    public:
        Families();
        void init (string25, string25, int, string25 []);
        void display (); // display the address book
        char * getFather();
        char * getMother();
        int getnumbKids ();
        char * getKid(int);// parameter is index to kid array
};
```

The two-dimensional array represented by the children array could be defined as either of the following:

```
char children [26][MAX_KIDS];
char children [MAX_KIDS][26];
```

In the first case, you get 26 rows, each of which is 10 columns across. The strings therefore run vertically. In the second case, you get 10 rows, each of which is 26 columns across, which conceptually stores the strings horizontally. When you are working with a two-dimensional array to handle strings, you have to pay special attention to the direction in which the strings are running so you use indexes properly. However, when you create a string data type with the typedef statement and then declare a one-dimensional array using the new data type, you can avoid having to worry about which index is which.

MANIPULATING AN ARRAY OF STRINGS

Most of the manipulation of the array of strings used by the Families class takes place in the program's member functions (Listing 10.9). As you study this listing, keep in mind that when you reference an element in this array of objects, the name of each element is a main memory address because each element is an array in itself.

For example, by including the following, the constructor is placing a null in the ith element of the array:

```
strcpy (children[i],"");
```

By the same token, the init function can place a value in an array element with:

```
strcpy (children[i],ikids[i]);
```

In this case, ikids[i] is the ith element in an array of strings used as an input parameter to the init function.

If this seems a bit of a contradiction with what you've already learned, don't forget that we're really working with a two-dimensional array in which the second dimension is hidden by a programmer-defined data type:

```
char children [MAX_KIDS][26];
```

This is the same as:

```
typedef char string25[26];
string25 children [MAX_KIDS];
```

Listing 10.9   Member functions for the Families program

```cpp
#include <string.h>
#include <iostream.h>
#include "families.h"

Families::Families ()
{
    strcpy (father,"");
    strcpy (mother,"");
    // handle each string in the array one at a time
    for (int i = 0; i < MAX_KIDS; i++)
        strcpy (children[i],"");
    numb_kids = 0;
}

void Families::init (string25 ifather, string25 imother, int inumb_kids,
        string25 ikids[])
{
    strcpy (father,ifather);
    strcpy (mother,imother);
    numb_kids = inumb_kids;
    // handle each string in the array one at a time
    for (int i = 0; i < numb_kids; i++)
        strcpy (children[i],ikids[i]);
}

void Families::display ()
{
    cout << "\n" << father << endl;
    cout << mother << endl;
    cout << "Kids: " << endl;
    // because children[i] is the starting address of a string,
    // cout can handle it just like the name of any other string
    for (int i = 0; i < numb_kids; i++)
        cout << "   " << children[i] << endl;
}

char * Families::getFather()
{ return father; }

char * Families::getMother()
    { return mother; }

int Families::getnumbKids()
    { return numb_kids; }

// use the array index to make sure you get the right kid
char * Families::getKid(int index)
    { return children[index]; }
```

Given that this is the case, the address of the beginning of the `i`th element could also be written:

```
&children[i][0]
```

The `strcpy` function call is equivalent to:

```
strcpy (&children[i][0], &kids[i][0]);
```

The `main` function for the Families program (Listing 10.10) also works with an array of strings: the array that captures the names of children so the names can be passed into the `init` function (`ikids`). This array is exactly the same as the `children` array in the `Families` class.

As you look at the `main` function, notice that it performs *array bounds checking*. In other words, it makes sure that the program doesn't overflow the array of `Families` objects or the array of strings that collects the names of the children. To makes sure that the `people` array doesn't overflow, the function lets users enter new families only while the last array index used (stored in `lastIndex`) is less than the number of elements in the array (stored in `NUM_FAMILIES`).

To make sure that the `kids` array doesn't overflow, the function asks the user to enter the number of children in the family. It keeps repeating the request for a value until the user enters something between 0 and the maximum number of children allowed (the constant `MAX_KIDS`).

It usually isn't a good idea to require users to indicate beforehand how many values they want to enter into an array; they may not have counted the values. However, in this case, it's reasonable to assume that the user knows before beginning data entry how many children there are.

The alternative is to accept a child's name into a temporary variable. If the length of the string is 0, the user has pressed Enter without typing anything. In that case, the user is through. Otherwise, you copy the input string into some other variable (for example, the `kids` array), where it won't be overwritten by the next `gets` statement.

The sequence of steps might appear as in Listing 10.11. Notice that to find the number of characters in a string, you use the `strlen` function, which returns an integer. Keep in mind that this integer isn't the same as the last index used in the array; it's the number of characters in the string, excluding the terminating null.

NOTE

If you look carefully at Listing 10.10, you'll notice that two statements have been commented out. They bear the note "kludge." In computer slang, a kluge is an inelegant but

Listing 10.10   The main function for the Families program

```
#include <string.h>
#include <ctype.h>
#include <stdio.h>
#include <iostream.h>
#include <fstream.h>
#include "families.h"
int read (Families []); // prototypes for program functions
void write (int, Families []);
const NUM_FAMILIES = 10;
void main ()
{
    Families people[NUM_FAMILIES]; // up to 10 people for this example
    char yes_no, dummy2[2];
    int lastIndex = -1; // last index used in array of objects
    int i,j; // general purpose index variables
    string25 ifather, imother, ikids[MAX_KIDS];
    int inumb_kids = MAX_KIDS + 1;
    yes_no = 'Y';
    lastIndex = read (people); // read the data
    while (lastIndex < NUM_FAMILIES && toupper(yes_no) == 'Y')
    {
        cout << "\nDo you want to add another family? ";
        cin >> yes_no;
        if (toupper(yes_no) == 'Y')
        {
//          gets(dummy2); //kludge
            cout << "\n\nFather: ";
            gets (ifather);
            cout << "Mother: ";
            gets (imother);
            while (inumb_kids > MAX_KIDS)
            {
                cout << "\nHow many children do they have? ";
                cin >> inumb_kids;
                if (inumb_kids > MAX_KIDS)
                    cout << "\nThis program is limited to " << MAX_KIDS
                         << " kids. Try again." << endl;
            }
//          gets(dummy2); //kludge
            for (i = 0; i < inumb_kids; i++)
            {
                cout << "Child #" << i+1 << ": ";
                gets (ikids[i]);
            }
            people[++lastIndex].init (ifather,imother,inumb_kids,ikids);
            inumb_kids = MAX_KIDS + 1;
        }
    }
```

Continued next page

Listing 10.10 (Continued)   The main function for the Families program

```
    for (i = 0; i <= lastIndex; i++)
    {
        people[i].display();
        if (i < lastIndex)
        {
            cout << "\nNext? ";
            cin >> yes_no;
            if (toupper(yes_no) == 'N')
                break;
        }
    }
    write (lastIndex, people); // write the data
}
```

Listing 10.11   An alternative method for filling a string array

```
string25 name;
int i = -1

while (++i < MAX_KIDS)
{
    cout << "Name: ";
    gets (name)
    if (strlen(name) > 0)
        strcpy (kids[i], name);
    else
    {
        i--; // otherwise, i won't reflect last index actually used
        break; // get out of the loop
    }
}
```

effective solution to a problem. On the author's computer (a PowerMac 8100/80), there is a persistent problem when a sequence of gets statements follow a cin; the computer somehow assumes that the user has pressed Enter and skips the first gets that follows a cin. (The problem occurs if the program uses the cin member function getline as well.) The solution is to insert a dummy gets that the computer can skip. The tech support people at Metrowerks have been unable to reproduce the problem; according to their reports, all code that exhibits the problem on the author's system works properly without the dummy gets. Therefore, try this code on your computer with the "kludge" statements commented out. If you seem to be skipping the first gets in each sequence (you'll see two prompts to the user on the same line), remove the comment marks.

Strings and Data Files

Strings present a challenge for text files because the spaces between words in a string will be interpreted by the stream extraction operator as delimiters between individual values. If you attempt to read a string with the string extraction operator, you'll read only the first word.

The solution to the problem comes in two parts. The first is to make sure that you write a null (`'\0'`) at the end of each string. The second is to use a library function—`getline`—to read the entire string.

WRITING STRINGS

In Listing 10.12 you will find a program function that writes data from the `people` array to a text file. The `write` function first opens an output file and then checks to make sure that the file was opened successfully. Since the `write` function is the last thing that happens in the program, the program simply exits with an error message to the user and a `return` statement if the file can't be opened.

Listing 10.12   Writing Families data from a text file

```
void write (int lastIndex, Families people[])
{
    int inumb_kids;

    ofstream peopleOut ("people");
    if (!peopleOut)
    {
        cout << "Problem opening output file.";
        return;
    }
    peopleOut << lastIndex << ' ';
    // write to file
    for (int i = 0; i <= lastIndex; i++)
    {
        peopleOut << people[i].getFather() << '\0';
        peopleOut << people[i].getMother() << '\0';
        inumb_kids = people[i].getnumbKids();
        peopleOut << inumb_kids << ' ';
        for (int j = 0; j < inumb_kids; j++)
            peopleOut << people[i].getKid (j) << '\0';
    }
}
```

If the file is opened successfully, the function enters a `while` loop that writes each object in the `people` array, one at a time. Notice that for each string, the stream insertion ends with a null (`'\0'`). When the function is writing an integer, it appends a blank (`' '`). With these terminators in place, the file has been written in a format that will ensure that the program can read the data accurately.

Reading Strings

To read a string, you must use the `ifstream` object's `getline` member function. The purpose of this function is to read a block of characters, ignoring embedded blanks and other punctuation. There are many versions of the `getline` function.

The version used when reading text from a file requires three input parameters: the name of a string variable into which the data will be stored, the maximum number of characters to read, and an optional terminating character. For example, the following syntax tells the computer to read no more than 80 characters and to stop when it reaches the first null, even if it has read fewer than 80 characters:

```
stream_name.getline (string,80,'\0');
```

If you have written strings with a terminating null, this will read in the strings up to that null. If you leave off the third parameter (the terminating character), the function call will read the total number of characters specified.

The other major thing to keep in mind is what needs to occur when you mix simple variables (integers, floating point numbers, single characters) with strings. When you are reading into a simple variable, the computer uses the blank after the value to determine where the value ends. However, the computer doesn't read the blank. If a string follows the simple value, you must step over the blank before reading the string. If you don't, the blank will appear as the first character in the string. The easiest way to do this is to set up a character variable (`dummy` in this case) and then use the input stream member function `get` to read it:

```
stream_name.get (dummy);
```

As you can see, `get` grabs a single character and stores it in the variable in its parameter list.

Listing 10.13   Reading Families data from a text file

```
int read (Families people[])
{
    int lastIndex, inumb_kids;
    char yes_no, dummy;
    string25 ifather, imother, ikids[MAX_KIDS];

    ifstream peopleIn ("people"); // input file

    if (!peopleIn)
    {
        cout << "Couldn't open input file. OK to continue? ";
        cin >> yes_no;
        if (toupper(yes_no) == 'N')
            return; // quit the program
    }
    else // read from file
    {
        peopleIn >> lastIndex; // get last array-of-objects index
        peopleIn.get (dummy); // skip over whitespace
        for (int i = 0; i <= lastIndex; i++)
        {
            peopleIn.getline (ifather,80,'\0');
            peopleIn.getline (imother,80,'\0');
            peopleIn >> inumb_kids;
            peopleIn.get (dummy); // skip over whitespace
            for (int j = 0; j < inumb_kids; j++)
                peopleIn.getline (ikids[j],80,'\0');
            people[i].init (ifather,imother,inumb_kids,ikids);
        }
        peopleIn.close();
    }
    return lastIndex;
}
```

NOTE

The process for reading and writing to a text file can be simplified enormously if it can be done in a member function. However, to do this you need to pass the file stream itself as a parameter to the member function. You'll therefore find out how to do this in the next chapter, when you learn a great deal more about pointers.

Programming Challenge Number 7

If the Families program were ever to be used as a genealogy program, it would need to include birthdates for all people. For this challenge, you'll be adding dates stored as strings. (You'll later replace the string storage with a more effective way of handling dates.) To add the dates, you'll have to do the following:

- Use the `typedef` statement to create a data type that holds a date (a nine-character string will do the trick).

- Add date variables to the class for the mother's birthdate and the father's birthdate.

- Add an array of dates for the children's birthdates.

- Modify constructors as necessary to include the added data.

- Modify all I/O code to allow entry of dates (both from a file and interactively) and output of dates (both in screen display and to a file). Keep in mind that once you've modified the code for file I/O, a data file that was written using the initial format won't be any good. Be sure to delete that file before attempting to run your modified code.

When you add the array of dates for the children's birthdates, you'll notice that there is no way to automatically ensure that a child's name and birthdate are entered in the same array element in both arrays. It will be up to your program to make sure that if a child's name is in array element 2 of the name array, for example, that the child's birthdate is also in array element 2 of the birthdate array.

To make the program even more complete, you may also want to include last names. Consider carefully how you will include the last names. Should there be separate variables for the last names, or can you store both first and last names in the same variable? If you choose to store them in one variable, what format should you use? Make your choice and then implement it. (Keep in mind that it's unreasonable to assume that every member of a family has the same last name.) As with the dates, you'll need to modify all I/O code as necessary to accommodate the added data. Depending on how you choose to handle the last names, you may also need to modify some of the constructors.

Pointers

As you have been reading, a pointer is a main memory address. Pointers make it possible to return multiple values from the same function. Pointers also let you use dynamic binding, which supports the creation and destruction of objects while a program is running. In general, pointers give you significant control over what is going on in main memory.

In this chapter you will learn about how pointers are used in a C++ program. You will be introduced to pointer variables and how they can be used to manipulate blocks of memory and how they can be passed into and out of functions. In addition, you will learn about dynamic binding and how to pass references to I/O streams into and out of functions.

Pointer Variables

A *pointer variable* is a variable that is declared to hold a pointer to some specific type of data. The contents of a pointer variable might point to a simple variable type, such as an integer or a floating point value, or it might point to an object. In this section you will learn about what pointer variables contain and how to declare pointer variables, initialize them, and gain access to the contents of memory locations pointed to by pointer variables.

> **NOTE**
>
> *Don't forget that the names of arrays are already pointer variables, in that they always hold the starting address of the array in main memory. We therefore set up separate pointer variables under very specific circumstances, one of which you will see shortly.*

How Pointer Variables "Point"

The contents of a pointer variable is an address in main memory. Other than that distinction, it is pretty much like any other variable. To make this a bit clearer, let's take a look at a simplified segment of main memory. In Figure 11.1 every value in main memory takes up the same amount of space: one memory location. (In a real computer the amount of space taken by a value depends on the type of data. The starting addresses of values therefore aren't equally spaced.)

The addresses in the simplified main memory segment run from **00512** to **00520**. Each address has been labeled with a variable name, which appears at the far right of the illustration. `Variable1`, `Variable4`, `Variable5`, `Variable7`, and `Variable9` are regular variables that hold data values. The remaining variables are pointer variables. If you examine their contents, you'll notice that `Variable2` and `Variable6` both contain the address of `Variable1`. In other words, they "point to" `Variable1`. By the same token, `Variable3` points to `Variable5` and `Variable8` points to `Variable9`.

Declaring and Initializing Pointer Variables

To declare a variable that will hold a pointer, you use the * operator with the following general syntax:

```
data_type * variable_name;
```

Figure 11.1   Pointer variables and memory

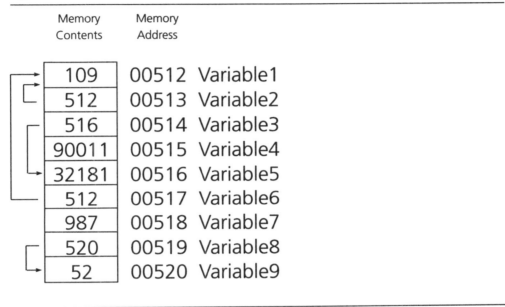

Memory Contents	Memory Address	
109	00512	Variable1
512	00513	Variable2
516	00514	Variable3
90011	00515	Variable4
32181	00516	Variable5
512	00517	Variable6
987	00518	Variable7
520	00519	Variable8
52	00520	Variable9

For example, to declare a variable that holds a pointer to an integer storage location, you could use the statement:

```
int * integerPtr;
```

Note that if you are including many pointer variables in the same declaration statement, you must use the * operator before each variable name:

```
int * integerPtr1, * integerPtr2;
```

You can also mix regular variables and pointer variables in the same declaration statement:

```
int integerValue, * integerPtr;
```

As a first example of the use of pointers, we'll be looking at a modified version of the Calculator program you first saw in Chapter 6. Rather than working directly with a floating point result value, this version of the program uses pointer variables, both in its member functions and in its main function.

The modified header file appears in Listing 11.1. There are two important things to notice. First, the class variables now include a pointer to a floating point value (resultPtr). Second, the member functions now return pointers to floating point values rather than to the pointers themselves.

Listing 11.1   Header file for the pointer-based version of the Calculator program

```
class Calculator
{
    private:
        float result, * resultPtr;
    public:
        Calculator ();
        float * Add (float, float);
        float * Subtract (float, float);
        float * Multiply (float, float);
        float * Divide (float, float);
        float * Exponentiate (float, float);
};
```

Like any other variable, the contents of a newly declared pointer variable aren't automatically initialized by the computer. You must explicitly place a main memory address in the pointer. There are two major ways to do so. One is to assign the pointer variable the result of a function that returns a pointer value. The other is to obtain the address of a regular variable using the & operator:

```
pointer_variable = &regular_variable;
```

For example, the constructor for the Calculator class initializes the resultPtr with:

```
resultPtr = &result;
```

ACCESSING DATA POINTED TO BY POINTER VARIABLES

When you use the name of a pointer variable, you are working with a main memory address, not the contents of that address. There must therefore be some way that you can tell the computer that you want the contents of the location pointed to by a pointer variable rather than the main memory address itself. To do this, you use the * operator to *dereference* the pointer.

The notation *`*pointer_variable`* asks for the contents of a pointer variable. As an example, consider the following statements:

```
int number, * numberPtr;
numberPtr = &number;
number = 10;
*numberPtr = *numberPtr + 6;
```

What will be stored in `number` after the statements have been executed? The answer is 16. The third statement initializes `number` to 10. The last statement adds 6 to it. In other words, `*numberPtr` and `number` both access the contents of the same storage location.

The member functions for the pointer-based version of the Calculator program use exactly this technique. As you can see in Listing 11.2, each arithmetic statement is of the form:

```
*resultPtr = arithemtic_operation;
```

Notice also in Listing 11.2 that each member function returns the contents of `resultPtr` without dereferencing. This is because the functions expect a pointer as the return data type.

If a function has a pointer as a return data type, what does this mean for a calling function? It means that the calling function must prepare a pointer variable to hold the result. As you can see in Listing 11.3, the `main` function for the Calculator program declares a pointer variable—`answerPtr`—that is initialized to point to the address of a floating point variable (`answer`). The pointer variable can then be used to hold the result of calls to a `Calculator` object's member functions.

Once `answerPtr` contains an address, that address can be used to display the contents of that memory location. The `cout` statement below the `switch` in Listing 11.3 includes `*answerPtr` to tell the computer to show the contents of the member location, not the main memory address itself.

Listing 11.2   Member functions for the pointer-based version of the Calculator program

```cpp
#include <math.h> // location of prototype for "pow" function
#include "Calculator.h"

Calculator::Calculator ()
{
    resultPtr = &result;
    *resultPtr = 0;
}

float * Calculator::Add (float value1, float value2)
{
    *resultPtr = value1 + value2;
    return resultPtr;
}

float * Calculator::Subtract (float value1, float value2)
{
    *resultPtr = value1 - value2;
    return resultPtr;
}

float * Calculator::Multiply (float value1, float value2)
{
    *resultPtr = value1 * value2;
    return resultPtr;
}

float * Calculator::Divide (float value1, float value2)
{
    *resultPtr = value1 / value2;
    return resultPtr;
}

float * Calculator::Exponentiate (float value1, float value2)
{
    *resultPtr = pow (value1, value2); // computes value1 to the value2 power
    return resultPtr;
}
```

NOTE

There is no compelling reason one way or the other for choosing to use pointers or regular variables for the Calculator program. Nonetheless, the program provides a good first example of the way in which pointers work.

Listing 11.3 The main function for the pointer-based version of the Calculator program

```cpp
#include <iostream.h>
#include "Calculator.h"


void main ()
{
    Calculator Calc; // declare a Calculator object named "Calc;

    char Operator; // arithmetic operator used in an expression
    char yes_no = 'Y';
    float first_value, second_value; // values used in computation
    float answer, * answerPtr;

    // initialize the pointer variable
    answerPtr = &answer;

    while (yes_no == 'Y' || yes_no == 'y')
    {
        cout << "\nArithmetic expression: ";
        cin >> first_value >> Operator >> second_value;
        switch (Operator)
        {
            case '+':
                answerPtr = Calc.Add (first_value, second_value);
                break;
            case '-':
                answerPtr = Calc.Subtract (first_value, second_value);
                break;
            case '*':
                answerPtr = Calc.Multiply (first_value, second_value);
                break;
            case '/':
                answerPtr = Calc.Divide (first_value, second_value);
                break;
            case '^':
                answerPtr = Calc.Exponentiate
                    (first_value, second_value);
                break;
            default:
                cout << "\nUnidentified operator";
        }
        cout << "\nAnswer: " << *answerPtr << endl;
        cout << "\nAnother? ";
        cin >> yes_no;
    }
}
```

USING POINTER ARITHMETIC

The use of pointers makes it easy to step through a block of memory, one element at a time. In other words, if you have an array of floating point values, pointers can make it easy to access all the elements of the array, in order. You can do this by manipulating the contents of the pointer variable using *pointer arithmetic*.

Assume, for example, that you've declared an array (intArray) to hold up to MAX_INT values. The contents of the first value in the array is represented by *intArray. If you want to access the second value, you could write:

```
*(++intArray)
```

The parentheses around the arithmetic operation tells the computer to first increment the pointer and then dereference it. The parentheses are necessary because the * operator has precedence over the preincrement operator.

When you increment or decrement a pointer, the computer takes into account the type of data to which the pointer is pointing. For example, if the pointer variable has been declared to point to 16-bit integer values, each time you increment the pointer variable by one, the variable's contents are increased by two bytes. However, if the pointer variable points to an object, incrementing the pointer variable by one adds the number of bytes occupied by the entire object to the pointer.

There is one drawback to using array names as pointer variables for pointer arithmetic. Once you've modified the pointer, you've lost the starting location of the array. We therefore often create pointer variables for arrays so we can modify the pointer variables and still retain the starting location of the array:

```
int * arrayPtr;
arrayPtr = intArray;
```

Notice that because the name of an array is an address, you can assign a value to the pointer variable without using the & operator.

As a further example, let's look at a program that sums that values in an array of up to 25 positive floating point values. The program lets you enter values until you enter a negative value and then reports the sum (see Figure 11.2). (To keep it short, this program doesn't include array bounds checking, so be careful when you run it!)

The Array Summing program is based on the floatArray class in Listing 11.4. In addition to the array, the only other variable is a count of the number of values in the array.

Figure 11.2   Output of the Array Summing program

```
====== Sum Array.out ======
SIOUX state: application has terminated.

Value #1:  50
Value #2:  60
Value #3:  90
Value #4:  100
Value #5:  78
Value #6:  15
Value #7:  88
Value #8:  90
Value #9:  10
Value #10: 25
Value #11: 88
Value #12: 167
Value #13: 25
Value #14: 30
Value #15: 25
Value #16: 109
Value #17: 18
Value #18: 15
Value #19: -1
The sum of the values in the array is 1083.
```

Listing 11.4   The header file for the Array Summing program

```
class floatArray
{
    private:
        float numberArray[25];
        int count;
    public:
        floatArray();
        void init(float [], int);
        double sum ();
};
```

Most of the work for the program takes place in the floatArray class's member functions (Listing 11.5). In particular, take a look at the sum function. The function first declares a pointer variable (arrayPtr) that is then initialized to the starting location of numberArray. The function can then manipulate the address of the array in arrayPtr without worrying about disrupting the class variable.

To perform the sum, the program places the following expression in a for loop:

```
total += *(arrayPtr++);
```

Listing 11.5   Member functions for the Array Summing program

```
#include "sum array.h"

floatArray::floatArray()
{
    for (int i = 0; i < 25; i++)
        numberArray[i] = 0;
    count = 0;
}

void floatArray::init (float iarray[], int icount)
{
    count = icount;
    for (int i = 0; i <= icount; i++)
        numberArray[i] = iarray[i];
}

double floatArray::sum ()
{
    float * arrayPtr; // pointer to class array
    double total;

    // use pointer variable so you don't disrupt value in numberArray
    arrayPtr = numberArray;

    for (int i = 0; i <= count; i++)
        total += *(arrayPtr++);
    return total;
}
```

The parentheses around the pointer variable name tell the computer that postincrement is to be applied to the pointer variable itself, not to the contents of the pointer variable. (Don't forget that the * operator has higher precedence than any of the arithmetic operators; if you were to omit the parentheses, the computer would first dereference the pointer, perform the addition and assignment to total, and then increment the dereferenced contents.)

Each time the loop repeats, the computer dereferences the pointer and provides the value stored at the pointer's current location. The value is added to the value currently stored in total. The computer completes the execution of the statement by incrementing the pointer variable, adding the number of bytes used by a floating point number.

The main function, which manipulates a floatArray object, can be found in Listing 11.6. All this function does is collect values for the array, initialize an object with the init member function, and then call the sum function by placing it in a cout statement.

Listing 11.6   The main function for the Array Summing program

```
#include <iostream.h>
#include "sum array.h"

void main ()
{
    floatArray oneArray;
    float iarray[25], iNumb;
    int icount = 0, sum;

    cout << "Value #" << icount + 1 << ": ";
    cin >> iNumb;
    while (iNumb > 0)
    {
        iarray[icount++] = iNumb;
        cout << "Value #" << icount + 1 << ": ";
        cin >> iNumb;
    }
    icount--; // want icount to be last array index used
    oneArray.init (iarray, icount);

    cout << "The sum of the values in the array is " << oneArray.sum() << ".";
}
```

As you look at this code, notice that when the user enters a negative number, the while loop that collects data for the array stops. However, because the array index is increased with a postincrement, at the point the loop stops, the index's value will be one too great. This is why the function decrements the icount variable immediately after the input loop finishes.

Pointer Arithmetic and String Functions

The string functions to which you were introduced in Chapter 10 are often implemented using a pointer arithmetic technique similar to that you just saw in the array summing program. As a first example, consider the strlen function in Listing 11.7. To find the length, the function scans the string, counting characters as it goes, until it reaches a null.

NOTE

This function uses a pointer to a character storage location as an input parameter. For the moment, don't worry about the nature of this parameter. We'll look at passing pointers as parameters a bit later in this chapter.

Listing 11.7   Using pointers to find the length of a string

```
int strlen (char * string)
{
    int len = 0;
    while (*(string++) != '\0')
        len++;
    return len;
}
```

Copying a string requires moving characters one at a time from the source string to the destination string. As you can see in Listing 11.8, copying begins with the first character of each string and ends when the computer encounters the null at the end of the source string. Because the `while` loop stops before transferring the terminating null, the function adds a null.

Listing 11.8   Using pointers to copy one string to another

```
char * strcpy (char * destination, char * source)
{
    destPtr; // need to save address of destination
    destPtr = destination;

    while (*source != '\0')
        *(destination++) = *(source++);
    *destination = '\0';
    return destPtr;
}
```

Notice in Listing 11.8 that the function pays absolutely no attention to the size of the destination string. It copies all the characters in the source string, without regard to what it might be overwriting in memory. This means that if the destination string has been declared to hold as many characters as the source string, copying will almost certainly destroy something in main memory that you want to keep.

To concatenate one string onto another, copying of the source string onto the destination string must begin with the null at the end of the destination string. In Listing 11.9, for example, the `strcat` function uses an empty `while` loop to scan the destination string, stopping at the null. Because the postincrement moves the pointer one byte beyond the null, the function then backs up the pointer so that the first character copied overwrites the null. At that point, the copying proceeds just as it did in the `strcpy` function.

Listing 11.9   Using pointers to concatenate strings

```
char * strcat (char * destination, char * source)
{
    destPtr; // need to save address of destination
    destPtr = destination;

    while (*(destination++) != '\0')
        ; // empty while to find end of destination string
    destination--; // back up to null

    while (*source != '\0')
        *(destination++) = *(source++);
    *destination = '\0';
    return destPtr;
}
```

Pointers and Parameter Passing

One of the most common uses of pointers in a C++ program is to "return" multiple values from a function. To be completely accurate, you can't use the return mechanism for more than one value. However, if you manipulate data directly in memory rather than working on a copy passed into a function, the modified data are available to any function—including the calling function—that happens to have access to the address where the data are located.

The trick is to use pass by reference, in which you send a function the address of a variable rather than the contents of the variable. The function receiving the addresses then can dereference the pointers to manipulate the data stored at those addresses.

To prepare a function to accept addresses rather than values, you declare parameters as pointer variables rather than as regular variables. For example, if a function should expect pointers to an integer value and a floating point value, the function's prototype would be written:

```
void function_name (int *, float *);
```

The asterisk following the data type tells the computer to expect a pointer rather than a data value. By the same token, the function's header must declare pointer variables as follows:

```
void function_name (int * intPtr, float * floatPtr);
```

NOTE

By convention, pointer variables are often named with the characters "Ptr" at the end of the name. There is no requirement that you do this, but doing so makes it easier to recognize pointer variables.

There are two ways to send addresses into a function. The first is to send the contents of a pointer variable; the second is to send the address of a regular variable. If you happen to have a pointer variable available, you can place it in a function's parameter list to send its contents to the function:

```
int integerValue, * intPtr;
float floatValue, * floatPtr;
intPtr = &integerValue;
floatPtr = &floatValue;
function_name (intPtr, floatPtr);
```

Alternatively, if you don't really need to use pointer variables, you can use the & operator with the name of a regular variable to send that variable's address, without ever storing the address in a pointer variable:

```
function_name (&integerValue, &floatValue);
```

Which you choose depends simply on whether you have a need for the pointer variables in the calling function. If you'll be using the pointer variables for other purposes, use them as function parameters. However, there's no point in creating the pointer variables if you don't have any other use for them; simply pass the addresses of regular variables.

As a first example of a function that returns multiple values, we'll be looking at a program that collects the distance a runner has run each day during a seven-day period. The program then finds the average distance run, the maximum distance, and the minimum distance (see Figure 11.3).

The Running Analysis program is based on the weeklyRuns class (Listing 11.10). This class contains an array that holds seven floating point values, a constructor, an

Figure 11.3   Output of the Running Analysis program

```
━━━━━━━━━━━━ Running.out ━━━━━━━━━━━━
SIOUX state: application has terminated.

Day #1: 2.6
Day #2: 3.1
Day #3: 2.5
Day #4: 3.3
Day #5: 7.2
Day #6: 5.0
Day #7: 2.5
Last week I ran an average of 3.74 miles per day.
My maximum distance was 7.20 miles.
My minimum distance was 2.50 miles.
```

Listing 11.10   Header file for the Running Analysis program

```cpp
const NUM_RUNS = 7;

class weeklyRuns
{
    private:
        float distance[NUM_RUNS];
    public:
        weeklyRuns();
        void init (float []);
        void analyze (float *, float *, float *);
};
```

initialization function, and a function to perform computations on the array. Notice that the prototype for this function includes three pointers to floating point values: one for the average, one for the minimum, and one for the maximum.

The member functions for the Running Analysis program can be found in Listing 11.11. Look first at the function header for the analyze function. The parameter list indicates that the function expects pointers. The variables declared in the parameter list are therefore pointer variables.

To assign values to the pointer variables, the analyze function uses the * operator to dereference the pointer variables. Keep in mind that every time the function dereferences a pointer, it is gaining access to the original data in main memory. For this reason, the function doesn't contain a return statement. When the function terminates, the modified values remain in memory, in the locations where the variables were declared by the main function (Listing 11.12).

In this particular example, the main function has no need to use pointer variables. It therefore declares three floating point variables, one for each of the values

Listing 11.11   Member functions for the Running Analysis program

```
#include "running.h"

weeklyRuns::weeklyRuns ()
{
     for (int i = 0; i < NUM_RUNS; i++)
          distance[i] = 0;
}

void weeklyRuns::init (float iArray[])
{
     for (int i = 0; i < NUM_RUNS; i++)
          distance[i] = iArray[i];
}

void weeklyRuns::analyze (float * average, float * minimum, float * maximum)
{
     float sum = 0;

     for (int i = 0; i < NUM_RUNS; i++)
          sum += distance[i];
     *average = sum / NUM_RUNS;

     *minimum = distance[0];
     *maximum = distance[0];

     for (i = 1; i < NUM_RUNS; i++)
     {
          if (distance[i] < *minimum)
               *minimum = distance[i];
          if (distance[i] > *maximum)
               *maximum = distance[i];
     }
}
```

computed by the `analyze` function. When the time comes to call `analyze`, the `main` function passes the addresses of the variables by preceding their names with the & operator. After the completion of the function call, the `main` function can use the contents of the modified regular variables directly.

Listing 11.12   The main function for the Running Analysis program

```
#include <iostream.h>
#include <iomanip.h>
#include "running.h"

void main ()
{
    float iArray[NUM_RUNS];
    float average, minimum, maximum;
    weeklyRuns myRuns;

    for (int i = 0; i < NUM_RUNS; i++)
    {
        cout << "Day #" << i + 1 << ": ";
        cin >> iArray[i];
    }

    myRuns.init (iArray);
    myRuns.analyze (&average, &minimum, &maximum);

    cout << setiosflags (ios::fixed) << setprecision(2);
    cout << "Last week I ran an average of " << average
         << " miles per day." << endl;
    cout << "My maximum distance was " << maximum << " miles." << endl;
    cout << "My minimum distance was " << minimum << " miles." << endl;
}
```

Dynamic Binding

Dynamic binding, in which functions are linked to objects while a program is running, makes it possible to create and destroy objects as needed, rather than needing to create all objects when a program begins its runs. There are two big advantages to dynamic binding. First, dynamic binding gives you better control over main memory because you don't need to consume memory with objects that are no longer needed. Second, you can collect the data needed to initialize an object and then pass that data into the class's constructor, thus eliminating the need for a separate initialization function.

To create an object for use with dynamic binding, first declare a variable that will hold a pointer to the object. Then use the new operator to create the object, including parameters for the class's constructor:

    objectPtr = new class_name (parameter list);

The new operator creates an object from the named class, runs a constructor using the values in the parameter list, and returns a pointer to the newly created object.

Once you've created an object for use with dynamic binding, you use the -> (arrow) operator to call member functions using the following general syntax:

```
objectPtr->function_name (parameter list);
```

The arrow operator dereferences the object pointer and turns the call into the dot notation (*object_name.function_name*) you have been using to this point.

When you have finished with an object created for dynamic binding, you can remove it from memory with the delete operator:

```
delete objectPtr;
```

NOTE

Using delete to remove an object automatically executes a special type of member function known as a destructor. A destructor has no return value. Its name is a tilde (~) followed by the name of the class. The job of a destructor is typically to release any other memory used by the object. For example, if the object has created other objects using new, those objects probably should be removed with the delete operator in the destructor. Because none of the classes you have seen allocate memory, no destructors have been required.

To show you how dynamic binding fits into a program, let's look at a revised version of the Families program you first saw in Chapter 10. The header file has been modified somewhat (see Listing 11.13). For the purposes of this discussion, the most important change is that the init function is gone. Instead, the interactive constructor contains the parameter from the init function. (The file input constructor and the write function will be discussed in the next section, when we talk about passing streams into functions.

The revised member functions can be found in Listing 11.14. Right now, look just at the first function, the interactive constructor. Notice that it contains the code that originally was part of the init function.

The program's main function (Listing 11.15) has been modified in several ways to support dynamic binding:

Listing 11.13 Revised header file for the Families program

```
typedef char string25[26];
const MAX_KIDS = 10;

class Families
{
    private:
        string25 father, mother;
        int numb_kids;
        string25 children[MAX_KIDS];
    public:
        // interactice constructor
        Families(string25, string25, int, string25 []);
        Families (ifstream &); // file input constructor
        void display (); // display the address book
        void write (ofstream &);
};
```

- The `people` array is now an array of pointers to `Families` objects rather than an array of the objects themselves.

  ```
  Families * people[NUM_FAMILIES];
  ```

- The program collects that data for a `Families` object and then uses the `new` operator to create the object.

  ```
  people[++lastIndex] = new Families
        (ifather,imother,inumb_kids,ikids);
  ```

  The program creates the object and executes the constructor whose function signature matches the parameter list that follows the name of the class. The pointer returned when the object is created is assigned to the `people` array.
- The call to the `display` function uses dynamic binding:

  ```
  people[i]->display();
  ```

Listing 11.14   Member functions for the revised Families program

```
#include <string.h>
#include <iostream.h>
#include <fstream.h>
#include "families.h"


Families::Families (string25 ifather, string25 imother, int inumb_kids,
                     string25 ikids[])
{
    strcpy (father,ifather);
    strcpy (mother,imother);
    numb_kids = inumb_kids;
    for (int i = 0; i < numb_kids; i++)
        strcpy (children[i],ikids[i]);
}


Families::Families (ifstream & Input)
{
    char dummy;

    Input.getline (father,80,'\0');
    Input.getline (mother,80,'\0');
    Input >> numb_kids;
    Input.get (dummy); // skip over whitespace
    for (int j = 0; j < numb_kids; j++)
        Input.getline (children[j],80,'\0');
}


void Families::display ()
{
    cout << "\n" << father << endl;
    cout << mother << endl;
    cout << "Kids: " << endl;
    for (int i = 0; i < numb_kids; i++)
        cout << "   " << children[i] << endl;
}


void Families::write (ofstream & Output)
{
    Output << father << '\0';
    Output << mother << '\0';
    Output << numb_kids << ' ';
    for (int i = 0; i < numb_kids; i++)
        Output << children[i] << '\0';
}
```

Listing 11.15 The main function for revised Families program

```
#include <string.h>
#include <ctype.h>
#include <stdio.h>
#include <iostream.h>
#include <fstream.h>
#include "families.h"
int read (Families * []); // prototypes of program functions
void write (int, Families * []);
const NUM_FAMILIES = 10;
void main ()
{
    Families * people[NUM_FAMILIES]; // up to 10 people for this example
    char yes_no, dummy2[2];
    int lastIndex = -1, i, j;
    string25 ifather, imother, ikids[MAX_KIDS];
    int inumb_kids = MAX_KIDS + 1;
    yes_no = 'Y';
    lastIndex = read (people);
    while (lastIndex < NUM_FAMILIES && toupper(yes_no) == 'Y')
    {
        cout << "\nDo you want to add another family? ";
        cin >> yes_no;
        if (toupper(yes_no) == 'Y')
        {
//          gets(dummy2); //kludge
            cout << "\n\nFather: ";
            gets (ifather);
            cout << "Mother: ";
            gets (imother);
            while (inumb_kids > MAX_KIDS)
            {
                cout << "\nHow many children do they have? ";
                cin >> inumb_kids;
                if (inumb_kids > MAX_KIDS)
                    cout << "\nThis program is limited to " << MAX_KIDS
                        << " kids. Try again." << endl;
            }
//          gets(dummy2); //kludge
            for (i = 0; i < inumb_kids; i++)
            {
                cout << "Child #" << i+1 << ": ";
                gets (ikids[i]);
            }
            people[++lastIndex] = new Families
                (ifather,imother,inumb_kids,ikids);
            inumb_kids = MAX_KIDS + 1;
        }
    }
```

Continued next page

Listing 11.15 (Continued)   The main function for revised Families program

```
    for (i = 0; i <= lastIndex; i++)
    {
        people[i]->display();
        if (i < lastIndex)
        {
            cout << "\nNext? ";
            cin >> yes_no;
            if (toupper(yes_no) == 'N')
                break;
        }
    }
    write (lastIndex, people);
}
```

Programming Challenge
Number 8

To get some practice with pointer variables, dynamic binding, and pass by reference, in this challenge you will be modifying the Exam Scoring program that you read about in Chapter 9. Make the following changes to the program:

- Use dynamic binding to create the Exam object.
- Modify the score member function so that it accepts a pointer to an integer variable as an input parameter (along with the existing input parameters). Use pointer notation to modify the contents of the integer variable directly in main memory. After these modifications, the function's return data type should be void.
- In the main function, use the pointer variable whenever you need to access a student's exam score (the program variable result).

Programming Challenge Number 9

In this challenge, you'll be modifying the Temperatures program from Chapter 9 so that it can handle weekly temperatures for an entire year. You'll be declaring an array of pointers to objects. The changes you need to make include the following:

- Add an integer variable to the `temps` class to hold a week number.
- Change all I/O routines to include the new class variable.
- Create an array of pointers to `temps` objects in the `main` function.
- Use dynamic binding to create `temps` objects.
- Include in the `main` function another loop that lets the user enter temperatures for more than one week. In this case, you can ask the user the week for which he or she is entering temperatures. (Hint: The user will enter weeks numbered from 1 to 52, but the indexes in your array of objects run from 0 to 51.)
- Modify display code so that the user can indicate the week for which he or she wants to see the average temperature.

If you want to make this program useful for keeping track of temperatures in your area, it should store its data in a text file. (You don't want to have to reenter an entire year's temperatures each time you run the program.) You should therefore add a constructor to read one `temps` object from a file and a member function to write one object to a file. Add code to the `main` function to manage file I/O. Be sure to use dynamic binding throughout.

References to I/O Streams

One of the problems with the original version of the Families program is that to read and write objects from the data file, the program must know the details of the internals of the class, as well as the layout of the file. To make the program more flexible, the details of the class and the file should be hidden from the main program. In other words, reading and writing a text file should be handled by member functions.

The problem that reading and writing from a member function presents is that a member function can handle only one object. If your program happens to be working with an array of objects, you can't open the I/O stream in the member function.

It needs to be opened in the main program and then passed into the member function.

When you pass an I/O stream into a member function, you pass a reference to the stream—the address in main memory where the stream's storage begins. The prototype for a function that has an I/O stream as a parameter looks like the following:

```
void function_name (stream_class &);
```

For example, the constructor that reads a Families object from a file is declared as:

```
Families (ifstream &);
```

Because this function is a constructor, it has no return data type.

> **NOTE**
>
> *The Families class now has two constructors. As you read earlier in this book, this is an example of function overloading, where two functions have the same name but different signatures. In other words, although the function names may be the same, their parameter lists are different, making it possible for the compiler to distinguish between them. When you create a new object, the computer calls the correct constructor based on the parameters you use. By the same token, if the compiler can't find a constructor with a matching signature, it will report an error.*

The member function that writes an object to a file is declared as:

```
void write (ofstream &);
```

All the function headers need to do is give the stream a name that can be used inside the member function:

```
Families::Families (ifstream & Input)
void Families::write (ofstream & Output)
```

The functions, which appeared in Listing 11.14, can then access the streams to read and write data. Notice that another benefit of reading and writing using member functions is that you no longer need to call functions that return object data. All of the get functions that were part of the first version of this program are no longer necessary.

Reading and writing files in member functions also has the benefit of shortening code in the main program. Rather than reading the data from the text file and then calling a function to initialize an object, the main program's read function (Listing 11.16) simply includes a new statement that creates an object and passes the name of the input file stream into the constructor. Notice that to pass the address of the stream, you simply place its name in the parameter list.

Listing 11.16   Revised function to read objects from a data file

```
int read (Families * people[])
{
    int lastIndex = -1, inumb_kids;
    char yes_no, dummy;
    string25 ifather, imother, ikids[MAX_KIDS];

    ifstream peopleIn ("people"); // input file

    if (!peopleIn)
    {
        cout << "Couldn't open input file. OK to continue? ";
        cin >> yes_no;
        if (toupper(yes_no) == 'N')
            return; // quit the program
    }
    else // read from file
    {
        peopleIn >> lastIndex; // get last array-of-objects index
        peopleIn.get (dummy); // skip over whitespace
        for (int i = 0; i <= lastIndex; i++)
        {
            people[i] = new Families (peopleIn);
        }
        peopleIn.close();
    }
    return lastIndex;
}
```

The write function (Listing 11.17) also is shorter than the same function in the original version. Rather than including code that retrieves data values from an object and writes those objects to the file, it uses dynamic binding to call the write member function:

```
people[i]->write (peopleOut);
```

Listing 11.17   Revised function to write object to a data file

```
void write (int lastIndex, Families * people[])
{
    int inumb_kids;

    ofstream peopleOut ("people");
    if (!peopleOut)
    {
        cout << "Problem opening output file.";
        return;
    }
    peopleOut << lastIndex << ' ';
    // write to file
    for (int i = 0; i <= lastIndex; i++)
        people[i]->write(peopleOut);
}
```

NOTE

Objects that can read and write themselves are known as "persistent" objects. Persistent objects form the basis of most of today's object-oriented database management systems.

Pulling It Together: The Checkbook Program

The programs you have seen to this point have been relatively short examples that demonstrate one or more features of the C++ language. None of these program have been designed to do real work. In this chapter we'll therefore take a look at a much longer program that in a relatively simple way manages checking accounts. This program uses all of the concepts we've discussed to this point and provides a good example of how all of these elements come together into a useful program. Along the way, you'll be introduced to a few issues that arise when you begin to work with more than one class and to some further pointer concepts.

What the Program Can Do

The Checkbook program lets a user maintain up to 25 checking accounts, each of which can hold up to 10,000 transactions. (These limits, however, can easily be changed by changing the sizes of arrays.) Program actions are controlled by the menu function in Listing 12.1. As you can see, you can use this program to store data about accounts and the transactions posted to them. You can also reconcile the checking account, indicating which transactions have appeared on your statement. The program then reports what the balance in your checkbook should be. The remaining menu options let you find a single transaction (using the check number or the payee and transaction date) and view a sequence of transactions based on the transaction date.

Listing 12.1   The simpleMenu function

```
int simpleMenu ()
{
    int menuchoice;
    char dummy[2]; // for bug fix

    cout << "\nPick an option:" << endl << endl;
    cout << " 1. Create a new acount" << endl;
    cout << " 2. Enter a transaction" << endl;
    cout << " 3. Reconcile an account" << endl;
    cout << " 4. Find a transaction" << endl;
    cout << " 5. View transactions" << endl;
    cout << " 9. Quit" << endl << endl;
    cout << "Enter your choice: ";
    cin >> menuchoice;
//  gets (dummy); // kludge around cin bug
    return menuchoice;
}
```

The Classes

Because the Checkbook program can handle more than one checking account, it requires two classes: one for accounts and one for transactions (deposits, checks, service charges, and ATM withdrawals) posted against those accounts. Pointers to objects created from the Trans class are stored in an array that is a variable belonging to the Account class. In this way, the program knows which transactions belong to which account.

The Account class, in Listing 12.2, stores the account number, the name of the bank, the current account balance, and an array of pointers to the account's transactions. In addition, it has two "housekeeping" variables: the last transaction number used and the number of transactions in the transaction array. Because a programmer may eventually want to add a member function that deletes transactions, the number of transactions in the transaction array may not always be the same as the highest transaction number.

Listing 12.2   The Account class

```
class Account
{
    private:
        string25 acc_numb;
        string50 bank_name;
        float balance;
        Trans * transactions[MAX_TRANS];
        int lastTrans_numb, Trans_count;
    public:
        // constructor for interactive input
        Account (string25, string50, float);
        Account (ifstream &); // constructor for file input
        int nextTrans_numb ();
        void insertTrans (Trans *); // insert transaction into array
        void Reconcile();
        Trans * find (char * ); // find by check/reference numb
        // find check by date and Payee/Source
        Trans * find (date_string, string80);
        // list transactions in date range
        void byDate (date_string, date_string);
        void write (ofstream &); // write to file
        char * getAcc_numb ();
        char * getBank_name();
        // set balance when transaction is posted
        void setBalance (int, float);
};
```

Why use an array of pointers to Trans objects rather than simply declare the array to hold the objects themselves? To make better use of main memory. The transactions array has been declared to hold 10,000 pointers, each of which takes up 32 bits of memory. When the program is running, the array occupies 320,000 bits, or 40,000 bytes (just under 40K). However, a Trans object takes up 188 bytes. An array to hold 10,000 of them would therefore consume 1,880,000 bytes (just under 2Mb).

If an account has only a few transactions posted, there's no need to waste memory by allocating nearly 2Mb for transactions. Instead the program allocates just enough space for the pointers and then uses the new operator to create transactions as they are needed, using only the amount of memory required for existing transactions.

Like the Families program that you saw in Chapter 11, the Account class has two constructors: one for interactive input and another for input from a text file. You'll be introduced to the rest of the member functions shortly.

The Trans class (Listing 12.3) appears first in the header file. It holds a transaction number, a check number (unused by noncheck transactions), the date of the transaction, the payee of a check or source of a deposit, a note about the transaction, the amount of the transaction, a flag to indicate whether the transaction has cleared, the type of transaction, and a pointer to the Account object to which the transaction belongs.

The presence of a pointer to an Account object in the Trans class presents a bit of a problem. Because Trans comes first in the header file, the compiler doesn't recognize the Account class as a data type, because it hasn't been declared. However, the Account class contains pointers to Trans objects. Therefore, placing the Account class first in the header file only reverses the problem.

The solution is a *forward declaration*, a statement that identifies a class to the compiler by name without defining the class:

```
class class_name;
```

The following statement therefore precedes the declaration of the Trans class in the header file:

```
class Account;
```

Like the Account class, the Trans class has two constructors: one for interactive input and another for input from a file. There are also two private member functions. These are used by other Trans class member functions to translate between the text of a transaction type and the number that is stored in an object. You will be introduced to the rest of the member functions as we explore the program further.

The Constructors

The constructors used by both the Account and Trans classes are similar in concept to those used by the Families program. One handles input from the user; the other reads data from a text file. Both sets of constructors use a special pointer, known as this, which we'll look at before examining the constructors in detail.

Listing 12.3   The Trans class

```
typedef char string80[81];
typedef char string50[51];
typedef char string25[26];
typedef char date_string[9];

const MAX_TRANS = 10000;
const CHECK = 1;
const DEPOSIT = 2;
const ATM = 3;
const SERVICE = 4;

class Account;

class Trans
{
    private:
        int trans_numb; // arbitrary unique identifier for each transaction
        char check_numb[6];  // used only for check transactions
        date_string trans_date;
        string80 PayeeSource, Note;
        float amount;
        int cleared; // Boolean set to true when check has cleared

        // 1 = check, 2 = deposit, 3 = ATM withdrawl, 4 = service charge;
        int trans_type;

        Account * owner; // pointer to account that owns the transaction

        // private functions not used outside class
        // translate transaction type string into integer
        int Text2Type (char *);
        char * Type2Text (); // translate integer type into string

    public:
        // constructor for interactive input
        Trans (Account *, char *, date_string, string80, string80,
            float, char *);
        // constructor to read from file
        Trans (ifstream &, Account *);

        void markCleared ();
        void write (ofstream &); // write to file
        void displayTrans ();
        char * getCheck_numb ();
        char * getDate ();
        char * getPS ();
        int getCleared ();
        int getType ();
        float getAmount ();
};
```

THE THIS POINTER

The this pointer is a pointer variable that contains a pointer to the current object. A program doesn't need to declare this. It is declared, and initialized and its contents kept current by the computer.

You can use the this pointer just like any other variable that points to an object. For example, if you are writing a member function and need to call another member function of the same class, you might write:

```
this->function_name (parameter list);
```

You can also pass this to a function as a parameter from within a member function:

```
function_name (this, other parameters);
```

THE ACCOUNT CLASS CONSTRUCTORS

As you can see in Listing 12.4, the interactive constructor for the Account class accepts data from the calling function and initializes the class variables. The values for the last transaction number and for the transaction count are set to 0.

The constructor for file input reads class data from the file. However, doing so isn't as straightforward as it was with the Families program. As transaction data are read from the file, the Account class's constructor must create transaction objects, storing pointers to the objects in the Account object's transactions array. The parameters in the new statement are the file input stream and a pointer to the Account object (the this pointer).

THE TRANS CLASS CONSTRUCTORS

The constructors for the Trans class and functions used by those constructors can be found in Listing 12.5. The file input constructor takes the pointer to the Account object to which the transaction belongs and assigns it to the owner variable. Then it reads the rest of the data from the file.

Listing 12.4   Constructors for the Account class

```
// interactive constructor
Account::Account (string25 iAcc_numb, string50 iBank_name, float iBalance)
{
    strcpy (acc_numb, iAcc_numb);
    strcpy (bank_name, iBank_name);
    balance = iBalance;
    for (int i = 0; i < MAX_TRANS; i++)
        transactions[i] = 0;
    lastTrans_numb = 0;
    Trans_count = 0;
}

// file input constructor
Account::Account (ifstream & fin)
{
    Account * owner;
    char dummy;

    fin.getline (acc_numb,80,'\0');
    fin.getline (bank_name,80,'\0');
    fin >> balance;
    fin >> lastTrans_numb;
    fin >> Trans_count;
    for (int i = 0; i < Trans_count; i++)
        transactions[i] = new Trans (fin, this);
    fin.get (dummy); // skip over blank between accounts
}
```

The Interactive Constructor

Because a transaction entered from the keyboard must be numbered and connected to the account to which it belongs, the interactive constructor is a bit more involved than the file input constructor. This constructor performs the following actions:

- Assigns the pointer to the Account object that owns the transaction to the owner variable.

- Calls the Account object's nextTrans_numb function to generate a number for the transaction and to increment the Account object's lastTrans_numb variable.

- Copies input parameters into class variables.

- Converts the text version of the transaction type to an integer code using the Text2Type function. (We will look at that function, along with the function that converts from an integer code back to text, shortly.

Listing 12.5   Constructors and functions used by the constructors for the Transaction class

```
Trans::Trans (Account * whichAccount, char * icheck_numb,
         date_string itrans_date, string80 iPayeeSource, string80 iNote,
         float iAmount, char * iType)
{
    owner = whichAccount;
    trans_numb = owner->nextTrans_numb();
    strcpy (check_numb, icheck_numb);
    strcpy (trans_date, itrans_date);
    strcpy (PayeeSource, iPayeeSource);
    strcpy (Note, iNote);
    amount = iAmount;
    trans_type = Text2Type (iType);
    if (trans_type == SERVICE)
        cleared = TRUE;
    else
        cleared = FALSE;
    owner->insertTrans (this);
    owner->setBalance (trans_type, amount); // change balance as needed
}

Trans::Trans (ifstream & fin, Account * whichAccount)
{
    char dummy;

    owner = whichAccount;
    fin >> trans_numb;
    fin.get (dummy); // skip over blank before string
    fin.getline (check_numb,80,'\0');
    fin.getline (trans_date,80,'\0');
    fin.getline (PayeeSource,80,'\0');
    fin.getline (Note,80,'\0');
    fin >> amount;
    fin >> cleared;
    fin >> trans_type;
}
// insert into array and increment count; used by interactive constructor
void Account::insertTrans(Trans * newTrans)
    { transactions[Trans_count++] = newTrans; }

void Account::setBalance (int trans_type, float amount)
{
    if (trans_type == DEPOSIT)
        balance += amount;
    else
        balance -= amount;
}
int Account::nextTrans_numb ()
    { return ++lastTrans_numb; }
```

- Inserts a pointer to this `Trans` object into the `transactions` array of the account that owns it by calling the `Account` object's `insertTrans` function. Notice in Listing 12.5 that the function's sole parameter is `this`, a pointer to the `Trans` object.
- Modifies the account balance to reflect the current transaction by calling the `Account` object's `setBalance` function.

The Transaction Type Conversion Functions

It's easier for a user to enter a type of transaction using a word (for example, *check* or *ATM*) than to remember which of a group of numeric codes to use. However, a `Trans` object takes up less space if it uses two bytes for an integer rather than eight or nine bytes for a string. The Checkbook program therefore stores an integer and converts to and from text for input and output.

The conversion functions, which are private to the `Trans` class because they aren't used outside the class, can be found in Listing 12.6. `Text2Type`, which translates from a string to an integer, uses the `strcmp` function and a set of nested `if` statements to identify the transaction type. `Type2Text`, because its decisions are based on an integer, can use a `switch` to decide which string to return to the calling function.

The main Function

The Checkbook program is managed by the `main` function in Listing 12.7. This function declares an array to hold pointers for up to 25 accounts. Just as with the `transactions` array in the `Account` class, this array holds pointers rather than objects to help conserve main memory.

The `main` function's first task is to call a program function that loads data from a text file into main memory. The function then enters a `while` loop that displays the menu (using the `simpleMenu` function you saw in Listing 12.1). The loop collects a menu choice and then enters a `switch` that chooses the program function that performs the selected action.

This is a typical structure for a long program: The `main` function is little more than a dispatcher. In fact, there is a school of thought that no function should be much longer than one page of code. The idea is that shorter blocks of code are easier to debug. Although the intent is laudable, it often isn't possible to keep your functions that short. Nonetheless, you should get into the habit of placing code that

Listing 12.6   Transaction type conversion member functions

```
int Trans::Text2Type (char * iType)
{
    if (strcmp("check",iType) == 0)
        return CHECK;
    else if (strcmp("deposit",iType) == 0)
        return DEPOSIT;
    else if (strcmp("ATM",iType) == 0)
        return ATM;
    else if (strcmp("service",iType) == 0)
        return SERVICE;
    else return 0; // type of transaction can't be identified
}

char * Trans::Type2Text ()
{
    static char type_string[8];
    switch (trans_type)
    {
        case CHECK:
            return strcpy(type_string,"check");
            break;
        case DEPOSIT:
            return strcpy(type_string,"deposit");
            break;
        case ATM:
            return strcpy(type_string,"ATM");
            break;
        case SERVICE:
            return strcpy(type_string,"service");
            break;
        default:
            return strcpy(type_string,"");
    }
}
```

performs a single task (for example, creating an account, creating a transaction, or reconciling an account) in a separate function. Notice that prototypes for all the program functions appear at the top of Listing 12.7.

NOTE

If a program is very long, you will probably want to separate functions into their own files. (It cuts down on the amount of scrolling you have to do.) When you do so, don't forget to add each file's name to the project file so that the compiler knows to link all the functions.

Listing 12.7   The main function for the checkbook program

```cpp
// function prototypes
int simpleMenu (); // display the simple text menu
int Load (Account * []); // load data from file; return number of accounts
void Unload (Account * [], int); // write data to file
int newAccount (Account * [], int); // create a new account
void enterTrans (Account * [], int); // enter a transaction
void reconcileAccount (Account * [], int); // reconcile an account
void findTrans (Account * [], int); // find a transaction
void viewTrans (Account * [], int); // look at transactions
Account * findAccount (Account * [], int); // find an account

void main ()
{
    int option = 0, acct_index;
    Account * Accounts[25]; // array to handle up to 25 accounts

    acct_index = Load (Accounts); // read data from file into array
    if (acct_index == -1)
        return; // no file; user asked to quit; exit program

    while (option != 9)
    {
        option = simpleMenu();
        switch (option)
        {
            case 1:
                acct_index = newAccount (Accounts, acct_index);
                break;
            case 2:
                enterTrans (Accounts, acct_index);
                break;
            case 3:
                reconcileAccount (Accounts, acct_index);
                break;
            case 4:
                findTrans (Accounts, acct_index);
                break;
            case 5:
                viewTrans (Accounts, acct_index);
                break;
            case 9:
                Unload (Accounts, acct_index);
                break;
            default:
                cout << "\nYou've entered an unavailable option." << endl;
                break;
        }
    }
}
```

Loading Data

To load data from the text file, the `main` function calls the program function `Load` (Listing 12.8), which first opens an input file. If the file was opened successfully, the function reads the number of accounts from the beginning of the file, skips over the blank between the number of accounts and the first account data, and then enters a `for` loop to read the accounts.

Listing 12.8   Loading stored data from the file

```
int Load (Account * Accounts[])
{
    int acct_index;
    char dummy, yes_no;

    ifstream ChecksIn ("Checkbook");
    if (ChecksIn) // load if file was opened successfully
    {
        ChecksIn >> acct_index; // read number of accounts
        ChecksIn.get(); // skip over blank
        for (int i = 0; i < acct_index; i++)
            Accounts[i] = new Account (ChecksIn);
        return acct_index;
    }
    else
    {
        cout << "Checkbook file couldn't be opened. OK to proceed? (y/n) ";
        cin >> yes_no;
        if (toupper(yes_no) == 'N')
            return -1; // quit the program
        else
            return 0;
    }
}
```

The content of this loop is a single `new` statement that creates an `Account` object, assigning the pointer to the new object to the `Accounts` array. Once the loop terminates, the function returns the number of accounts. Keep in mind that because the account pointers are stored in an array, there is no need to explicitly pass that array back to the calling function; arrays are always passed by reference.

If something goes wrong and the `Load` function can't open the input file, the user has a choice of continuing with the program or exiting. (Continuing means that the user will be working with no existing accounts.) When the user chooses to quit the program, the `main` function in Listing 12.7 identifies the -1 and issues a `return`. (A `return` from a `main` function exits the program.)

Creating a New Account

Creating a new account is a combination of a program function and the interactive `Account` class constructor you saw earlier. The `newAccount` function (Listing 12.9) collects the data for the account (Figure 12.1) and then uses the `new` operator to create the new account, passing the data collected into the interactive constructor.

Listing 12.9   Creating a new account

```
int newAccount (Account * Accounts[], int acct_index)
{
    string25 iacc_numb;
    string50 ibank_name;
    float ibalance;

    cout << "\nBank name: ";
    gets (ibank_name);
    cout << "\nAccount number: ";
    gets (iacc_numb);
    cout << "\nCurrent account balance: ";
    cin >> ibalance;
    Accounts[acct_index++] = new Account (iacc_numb, ibank_name, ibalance);
    return acct_index;
}
```

As the new account is created, the function also increments the `acct_index` variable, which keeps track of how many accounts are in existence. This value is passed back to the `main` function so that it is always up to date for use by other program functions.

Figure 12.1   The user's view: creating a new account

Entering Transactions
===================

From the user's point of view, entering a new transaction requires identifying the checking account with the bank name and account number and then entering transaction data (see Figure 12.2). Underneath what the user sees is a group of program and member functions.

The process is controlled by the `enterTrans` function (Listing 12.10). Because the program handles more than one account, the function's first job is to verify that the account is on file. Finding an account is performed by the `findAccount` function in Listing 12.11. This function is used throughout the program to locate an account, either to verify that the account exists or to provide access to the transactions that are part of an account. Because the possibility exists that two banks could have the same account numbers, the `findAccount` function bases its search on both

Figure 12.2   The user's view: entering a transaction

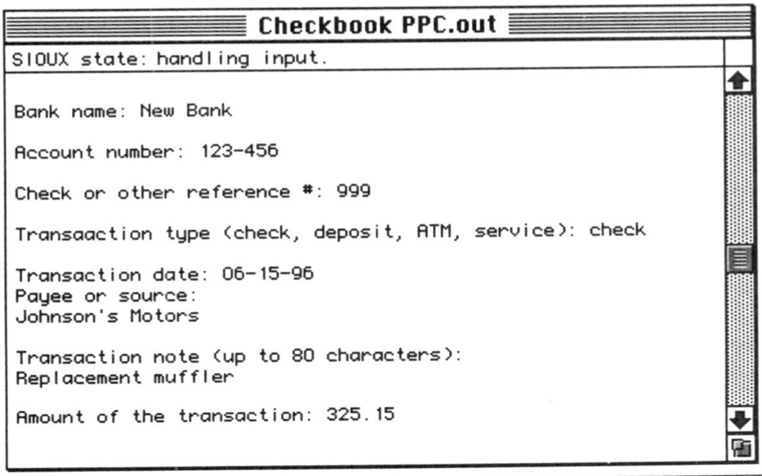

```
=============== Checkbook PPC.out ===============
SIOUX state: handling input.

Bank name: New Bank

Account number: 123-456

Check or other reference #: 999

Transaaction type (check, deposit, ATM, service): check

Transaction date: 06-15-96
Payee or source:
Johnson's Motors

Transaction note (up to 80 characters):
Replacement muffler

Amount of the transaction: 325.15
```

the bank name *and* the account number. (If you're convinced that no two banks would ever have duplicate account numbers, you could get by without the bank name.)

To perform its search, the findAccount function enters a for loop that checks each account, one by one, to see whether the bank name and account number match. The strcmp operations are based on data returned by two utility functions that retrieve private data from an Account object (Listing 12.12).

The search technique used by findAccount is known as a *sequential search* because it begins at the first item to be searched and looks through all items, in order. As the number of items to be searched becomes large, it is a very inefficient search method. However, because there will never be more than 25 accounts, it is adequate for use in this program.

The findAccount function returns a pointer to the Account object as soon as it finds a match. However, if the for loop finishes, the function wasn't able to locate a matching account. The function therefore returns a 0, telling the calling function that the search was unsuccessful.

Once the existence of the checking account has been verified, all the enterTrans function needs to do is to collect the transaction information and then use the new operator to create the Trans object. The pointer to the Account object that was located earlier is passed into the Trans object's constructor along with the rest of the transaction data.

Listing 12.10   Entering a transaction

```
void enterTrans (Account * Accounts[], int acct_index)
{
    Account * whichAccount;
    Trans * newTrans;
    char icheck_numb[6], iType[8];
    date_string itrans_date;
    string80 iPayeeSource, iNote;
    float iAmount;

    whichAccount = findAccount (Accounts, acct_index);
    if (whichAccount == 0)
    {
        cout << "\nThat account isn't in the database." << endl;
        return;
    }

    cout << "\nCheck or other reference #: ";
    cin.getline (icheck_numb,6);
    cout << "\nTransaaction type (check, deposit, ATM, service): ";
    gets (iType);
    cout << "\nTransaction date: ";
    cin.getline (itrans_date,10);
    cout << "\Payee or source:" << endl;
    cin.getline (iPayeeSource,80);
    cout << "\nTransaction note (up to 80 characters):" << endl;
    cin.getline (iNote,80);
    cout << "\nAmount of the transaction: ";
    cin >> iAmount;
    newTrans = new Trans (whichAccount, icheck_numb, itrans_date,
        iPayeeSource, iNote, iAmount, iType);
}
```

Listing 12.11   Finding an account

```
Account * findAccount (Account * Accounts[], int acct_index)
{
    string25 iacc_numb;
    string50 ibank_name;
    cout << "\nBank name: ";
    gets (ibank_name);
    cout << "\nAccount number: ";
    gets (iacc_numb);
    for (int i = 0; i < acct_index; i++)
        if ((strcmp (ibank_name,Accounts[i]->getBank_name()) == 0) &&
            (strcmp(iacc_numb,Accounts[i]->getAcc_numb()) == 0))
                return Accounts[i];
    return 0;
}
```

Listing 12.12   Utility functions to retrieve account data

```
char * Account::getAcc_numb ()
    { return acc_numb; }

char * Account::getBank_name ()
    { return bank_name; }
```

Reconciling a Checking Account

The process of reconciling a checking account involves letting the user indicate which transactions have appeared on an account statement, calculating the amount of uncleared withdrawals and deposits, and then letting the user know what the balance in the checkbook should be. The program function that controls reconciliation (Listing 12.13) first locates the account. If the account exists, it then calls the Account object's Reconcile member function.

Listing 12.13   Reconciling an account

```
void reconcileAccount (Account * Accounts[], int acct_index)
{
    Account * whichAccount;

    whichAccount = findAccount (Accounts, acct_index);
    if (whichAccount == 0)
    {
        cout << "\nThat account isn't in the database." << endl;
        return;
    }

    whichAccount->Reconcile();
}
```

The Reconcile member function (Listing 12.14) has several tasks:

- Examine all the transactions for this account, showing the user each transaction that hasn't been marked as cleared. Ask the user whether the transaction has

Listing 12.14   Member function to reconcile a checking account

```
void Account::Reconcile ()
{
    char yes_no;
    float statementBalance, outstandingDebits = 0, outstandingCredits = 0;

    // first let user mark transactions on statement
    for (int i = 0; i < Trans_count; i++)
        if (transactions[i]->getCleared() == FALSE)
        {
            transactions[i]->displayTrans();
            cout << "\nPart of this statement? (y/n) ";
            cin >> yes_no;
            if (yes_no == 'Y' || yes_no == 'y')
                transactions[i]->markCleared();
        }
    // sum outstanding debits and credits
    for (i = 0; i < Trans_count; i++)
        if (transactions[i]->getCleared() == FALSE)
            if (transactions[i]->getType() != DEPOSIT)
                outstandingDebits += transactions[i]->getAmount();
            else
                outstandingCredits += transactions[i]->getAmount();
    // ask for statement balance
    cout << "\nStatement balance: ";
    cin >> statementBalance;
    cout << "\nCheckbook balance should be: " <<
        statementBalance + outstandingCredits - outstandingDebits
        << endl << endl;
}

void Trans::markCleared ()
    { cleared = TRUE; }
```

cleared. If it has, call the Trans class member function markCleared, which appears at the bottom of Listing 12.14.

• Add up outstanding debits (checks, ATM withdrawals, service charges) and credits (deposits).
• Ask the user for the statement balance.
• Compute the correct checking account balance by adding the statement balance to uncleared credits and subtracting uncleared debits. Show the user what the checking account balance should be.

From the user's point of view, the process appears like the example in Figure 12.3. Unless the account has a large number of transactions, verifying which transactions have cleared takes only a minute or two. However, it is true that as the number of

Figure 12.3 The user's view: reconciling an account

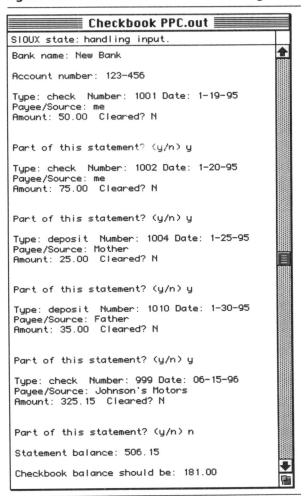

```
≡≡≡≡≡≡≡ Checkbook PPC.out ≡≡≡≡≡≡≡
SIOUX state: handling input.

Bank name: New Bank

Account number: 123-456

Type: check   Number: 1001 Date: 1-19-95
Payee/Source: me
Amount: 50.00   Cleared? N


Part of this statement? (y/n) y

Type: check   Number: 1002 Date: 1-20-95
Payee/Source: me
Amount: 75.00   Cleared? N


Part of this statement? (y/n) y

Type: deposit   Number: 1004 Date: 1-25-95
Payee/Source: Mother
Amount: 25.00   Cleared? N


Part of this statement? (y/n) y

Type: deposit   Number: 1010 Date: 1-30-95
Payee/Source: Father
Amount: 35.00   Cleared? N


Part of this statement? (y/n) y

Type: check   Number: 999 Date: 06-15-96
Payee/Source: Johnson's Motors
Amount: 325.15   Cleared? N


Part of this statement? (y/n) n

Statement balance: 506.15

Checkbook balance should be: 181.00
```

transactions increases, the amount of time needed to find uncleared transactions will go up as well.

Finding and Viewing Transactions

The Checkbook program has two ways to look at existing transactions. One is to locate a single transaction, based on either a check number or a combination of the date and payee or source of the transaction. The second is to view all transactions with a range of dates.

FINDING A SINGLE TRANSACTION

The Checkbook program uses the findTrans function (Listing 12.15) to locate one specific transaction. This function first asks the user for account information. If the account is present, the function then asks for data to identify the transaction.

If the transaction is a check and the user knows the check number, the easiest way to find the transaction is to enter the check number, as in Figure 12.4. Because the check number is stored as a string, findTrans can check the length of the input string to determine whether a check number has been entered. If the length is greater than 0, something was typed as a check number.

If the user enters a check number, findTrans calls a member function of the Account class (see the first function in Listing 12.16). This find function has one input parameter: a character string containing the check number. The function performs a sequential search on the transactions array. When a match is found, the function returns a pointer to the transaction. However, if the function's for loop terminates, the search was unsuccessful and the function returns a 0.

If the transaction is something other than a check or the user doesn't know the check number, he or she can press Enter to the request for the check number; the length of the input string will be 0. In that case, the findTrans function asks for the source or payee of the item and the transaction date (see Figure 12.5).

The findTrans function then uses the second find function in Listing 12.16. This function also performs a sequential search, comparing both the transaction date and the contents of the Payee/Source variable in each transaction to the function's input parameters. Like the find function that is based on the check number, this function returns a pointer to the transaction as soon as a match is found. If no match is found, it returns 0.

Listing 12.15   Finding a transaction

```
void findTrans (Account * Accounts[], int acct_index)
{
    Account * whichAccount;
    Trans * whichTrans;
    char icheck_numb[6];
    date_string idate;
    string80 iPayeeSource;

    whichAccount = findAccount (Accounts, acct_index);
    if (whichAccount == 0)
    {
        cout << "\nThat account isn't in the database." << endl;
        return;
    }

    cout << "\nCheck or other reference #: ";
    gets (icheck_numb);
    if (strlen(icheck_numb) == 0)
    {
        cout << "Transaction date: ";
        gets (idate);
        cout << "Payee or Source: ";
        gets (iPayeeSource);
        whichTrans = whichAccount->find (idate, iPayeeSource);
    }
    else
        whichTrans = whichAccount->find (icheck_numb);
    if (whichTrans == 0)
    {
        cout << "\nThat transaction isn't a part of this account." << endl;
        return;
    }

    whichTrans->displayTrans ();
}
```

NOTE

The two "find" functions are another example of function overloading. Because they have different parameter lists, the compiler has no difficulty in telling them apart. In fact, it sees them as two entirely different functions. The benefit of using overloading in this case is that the programmer has to know only one function name—find—to locate transactions, regardless of what input data the programmer has available.

Regardless of which find function is used to locate a transaction, the findTrans function uses the displayTrans member function (Listing 12.17) to display data on

Figure 12.4   The user's view: finding a transaction using a check number

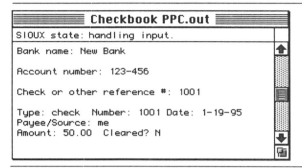

```
Checkbook PPC.out
SIOUX state: handling input.

Bank name: New Bank

Account number: 123-456

Check or other reference #: 1001

Type: check   Number: 1001 Date: 1-19-95
Payee/Source: me
Amount: 50.00   Cleared? N
```

Listing 12.16   Member functions to find transactions

```
Trans * Account::find (char * icheck_numb)
{
    for (int i = 0; i < Trans_count; i++)
        if (strcmp(transactions[i]->getCheck_numb(),icheck_numb) == 0)
            return transactions[i];
    return 0;
}

Trans * Account::find (date_string idate, string80 iPS)
{
    for (int i = 0; i < Trans_count; i++)
        if (strcmp(transactions[i]->getDate(),idate) == 0 &&
strcmp(transactions[i]->getPS(),iPS) == 0)
            return transactions[i];
    return 0;
}
```

the screen. The body of the function consists of a series of cout statements that display all transaction information.

VIEWING MULTIPLE TRANSACTIONS

Viewing transactions dated within a given range is handled by the program function viewTrans (Listing 12.18) and the Account class member function byDate (Listing 12.19). Like several of the other functions you have seen, viewTrans begins by searching for the account. If the search for the account is successful, the function collects a starting and ending date, and then calls byDate.

Figure 12.5   The user's view: finding a transaction using payee/source and date

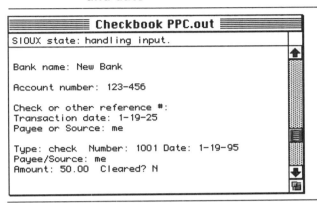

Listing 12.17   Displaying transaction information

```
void Trans::displayTrans ()
{
    char Type[8];

    strcpy (Type,Type2Text());
    cout << "\nType: " << Type << "  Number: " << check_numb << " Date: " <<
        trans_date << endl;
    cout << "Payee/Source: " << PayeeSource << endl;
    cout << setprecision(2) << setiosflags (ios::fixed);
    cout << "Amount: " << amount << "  Cleared? ";
    if (cleared == TRUE)
        cout << "Y" << endl;
    else
        cout << "N" << endl;
    cout << endl; // extra blank line
}
```

The byDate function conducts a sequential search on the transactions array. In this case, the function looks for transaction dates within the range indicated by the function's input parameters. There is one very important limitation to this function. Because dates are stored as strings, the format in which the dates are stored has a major impact on whether the search is accurate. If the dates are stored in MM-DD-YY format, the date range will be accurate only within the same month in the same year. If you want all date ranges to work correctly, you must store dates as YY-MM-DD.

Listing 12.18   Viewing transactions

```
void viewTrans (Account * Accounts[], int acct_index)
{
    Account * whichAccount;
    date_string startDate, endDate, transDate;
    int howMany;

    whichAccount = findAccount (Accounts, acct_index);
    if (whichAccount == 0)
    {
        cout << "\nThat account isn't in the database." << endl;
        return;
    }

    cout << "Starting date: ";
    gets (startDate);
    cout << "Ending date: ";
    gets (endDate);

    whichAccount->byDate (startDate, endDate);
}
```

Listing 12.19   Member function to view transactions in a date range

```
void Account::byDate (date_string start, date_string end)
{
    for (int i = 0; i < Trans_count; i++)
        if (strcmp(transactions[i]->getDate(), start) >= 0 &&
            strcmp (transactions[i]->getDate(),end) <= 0)
                transactions[i]->displayTrans();
}
```

NOTE

The YY-MM-DD format isn't very natural for people in the U. S. We're much more familiar with the MM-DD-YY format. In Chapter 13 you'll be introduced to a date class that can handle dates accurately in that format.

Exiting the Program

When the user decides to quit the Checkbook program, the program calls the Unload function to write account and transaction data back to the text file. The process begins by opening the output file stream. The function then writes the number of accounts to the file. The data are then written by calling the `Account` class's `write` function once for each account.

Listing 12.20   Storing data in a text file

```
void Unload (Account * Accounts[], int acct_index)
{
    ofstream ChecksOut ("Checkbook"); // opens file for text output
    ChecksOut << acct_index << ' '; // save number of accounts
    for (int i = 0; i < acct_index; i++)
        Accounts[i]->write (ChecksOut);
}
```

The `Account` class's `write` function (Listing 12.21) accepts the file output stream as an input parameter and then writes the account information to the file. Transaction information immediately follows each account's data. To write the transaction data, the `Account` class's `write` function calls the `Trans` class's `write` function (Listing 12.22)

Listing 12.21   Writing Account data

```
void Account::write (ofstream & fout)
{
    fout << acc_numb << '\0';
    fout << bank_name << '\0';
    fout << balance << ' ';
    fout << lastTrans_numb << ' ';
    fout << Trans_count << ' ';
    for (int i = 0; i < Trans_count; i++)
        transactions[i]->write(fout);
}
```

There is one final important thing to keep in mind about the Checkbook program. To read and write the text file that stores the program's data, the program must know exactly how the data are formatted in the file. If you need to change the structure of the program's classes, you will also have to change all the code that manipulates the file. Your existing data file will then be unusable. The structure of the data handled by a program of this type therefore isn't very flexible.

Listing 12.22   Writing Trans class data

```
void Trans::write (ofstream & fout)
{
    fout << trans_numb << ' ';
    fout << check_numb << '\0';
    fout << trans_date << '\0';
    fout << PayeeSource << '\0';
    fout << Note << '\0';
    fout << amount << ' ';
    fout << cleared << ' ';
    fout << trans_type << ' ';
}
```

Operator Overloading

13

Overloading is a way of giving multiple meanings to the same operation. So far, you have seen that you can overload member functions by giving two functions in the same class the same name but different signatures. Because the compiler uses the entire signature to identify a function, the two functions appear as distinct, separate functions.

As well as overloading functions, a C++ program can overload operators. In other words, operators such as the comparison operators (for example, ==, <, or >) and the arithmetic operators (for example, + or -) can be given additional meanings so that they behave in different ways, depending on the objects with which they are used.

Why would you bother to do this? Because it can make programming with objects much more intuitive. Assume, for example, that you have a class named date and that you've declared two objects from that class, date1 and date2. It makes sense to a programmer to be able to write expressions such as:

```
date1 == date2
date > date2
```

Perhaps you want to add 30 days to a date so you can quickly print the due date of an invoice. It makes sense to a programmer to write:

```
date1 + 30
```

If you've implemented your dates as strings, none of these expressions are permissible. However, operator overloading makes them possible.

In this chapter you will be introduced to the concepts behind operator overloading and to the date class we have just been using as an example. Then, once you understand how the date class works, you'll see how it can be used to solve the transaction date problem that exists in the Checkbook program.

Declaring Overloaded Operators

Operator overloading is more restrictive than anything we have discussed so far. This characteristic also makes it a bit trickier to work with than other aspects of C++. Nonetheless, if you pay attention to all the rules, you can simplify many of the programs you write.

Overloaded operators are implemented as functions whose name is the keyword operator followed by the operator itself. For example, if you want to overload the assignment operator, the function's name is operator=; a function to overload the equality operator is named operator==.

Functions that overload operators can be implemented as member functions or as *friend* functions. A friend function is a function that is given access to all private elements of a class in which it isn't a member function. Although you can declare friend functions in many circumstances, using them violates the object-oriented principle of information hiding. For that reason, many programmers prefer to use them only when absolutely necessary. Operator overloading is one of those situations.

When a function that overloads an operator is declared as a member function, it can have only one input parameter. For example, if you are declaring a member function that checks to see whether two dates are equal, the function prototype might appear as:

```
int operator>= (date);
```

The function that accompanies this prototype is triggered by the syntax:

```
date1 >= date2
```

The object `date1` is the object that executes the function; `date2` is the input parameter to the function.

This illustrates the major limitation to declaring overloaded operators as member functions: They aren't commutative. In other words, the object on the left of the operator is always the object that runs the overloaded operator function. The object or value on the right of the operator is always the input parameter.

However, if you implement an overloaded operator as a friend function, it can have two input parameters. Assume that you want to overload the addition operator to add an integer to a date. You could declare two friend functions:

```
friend date operator+ (date, int);
friend date operator+ (int, date);
```

To indicate that a function is a friend to a class, just place the word `friend` in front of the function's prototype within the class declaration.

The first of the preceding friend functions is triggered by the syntax:

```
date1 + 14
```

The second is triggered by:

```
14 + date1
```

In this case, we are combining function overloading with operator overloading to make it appear to the programmer as if the addition operation works in both ways.

The header file for the `date` class can be found in Listing 13.1. The three parts of a date (month, day, and year) are stored as individual integers. The class also includes a private function that converts those integers back into a string (`itoa`), a constructor, three `get` functions, and a function that reassembles the date into a string for output (`showDate`).

The `date` class has two friend functions to overload the addition operator. The class also overloads all the relationship operators and the assignment operator as member functions. Before looking at the overloaded operators in depth, however, let's examine the constructor and the `showDate` function.

Listing 13.1   Header file for the date class

```
class date
{
     friend date operator+ (int, date);
     friend date operator+ (date, int);

     private:
          int month, day, year;
          void itoa (int, char *); // convert two-digit integer back to ASCII
     public:
          date (char *);
          int getMonth ();
          int getDay ();
          int getYear ();
          char * showDate (char *);

          // overloaded operators
          int operator== (date);
          int operator!= (date);
          int operator> (date);
          int operator>= (date);
          int operator< (date);
          int operator<= (date);
          // assignment--lets you copy one date to another
          void operator= (date);
};
```

THE NONOVERLOADED MEMBER FUNCTIONS

Whenever a program creates a date object, the constructor takes a date in string form and converts it into three integers. To see how this is done, take a look at Listing 13.2, which contains all the date class member functions that don't overload operators.

The date class's constructor copies characters, two at a time, from the input string into a temporary string. Then it uses a C library function—atoi (ASCII to integer)—to convert the string into an integer and assign it to the correct class variable. The atoi function, whose prototype appears in stdlib.h, takes only one parameter: the string to be converted. Conversion is successful only if the characters in the string make up an integer. For example, if the string contains a letter, you won't get a legal integer back from the function call.

Because dates will be output as strings, the date class must also contain a function that converts the three integers back into a single string. This conversion is performed by the showDate function, which must take each integer and transform it back into a string.

Listing 13.2   Nonoperator member functions

```c
#include <string.h>
#include <stdlib.h>
#include "date.h"

date::date (char * stringDate)
{
    char Tstring[3];

    strncpy (Tstring, stringDate, 2); // get month
    month = atoi (Tstring); // convert to integer
    strncpy (Tstring, &stringDate[3], 2); // get day
    day = atoi (Tstring); // convert to integer
    strncpy (Tstring, &stringDate[6], 2);
    year = atoi (Tstring); // convert to ingeter
}

void date::itoa (int integer, char * string)
{
    char numbers[] = {'0','1','2','3','4','5','6','7','8','9'};
    int digit, i;

    digit = integer / 10;
    string[0] = numbers[digit];
    digit = integer % 10;
    string[1] = numbers[digit];
}

int date::getMonth()
    { return month;}

int date::getDay()
    { return day; }

int date::getYear()
    { return year; }

char * date::showDate (char * stringDate)
{
    char Tstring[3];

    itoa (month, Tstring);
    strcpy (stringDate, Tstring);
    strcat (stringDate, "/");
    itoa (day,Tstring);
    strcat (stringDate,Tstring);
    strcat (stringDate,"/");
    itoa (year,Tstring);
    strcat (stringDate,Tstring);
    return stringDate;
}
```

The conversion is performed by the itoa (integer to ASCII) function. As you can see in Listing 13.2, it first divides a two-digit number by 10 to isolate the lefthand digit and then looks up that digit in an array of characters. (The numbers array is an array of individual characters, not a string; it has no terminating null.) To isolate the righthand digit, it performs a modulo division by 10 on the integer and looks up the value in the numbers array. The last step is to append a null to the string.

NOTE

Some implementations of C and C++ do supply an itoa function as part of stdlib.h. However, the function is not part of the ANSI standard and therefore isn't available with CodeWarrior.

The showDate function calls itoa for each part of the date. As the converted strings are returned, it copies them onto the end of the string that is returned to the calling function.

Although strings are always passed by reference, showDate explicitly returns the address of the string. This makes it possible to place a call to showDate in other statements—especially stream output statements—that require a pointer to a string to act on the contents of a string.

Overloading with Member Functions

Writing functions to overload operators isn't terribly different from writing other types of functions. As you can see in Listing 13.3, the body of the member functions that overload operators perform the actions that the operators represent. For example, the overloaded == operator function compares each part of the date stored in the current object against each part of the date stored in the object that arrives as an input parameter.

The inequality operators (> and so on) are a bit more complicated because there is no simple logical expression that can determine the relationship between two dates. Instead, each of the inequality functions first looks at the year. If the years are different, the function can make its decision based on the year alone. However, if the years are the same, the function needs to look at the month. If the months are different, the day is irrelevant. However, if the months are the same, the function also considers the month.

Listing 13.3   Operators overloaded as member functions

```cpp
int date::operator== (date inDate)
{
    if (month == inDate.getMonth() && day == inDate.getDay()
        && year == inDate.getYear())
            return TRUE;
    return FALSE;
}

int date::operator!= (date inDate)
{
    if (month == inDate.getMonth() && day == inDate.getDay()
        && year == inDate.getYear())
            return FALSE;
    return TRUE;
}

int date::operator> (date inDate)
{
    if (year > inDate.getYear())
        return TRUE;
    if (year == inDate.getYear())
    {
        if (month > inDate.getMonth())
            return TRUE;
        if (month == inDate.getMonth() && day > inDate.getDay())
            return TRUE;
    }
    return FALSE;
}

int date::operator>= (date inDate)
{
    if (*this > inDate)
        return TRUE;
    if (*this == inDate)
        return TRUE;
    return FALSE;
}

int date::operator<= (date inDate)
{
    if (*this < inDate)
        return TRUE;
    if (*this == inDate)
        return TRUE;
    return FALSE;
}
```

Continued next page

Listing 13.3 (Continued)   Operators overloaded as member functions

```
int date::operator< (date inDate)
{
    if (year < inDate.getYear())
        return TRUE;
    if (year == inDate.getYear())
    {
        if (month < inDate.getMonth())
            return TRUE;
        if (month == inDate.getMonth() && day < inDate.getDay())
            return TRUE;
    }
    return FALSE;
}

void date::operator= (date inDate) // copy
{
    month = inDate.getMonth();
    day = inDate.getDay();
    year = inDate.getYear();
}
```

NOTE

Because the equality and inequality operators always compare two dates, there is no reason to implement them as friend functions: There will always be date objects on both sides of the operator. However, there would be no harm in using a friend function rather than a member function.

The overloaded assignment operator is relatively simple. It takes each value from the input date object and copies it into the corresponding variables in the current object. In this case, you shouldn't attempt to implement the function as a friend function, because assignment always requires that the destination be on the lefthand side of the operator. In other words, assignment isn't commutative.

Overloading with Friend Functions

When you overload operators using friend functions, the friend functions aren't part of the class. The functions in Listing 13.4, for example, although physically in the same file as the date class's member functions, don't include the name of a class and the scope resolution operator. In other words, these are program functions much like any other function that isn't a part of a class.

The two functions that overload the addition operator are identical, with the exception of their input parameters. As you can see from the listing, adding dates is a bit more complicated than adding other quantities, because the "carrying" from days to months to years is based on the varying number of days in a month.

An overloaded addition operator function therefore first adds the number of days that come in as an input parameter to the days in the current date object. Then, based on the current month, the function decides whether to adjust the value in the day and month. Finally, the function examines the month and decides whether to adjust the month and increment the year.

The functions return an entire date object. In this case, the object returned is the same object that arrives in the functions as an input parameter. This is because the functions actually modify the input object.

Using Overloaded Operators

Using overloaded operators is relatively straightforward if you are using static binding and a little more involved when you have declared objects for use with dynamic binding. To show you how this works, consider the demonstration main function in Listing 13.5.

This function really doesn't do any useful work; its only purpose is to test the member functions in the date class. As you can see in Figure 13.1, the program first asks for two dates and then reports on their relationship (greater than, less than, or equal to each other). Next, the program copies the first date into the second and reports the results. It finishes by adding 30 to the first date and showing the user the modified date.

The function in Listing 13.5 creates date objects for use with dynamic binding. However, the overloaded operators need date objects rather than pointers to date objects. This means that the function must dereference the pointers when they are used with the overloaded operators. The only case in which the pointers aren't dereferenced is when the function calls showDate, which, of course, is a regular member function and not an overloaded operator.

Listing 13.4   Operators overloaded as friend functions

```
date operator+ (int days2add, date inDate) {
    inDate.day += days2add;
    if (inDate.month == 2 && inDate.day > 28)
    {
        inDate.day -= 28;
        inDate.month++;
    }
    else if ((inDate.month == 4 || inDate.month == 6 || inDate.month == 9
        || inDate.month == 11) && inDate.day > 30)
    {
        inDate.day -= 30;
        inDate.month++;
    }
    else if (inDate.day > 31)
    {
        inDate.day -= 31;
        inDate.month++;
    }
    if (inDate.month > 12)
    {
        inDate.month--;
        inDate.year++;
    }
    return inDate; }

date operator+ (date inDate, int days2add) {
    inDate.day += days2add;
    if (inDate.month == 2 && inDate.day > 28)
    {
        inDate.day -= 28;
        inDate.month++;
    }
    else if ((inDate.month == 4 || inDate.month == 6 || inDate.month == 9
        || inDate.month == 11) && inDate.day > 30)
    {
        inDate.day -= 30;
        inDate.month++;
    }
    else if (inDate.day > 31)
    {
        inDate.day -= 31;
        inDate.month++;
    }
    if (inDate.month > 12)
    {
        inDate.month--;
        inDate.year++;
    }
    return inDate; }
```

Listing 13.5   Sample main function to test the date class

```
#include <iostream.h>
#include <stdio.h>
#include "date.h"

void main()
{
    date * date1, * date2;
    char dateString[9];

    cout << "Enter a date (MM/DD/YY): ";
    gets (dateString);
    date1 = new date (dateString);
    cout << "Enter a second date (MM/DD/YY): ";
    gets (dateString);
    date2 = new date (dateString);

    if (*date1 == *date2)
        cout << "The dates are equal.";
    else if (*date1 > *date2)
        cout << "The first date is greater than the second.";
    else if (*date2 > *date1)
        cout << "The second date is greater than the first.";

    *date2 = *date1;
    cout << "\nSecond date is now " << date2->showDate(dateString);
    *date1 = *date1 + 30;
    cout << "\nThirty days further on is " << date1->showDate(dateString);
}
```

Figure 13.1   Output of the dates program

```
┌──────────────── dates.out ────────────────┐
├────────────────────────────────────────────┤
│ SIOUX state: application has terminated.   │
│                                          ┌─┐│
│ Enter a date (MM/DD/YY): 10/15/96        │⇧││
│ Enter a second date (MM/DD/YY): 06/12/95 │ ││
│ The first date is greater than the second.│ ││
│ Second date is now 10/15/96              ├─┤│
│ Thirty days further on is 11/14/96       │⇩││
│                                          ├─┤│
│                                          │▤││
└──────────────────────────────────────────┴─┘
```

Fixing the Checkbook Program

The operator overloading in the date class can be used to fix the problem with transaction dates that arose in the Checkbook program. To make the change, we need to first replace the string version of the transaction date with a pointer to a date object. As you can see in Listing 13.6, the return type of the getDate function has also been changed. It now returns a pointer to a date object.

Listing 13.6   The Trans class modified to use a date object

```
class Trans
{
    private:
        int trans_numb; // arbitrary unique identifier for each transaction
        char check_numb[6];  // used only for check transactions
        date * trans_date;  // pointer to date objec
        string80 PayeeSource, Note;
        float amount;
        int cleared; // Boolean set to true when check has cleared
        // 1 = check, 2 = deposit, 3 = ATM withdrawl, 4 = service charge;
        int trans_type;
        Account * owner; // pointer to account that owns the transaction

        // private functions not used outside class
        // translate transaction type string into integer
        int Text2Type (char *);
        char * Type2Text (); // translate integer type into string

    public:
        Trans (Account *, char *, date_string, string80, string80,
            float, char *); // constructor for interactive input
        Trans (ifstream &, Account *); // constructor to read from file
        void markCleared ();
        void write (ofstream &); // write to file
        void displayTrans ();
        char * getCheck_numb ();
        date * getDate ();
        char * getPS ();
        int getCleared ();
        int getType ();
        float getAmount ();
};
```

Both constructors for the Trans class must also change. Rather than simply copying a string date into a variable, they must create a date object, passing the date string that comes into each function as a parameter to the date object's constructor (see Listing 13.7).

Listing 13.7 Modified constructors for the Trans class

```
Trans::Trans (Account * whichAccount, char * icheck_numb,
    date_string itrans_date, string80 iPayeeSource, string80 iNote,
    float iAmount, char * iType)
{
    owner = whichAccount;
    trans_numb = owner->nextTrans_numb();
    strcpy (check_numb, icheck_numb);
    trans_date = new date (itrans_date); // create the date object
    strcpy (PayeeSource, iPayeeSource);
    strcpy (Note, iNote);
    amount = iAmount;
    trans_type = Text2Type (iType);
    if (trans_type == SERVICE)
        cleared = TRUE;
    else
        cleared = FALSE;
    owner->insertTrans (this);
    owner->setBalance (trans_type, amount); // change balance as needed
}

Trans::Trans (ifstream & fin, Account * whichAccount)
{
    char dummy;
    date_string Tdate;

    owner = whichAccount;
    fin >> trans_numb;
    fin.get (dummy); // skip over blank before string
    fin.getline (check_numb,80,'\0');
    fin.getline (Tdate,80,'\0');
    trans_date = new date (Tdate); // create a date object
    fin.getline (PayeeSource,80,'\0');
    fin.getline (Note,80,'\0');
    fin >> amount;
    fin >> cleared;
    fin >> trans_type;
}
```

When you write the file, you don't want to write the pointer to a date object; you want to write the date itself. Why? Because when you quit the program, the contents of the memory it used are lost. The next time you come back to the program, it is extremely unlikely that the contents of memory the last time you used the program are still intact. You may have shut down the computer or loaded some other program in the interim. Even if you quit the program and run it again immediately, there's no guarantee that it will load in exactly the same place twice. The solution is therefore to write the date as a text string and convert it back to a date object when you read the file, just as the file input constructor in Listing 13.7 does. The Trans class's modified write function (Listing 13.8) therefore includes a call to the date class's show-Date function, which reassembles the date into a string.

Listing 13.8   Modified write function for the Trans class

```
void Trans::write (ofstream & fout)
{
    date_string Tdate;

    fout << trans_numb << ' ';
    fout << check_numb << '\0';
    fout << trans_date->showDate (Tdate) << '\0'; // write text of date
    fout << PayeeSource << '\0';
    fout << Note << '\0';
    fout << amount << ' ';
    fout << cleared << ' ';
    fout << trans_type << ' ';
}
```

There are two other places in the Checkbook program where the switch to date objects occur: the routines that look for transactions by date. Using the overloaded comparison operators, these functions now work properly for dates stored in MM/DD/YY format. The functions affected are Account class's find function (the one that finds by date and payee/source) and byDate function, both of which appear in Listing 13.9).

Listing 13.9   Modified Account class functions using overloaded date class operators

```
Trans * Account::find (date_string idate, string80 iPS)
{
    date cDate (idate); // create and initialize a date object
    date tDate (idate);
    for (int i = 0; i < Trans_count; i++)
    {
        tDate = *(transactions[i]->getDate());
        if (tDate == cDate && strcmp(transactions[i]->getPS(),iPS) == 0)
            return transactions[i];
    }
    return 0;
}

void Account::byDate (date_string start, date_string end)
{
    date sDate (start), eDate (end),tDate (start); // two date objects
    for (int i = 0; i < Trans_count; i++)
    {
        tDate = *(transactions[i]->getDate());
        if (tDate >= sDate && tDate <= eDate)
            transactions[i]->displayTrans();
    }
}
```

Programming Challenge Number 10

The `date` class has access to overloaded assignment and addition operators, supporting statements in the format:

```
date1 = date1 + 30;
```

However, this doesn't mean that you can use the `+=` operator. To begin this challenge, overload the `+=` operator. (Hint: Make it a friend function and take advantage of the existing overloaded assignment and addition operators.)

Another limitation to the overloaded addition operator is that it doesn't take leap years into account. Add code to each of the overloaded addition operator functions that will identify and handle leap years. (Hint: Leap years are divisible by 4.)

A final limitation to the overloaded addition operator is that it will work with an integer constant but not a value stored in a variable. To complete this challenge, add overloaded functions that let the user use both variables and constants. (Hint: You'll end up with four overloaded friend functions for the addition operator.) Add code to the main function to test your new overloading.

Programming Challenge
Number 11

As written, the date class's constructor will work properly only if each month and day are entered as two digits. If a user enters something like 1/1/96, the conversion to integers will fail. Your job in this challenge is to fix the constructor so that it accepts either one or two characters for month and day.

Rather than using strncpy to get fixed-size chunks of the input string, consider scanning the string one character at a time with a for loop. You can detect the end of a number by encountering a '/' or '-' (the characters typically used to separate the parts of a date).

The date class also has a problem with the year. Right now, it handles only two-digit years, but once years beginning with 2000 come into the picture, comparisons based on just two digits for the year won't work properly. If you've done the scanning technique properly, your code should work for four-digit years as well.

When you allow for a one digit month and day and a four-digit year, the itoa function won't work properly. Consider carefully how you should modify that function so that it will work for an integer of any length. (The best strategy is based on the idea of repeatedly dividing by 10 and perfoming a modulo division by 10 on a number to isolate each digit in the integer.) Make those modifications and then test your modifications by running the main function that tests the date class.

Programming Challenge Number 12

In Chapter 10 you added birthdates to the Families program as strings. As you now know, storing dates as strings isn't particularly efficient when it comes to working with those dates. For this challenge, you'll be replacing the string dates with objects of the date class and adding functions to use those dates.

The modifications you should make include:

- Replace all string dates with pointers to objects of the date class.
- Pass the birthdate into a constructor as a string. Use that parameter as input to the date class constructor. (If you completed Programming Challenge Number 11, use your modified date class; it's more flexible than the original.)
- Add to the main program a function that searches for all people who have birthdates before a date the user enters. To do this, you'll need a date object into which the main program can store the user's comparison date. Then retrieve all birthdates (parents and kids)—one by one—and use the overloaded operators to make the requested comparison.

Consider carefully how you're going retrieve the dates for comparison. There is usually more than one date in each families object; you'll need to get father, mother, and all the kids!

Data Structures: Arrays

14

A *data structure* is a program structure that organizes data. The simplest data structure is an array, which organizes multiple items of the same type. Object-oriented programs, which often make use of arrays of objects, have special ways of managing such arrays. This chapter therefore begins by looking at special objects that exist only to manage arrays of other objects. You won't be learning any new language elements but will be seeing new ways to use what you already know.

One of the drawbacks to the way in which we have been handling arrays of objects is that the function that manipulates the array must know a great deal about the objects handled by the array. The functions using the array must know exactly what data to collect when a new object is created; they must know how many objects are in the array when they attempt to add a new object or access all the objects. If the structure of the objects in the array changes, the functions using the array must also change. In the first part of this chapter, you'll look at the object-oriented way of managing an array object to get around this problem.

Another drawback to the way we've been handling arrays is that the elements are always added to the bottom of an array. There hasn't been any way to change the order of those elements. However, many times you want to see array items in date, value, or alphabetical order. In other words, you need to sort the array. The second part of this chapter therefore looks at one technique for changing the order of elements in an array so that you can produce output in any order you desire.

Once you have a sorted array, you also have access to a variety of techniques for quickly searching an array. At the very end of this chapter you'll be introduced to a binary search, one of the fastest and most efficient ways to search an ordered array.

Objects to Manage Arrays

Object-oriented programs avoid much of the impact of changes in objects by hiding the internal structure of an object from the functions that use the object. Requiring a function to manipulate an array of objects therefore violates this principle and makes maintaining a program more difficult.

The solution is to create a special object whose sole job is to manage an array of another type of object. To show you how objects that manage arrays of objects work, we'll be modifying the Families program once again, this time introducing a new arrayMgr class that takes care of the array of families that was previously managed by the program's main function.

The arrayMgr class (Listing 14.1) has two class variables: an integer to keep track of how many families are in the array and the array of Families objects. In addition to the constructor, the class has four member functions. The insert function collects data for a new Families object, creates the object, and inserts it into the array. The read function handles reading data from a file; the write function does just the opposite. The list function displays all the data in the array.

Listing 14.1   The arrayMgr class

```
class arrayMgr
{
    private:
        int numb_families;
        Families * familyArray[MAX_FAMILIES];
    public:
        arrayMgr();
        int insert(); // create new object and insert into array
        int read ();
        void write ();
        void list ();
};
```

Much of the code in the member functions formerly appeared in the main function. If you look at Listing 14.2, you'll see that the insert function takes care of determining whether there is enough space in the array to insert another family, collecting all the data for a new Families object, creating the object, and adding it to the arrayMgr object's array. The insert function returns TRUE if the function was able to insert a new family or FALSE if it was not.

The arrayMgr class's read and write functions look almost identical to the program functions by the same name. (In fact, the changes to the program were made by simply copying the contents of the program functions into the member functions.) Both functions open a file and then perform the needed I/O operations. Keep in mind, however, that in this case, the main function doesn't need to know anything about how these operations are taking place, because they're hidden within the member functions of the arrayMgr object.

Listing all the objects in the array (Listing 14.4) also looks much like it did when the listing was handled by the main function. The only difference is that in this case the access to the contents of the array is handled by the arrayMgr object.

So what does this all mean for the main function and its program functions? As you can see in Listing 14.5, it doesn't leave much for the main function to do. It first creates one object from the arrayMgr class. (Because the program manipulates just one array, it needs only one array manager object.)

If reading the file fails, the read function returns FALSE and the program ends. However, if reading is successful, the main function enters a while loop for entering new families. The insert function returns TRUE when it was able to successfully add a new family. In that case, the loop continues. However, if the array is full or the user decided not to enter any more data, the loop stops and the program then executes the list function. The program finishes by calling the write function to store the data in the text file.

Notice throughout that the main function has no idea how many Families objects are in the array of objects. It also has no idea of what data are needed to create a new Families object or to display a Families object. You can change the size of the array or the elements of a Families object, without ever needing to modify the main function. You can also reuse the arrayMgr and Families classes in many programs, none of which need to be concerned with the details of the classes. This is therefore a good example of the object-oriented principle of information hiding.

Listing 14.2   Constructor and insert member functions for the arrayMgr class

```
arrayMgr::arrayMgr()
{
    numb_families = -1; // empty array
    for (int i = 0; i < MAX_FAMILIES; i++)
        familyArray[i] = 0; // initialze pointers to 0
}


int arrayMgr::insert ()
{
    char yes_no, dummy2[2];
    string25 ifather, imother, ikids[MAX_KIDS];
    int inumb_kids = MAX_KIDS + 1;

    if (numb_families + 1 >= MAX_FAMILIES)
    {
        cout << "\nThe families array is full";
        return FALSE;
    }

    cout << "\nDo you want to add another family? ";
    cin >> yes_no;
    if (toupper(yes_no) == 'N')
        return FALSE;
    gets(dummy2); //kludge
    cout << "\n\nFather: ";
    gets (ifather);
    cout << "Mother: ";
    gets (imother);
    while (inumb_kids > MAX_KIDS)
    {
        cout << "\nHow many children do they have? ";
        cin >> inumb_kids;
        if (inumb_kids > MAX_KIDS)
            cout << "\nThis program is limited to " << MAX_KIDS
                << " kids. Try again." << endl;
    }
    gets(dummy2); //kludge
    for (int i = 0; i < inumb_kids; i++)
    {
        cout << "Child #" << i+1 << ": ";
        gets (ikids[i]);
    }
    familyArray[++numb_families] = new Families (ifather, imother,
        inumb_kids, ikids);
    return TRUE;
}
```

Listing 14.3   The arrayMgr member functions to read from and write to a text file

```
int arrayMgr::read ()
{
    char yes_no, dummy;

    ifstream peopleIn ("people"); // input file
    if (!peopleIn)
    {
        cout << "Couldn't open input file. OK to continue? ";
        cin >> yes_no;
        if (toupper(yes_no) == 'N')
            return FALSE; // quit the program
    }
    else // read from file
    {
        peopleIn >> numb_families; // get last array-of-objects index
        peopleIn.get (dummy); // skip over whitespace
        for (int i = 0; i <= numb_families; i++)
        {
            familyArray[i] = new Families (peopleIn);
        }
        peopleIn.close();
    }
    return TRUE;
}

void arrayMgr::write()
{
    ofstream peopleOut ("people");
    if (!peopleOut)
    {
        cout << "Problem opening output file.";
        return;
    }
    peopleOut << numb_families << ' ';
    // write to file
    for (int i = 0; i <= numb_families; i++)
        familyArray[i]->write(peopleOut);
}
```

NOTE

If the Families program's main function is only what you see in Listing 14.5, why does it need to have the fstream.h header file included? Because some of the member functions in families.h, which contains both the Families and the arrayMgr classes, use file stream objects as parameters. The main function therefore won't compile unless it knows about file stream objects, which are declared in fstream.h.

**Listing 14.4   The arrayMgr member function that lists the contents
                    of its array**

```
void arrayMgr::list()
{
    char yes_no;

    for (int i = 0; i <= numb_families; i++)
    {
        familyArray[i]->display();
        if (i < numb_families)
        {
            cout << "\nNext? ";
            cin >> yes_no;
            if (toupper(yes_no) == 'N')
                break;
        }
    }
}
```

Listing 14.5   Modified main function for the Families program

```
#include <fstream.h>
#include "families.h"

void main ()
{
    arrayMgr familyGroup; // create an array manager object
    int response;

    response = familyGroup.read ();
    if (response == FALSE)
        return; // exit program

    response = TRUE;
    while (response == TRUE)
        response = familyGroup.insert(); // add new ones

    familyGroup.list ();
    familyGroup.write ();
}
```

Sorting an Array: The Bubble Sort

The many techniques for sorting arrays vary widely in efficiency (how quickly they work) and simplicity (the complexity of the logic). To introduce you to the idea of sorting, we're going to be looking at a logically simple sort technique that is efficient if an array is mostly in order (only a few elements are out of order) but whose efficiency degrades for large arrays that are in relatively random order. This sorting method is known as a *bubble sort*.

The bubble sort works by comparing successive pairs of values in an array. If the values are in the wrong order, the program swaps them. Each pass through the array moves the largest value that is out of order toward the bottom of the array. The sort makes repeated passes through the array until it scans the array without needing to swap any elements.

To see exactly how this works, take a look at Figure 14.1. For this example, we will be sorting an array of five integers. The original array appears at the top left of the figure. The first comparison is between the numbers in element 0 and element 1. Because these values are out of order, the program swaps them. The second comparison is between elements 1 and 2. Because these are in the correct order, the program doesn't move them. However, when the program compares elements 2 and 3, it must make a swap. The same occurs for elements 3 and 4. Notice that the effect of this first pass is to move the 16, the highest value in the array, to the very bottom.

For the second pass, the program begins by again comparing elements 0 and 1. During this second pass, elements 1 and 2, as well as elements 2 and 3, are out of order. Only two swaps are made, placing the last three elements in order.

The third pass requires only one swap. At the end of this pass, the entire array is in order, but the computer doesn't know it. It must make one final pass—a scan of the array without any swaps—to detect that the sort is complete.

A First Bubble Sort Example

As a very simple first example of a bubble sort, let's look at a program that accepts an array of 10 integers, sorts them in ascending numeric order, and then displays the sorted array. The program is based on the `integers` class in Listing 14.6, which has only one class variable (the array of integers) and three member functions in addition to the constructor, each of which does exactly what its name suggests (loads the array, sorts the array, and displays the array).

Figure 14.1 Performing a bubble sort

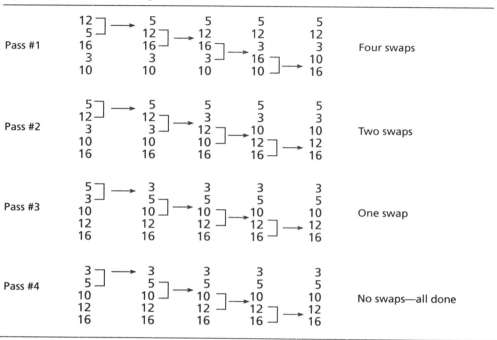

The member functions for the Bubble Sort program can be found in Listing 14.7. To see how you can implement a bubble sort, let's look at the sort function. The first thing a bubble sort must do is set up a variable to keep track of whether any elements have been swapped during a pass through the array. In this example, that variable is called flip_flag. It is initialized to TRUE so that the while loop that controls passes through the array will be executed at least once.

After initializing flip_flag, the sort enters the while loop. The program immediately sets flip_flag to FALSE. (In other words, the program makes the assumption that no swaps will be made.) Then the program enters a for loop that makes one pass through the array.

When setting up this loop, you must pay attention to the loop's terminating condition. Because the comparison is made between the element at the current loop index and the element below (loop index + 1), you want to stop the loop one value less than the highest array element's index. This will prevent you from looking at an element beyond the end of the array. In the program we are examining, the constant ARRAY_SIZE is the total number of elements in the array. The highest array index is

Figure 14.2   Output of the Bubble Sort program

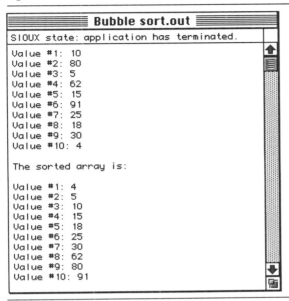

Listing 14.6   Header file for the Bubble Sort program

```
const ARRAY_SIZE = 10;

class integers
{
    private:
        int integerArray[ARRAY_SIZE];
    public:
        integers ();
        void load ();
        void sort ();
        void display ();
};
```

ARRAY_SIZE - 1. The loop should continue as long as the loop's index is less than this value. You could also write the terminating condition as i <= ARRAY_SIZE - 2.

Inside the for loop, the sort compares the current array element (integers[i]) with the following array element (integers[i+1]). If the current element is larger than the following element, the program must swap the position of the elements in the array.

Listing 14.7   Member functions for the Bubble Sort program

```cpp
#include <iostream.h>
#include "bubble sort.h"


integers::integers ()
{
    for (int i = 0; i < ARRAY_SIZE; i++)
        integerArray[i] = 0;
}


void integers::load ()
{
    for (int i = 0; i < ARRAY_SIZE; i++)
    {
        cout << "Value #" << i + 1 << ": ";
        cin >> integerArray[i];
    }
}


void integers::sort()
{
    int flip_flag = TRUE;
    int temp, i;

    while (flip_flag)
    {
        flip_flag = FALSE;
        for (i = 0; i < ARRAY_SIZE - 1; i++)
        {
            if (integerArray[i] > integerArray[i+1])
            {
                temp = integerArray[i];
                integerArray[i] = integerArray[i+1];
                integerArray[i+1] = temp;
                flip_flag = TRUE;
            }
        }
    }
}


void integers::display ()
{
    cout << "\nThe sorted array is:" << endl << endl;
    for (int i = 0; i < ARRAY_SIZE; i++)
        cout << "Value #" << i + 1 << ": " << integerArray[i] << endl;
}
```

To effect the swap, the program must store one of the two values in a temporary variable. If it doesn't, moving one value on top of the other destroys the original value. The swap therefore moves one value into `temp`, replaces that value with the other value, and copies the saved value in `temp` to its new location. Although this particular sort saves the current element in the temporary variable, it makes no difference which one you save. Just be sure that you replace the saved variable first. In other words, if you save the current element, move the current element + 1 into the current element. Then replace the current element + 1 with the contents of the temporary variable.

After making a swap, the sort sets `flip_flag` to `TRUE`. This assignment occurs every time a swap is made during a single pass, regardless of the number of swaps. Therefore, if even a single swap is made, the sort function will know that it has to make at least one more pass through the array.

When the sort function makes a pass through the array without making any swaps, `flip_flag` retains its value of `FALSE`. The `while` loop then stops and the sort is finished.

Just to be complete, you can find the `main` function for the bubble sort demonstration program in Listing 14.8. All this function needs to do is call the `load`, `sort`, and `display` member functions, one after the other.

Listing 14.8   Main function for the Bubble Sort program

```
#include "bubble sort.h"

void main ()
{
     integers myInts; // declare object

     myInts.load ();
     myInts.sort ();
     myInts.display ();
}
```

SORTING ARRAYS OF POINTERS

In the bubble sort example we just examined, the sort function swapped data values. However, when the items you want to sort are objects, moving entire objects in main memory can have undesirable consequences. First, it slows down a program because the swap involves many values. Second, it tends to fragment memory as you move objects around, leading to possible memory problems. It is therefore more efficient and reliable to sort an array of pointers to objects, rather than to sort the objects themselves.

When you sort an array of pointers, the comparisons between items is made using data from the objects. However, when you decide to move something, you move just the pointers to the objects, not the objects themselves. Then, when you want to access the objects in order, you access them via their ordered pointers.

NOTE

It may help to think of an array of pointers as something akin to the index in a book. A book's index is ordered by topic and includes pointers (page numbers) to the text in the body of the book. You look up a topic in the index and then follow the pointer to where the data can be found. You use an array of pointers in the same way: by following the pointer in the array to the object it represents.

As an example of how you can sort an array of pointers, we'll be adding sorted output capabilities to the Families program. Before displaying the families stored by the program, the user will have the choice of listing them alphabetically by the father's name or the mother's name.

The modified `list` function can be found in Listing 14.9. Notice first that the `list` function declares a temporary variable (`temp`) to store a pointer to a `Families` object. (Keep in mind that we will be swapping pointers, not objects.) Before entering the sort, the function also asks the user to choose between mother and father ordering. The sort then enters the `while` loop, which controls passes through the array.

There are two major differences between this sort and the sort of the integer array you saw earlier. The first is in the comparison made within the `for` loop to determine whether a swap of array elements is needed. Notice that the comparison is made on values retrieved from `Families` objects, not from values stored in the array. (Comparing pointers wouldn't be particularly meaningful.) In addition, because the data being matched are strings, the comparison uses the `strcmp` function.

NOTE

If you wanted to sort in chronological order, you might use objects of the date class presented in Chapter 13. Then you could make comparisons using the overloaded operators that are part of that class's member functions.

The second major difference between this sort and the sort of the integer array is simply that when the program decides that a swap is required, it manipulates the

Listing 14.9   The modified listing routine for the Families program

```
void arrayMgr::list()
{
    char yes_no;
    Families * temp;
    int flip_flag = TRUE, i;

    cout << "Alphabetical by father or mother (m/f)? ";
    cin >> yes_no;

    while (flip_flag == TRUE)
    {
        flip_flag = FALSE;
// note: numb_families is last index used in array
// Therefore don't need to subtract 1 to avoid overflowing array
        for (i = 0; i < numb_families; i++)
        {
            if ((toupper(yes_no) == 'M' &&
                strcmp (familyArray[i]->getMother(),
                    familyArray[i+1]->getMother()) > 0)
                || (toupper(yes_no) == 'F' &&
                strcmp (familyArray[i]->getFather(),
                    familyArray[i+1]->getFather()) > 0))
            {
                temp = familyArray[i];
                familyArray[i] = familyArray[i+1];
                familyArray[i+1] = temp;
                flip_flag = TRUE;
            }
        }
    }

    for (i = 0; i <= numb_families; i++)
    {
        familyArray[i]->display();
        if (i < numb_families)
        {
            cout << "\nNext? ";
            cin >> yes_no;
            if (toupper(yes_no) == 'N')
                break;
        }
    }
}
```

pointers in the array. The objects whose data were used in the comparison aren't touched.

NOTE

Because an array of pointers provides an index to a group of objects floating around in main memory, you could keep more than one array of pointers to the same group of objects. Each array could be sorted in a different order. This approach makes it easier and faster to output the array elements in the desired order. However, you must modify all arrays of pointers each time you add an object. The trade-off is between fast output speed and fast creation of new objects.

Searching Arrays: The Binary Search

Arrays are a "random access" data structure, meaning that you can access the elements in any order you want, just by supplying an element's index. However, up to this point we really haven't been taking advantage of that fact. We've been searching arrays sequentially (first element, to next element, to next element, and so on).

A sequential search is easy to implement but rather inefficient. For example, assume that you have an array of 1000 elements. In the worst case—where the element you want isn't in the array—you'll have to look at all 1000 elements to find out that your search is unsuccessful. On average, you'll have to look at 500 elements for a successful search.

A number of search techniques are much more efficient than a sequential search. If your array is ordered by the value on which you want to search, you can use a binary search. A binary search is one of the most efficient search techniques available for an array. If you have that same array of 1000 elements, an unsuccessful binary search will have to look at 12 elements at most. A successful search will need to consult only five or six elements.

Seem impossible? Not when you consider how the binary search works. The basic principle is to look at the middle element in the array. If the element you're seeking precedes the middle element, you know that you can eliminate the bottom half and concentrate on just the top half. By the same token, if the element you're seeking follows the middle element, you can eliminate the top half of the array from your search. Each time a binary search checks the middle of a range of array elements to see whether it has found the correct element, it eliminates half the remaining elements from the search.

To explore how a binary search works, we're going to make one final set of modifications to the Families program. These modifications will make it possible to quickly search for one family, based on either the father's name or the mother's name.

SETTING UP THE SORTED ARRAYS

To support binary searching by either the father's name or the mother's name, this final version of the Families program contains two arrays of pointers to Families objects. As you can see in the modified arrayMgr class, which appears in Listing 14.10, the original familyArray has been replaced by byFather and byMother.

Listing 14.10   The modified arrayMgr class

```
class arrayMgr
{
    private:
        int numb_families;
        Families * byFather[MAX_FAMILIES];
        Families * byMother[MAX_FAMILIES];
        void sortFather ();
        void sortMother ();
    public:
        arrayMgr();
        int insert(); // create new object and insert into array
        int read ();
        void write ();
        void list ();
        void search (); // find one family
        Families * searchFather (string25);
        Families * searchMother (string25);
};
```

Every time a new Families object is created, the arrayMgr object will sort both arrays to keep them in order. The objects themselves are scattered throughout main memory. The arrays of pointers are therefore acting as indexes to those arrays, each ordering the points differently.

The arrayMgr class also has five new functions. The sort functions (sortFather and sortMother) are private functions because they are never going to be used outside the class. The three search functions (search, searchFather, and searchMother) are public. Although currently searchFather and searchMother are used only by the search function, they are public so that they are accessible should someone want to use them when adding features to the program.

To maintain the sorted arrays, some changes need to be made to the `arrayMgr` class's `insert` function. As you can see in Listing 14.11, the single line that stored a pointer in the original `familyArray` has been replaced. When the `Families` object is created, its pointer is stored directly in the `byFather` array. That pointer is then copied into the `byMother` array.

Listing 14.11   Maintaining the sorted arrays

```
Original code from the insert function:

familyArray[++numb_families] = new Families (ifather, imother,
        inumb_kids, ikids);

Replacement code to support sorted arrays:

byFather[++numb_families] = new Families (ifather, imother,
        inumb_kids, ikids);
byMother[numb_families] = byFather[numb_families];
sortFather ();
sortMother ();
```

New elements are always added to the bottom of the array. This means that they probably aren't in their correct places. The function therefore calls `sortFather` to sort the `byFather` array and `sortMother` to sort the `byMother` array.

As you can see in Listing 14.12, both sort routines use a bubble sort, just like the sort to which you were introduced earlier in this chapter, although the comparison logic is a bit simpler because each sort function works with only a single array and a single sort order. In this case, a bubble sort is as efficient as just about any other sort method. This is because the array is completely in order except for the new element added at the bottom.

WRITING THE SEARCHES

The binary search functions can be found in Listing 14.13. As you can see, each search needs three variables to keep track of where it is.

- `top`: The lowest array index in the portion of the array being searched. It is initialized to one less than the lowest index in the array (in this case, -1).
- `bottom`: The highest array index in the portion of the array being searched. It is initialized to one higher than the highest index in the array (in this case, the value

Listing 14.12   Sorting the arrays

```
void arrayMgr::sortMother ()
{
     int flip_flag = TRUE;
     Families * temp;

     while (flip_flag == TRUE)
     {
          flip_flag = FALSE;
          // note: numb_families is last index used in array
          for (int i = 0; i < numb_families; i++)
          {
               // make comparison based on mother
               if (strcmp(byMother[i]->getMother(),
                    byMother[i+1]->getMother()) > 0)
               {
                    // swap elements just in the byMother array
                    temp = byMother[i];
                    byMother[i] = byMother[i+1];
                    byMother[i+1] = temp;
                    flip_flag = TRUE;
               }
          }
     }
}

void arrayMgr::sortFather ()
{
     int flip_flag = TRUE;
     Families * temp;

     while (flip_flag == TRUE)
     {
          flip_flag = FALSE;
          // note: numb_families is last index used in array
          for (int i = 0; i < numb_families; i++)
          {
               // make comparison based on father
               if (strcmp(byFather[i]->getFather(),
                    byFather[i+1]->getFather()) > 0)
               {
                    // swap elements just in the byFather array
                    temp = byFather[i];
                    byFather[i] = byFather[i+1];
                    byFather[i+1] = temp;
                    flip_flag = TRUE;
               }
          }
     }
}
```

Listing 14.13   The binary search functions

```
Families * arrayMgr::searchFather (string25 ifather)
{
    int top, bottom, mid, test;

    top = -1; // top is one less than lowest array index
    bottom = numb_families; // bottom is one greater than highest array index

    mid = (top + bottom) / 2; // find middle of range

    // search fails when top crosses middle
    while (top < mid)
    {
        test = strcmp (ifather, byFather[mid]->getFather());
        if (test == 0) // correct one found
            return byFather[mid];
        if (test < 0) // search value is above middle
            bottom = mid; // move up bottom
        else // search value is below middle
            top = mid; // move down top
        mid = (top + bottom) / 2; // compute new middle
    }
    return 0; // wasn't found
}

Families * arrayMgr::searchMother (string25 imother)
{
    int top, bottom, mid, test;

    top = -1; // top is one less than lowest array index
    bottom = numb_families; // bottom is one greater than highest array index

    mid = (top + bottom) / 2; // find middle of range

    // search fails when top crosses middle
    while (top < mid)
    {
        test = strcmp (imother, byMother[mid]->getMother());
        if (test == 0) // correct one found
            return byMother[mid];
        if (test < 0) // search value is above middle
            bottom = mid; // move up bottom
        else // search value is below middle
            top = mid; // move down top
        mid = (top + bottom) / 2; // compute new middle
    }
    return 0; // wasn't found
}
```

in `numb_families`).

- `mid`: The array index of the element that is in the middle of the array being searched. Its value is computed with:

```
mid = (top + bottom) / 2;
```

The search is controlled by a `while` loop that stops when an unsuccessful search is detected. There are two methods for identifying an unsuccessful search. If `top` becomes greater than or equal to `mid`, the search has failed. By the same token, if `bottom` becomes less than or equal to `mid`, the search has failed. In this case, we are using the first method.

Inside the `while`, the search function first compares the name for which the user is searching with the name in the `mid` element of the portion of the array being searched. The result is stored in the variable `test`. Although you could get away without this variable by placing the call to `strcmp` in the `if` statements, the code is cleaner (and shorter) if the result of the `strcmp` is stored.

If the two names match (`test == 0`), the search is successful and the function returns a pointer to the `Families` object that is at the `mid` position in the array. However, if the correct element hasn't been found, the search must decide whether to eliminate the top or bottom half of the current range of elements.

If the search value came alphabetically prior to the name at the `mid` position in the array (`test < 0`), the search value can't be in the bottom half of the array. The function therefore moves `bottom` up to equal `mid`. However, if the search value was alphabetically greater than the value at element `mid` (`test > 0`), the search value can't be in the top half of the current range of elements. The function therefore moves `top` down to equal `mid`. In either case, after moving either `top` or `bottom`, the function computes a new `mid` for the modified range of elements. The search can then check the middle element in the new range, repeating this process until either the correct element is found or `top` crosses `mid` and the search is unsuccessful.

The binary search functions are used by the `arrayMgr` class's `search` member function. As you can see in Listing 14.14, this function asks the user whether the search should be by father's name or mother's name. The function then collects the name that the user wants to find and, based on which name should be searched, calls either the `searchFather` or the `searchMother` function. If the search is unsuccessful (the return value is 0), the user sees an error message indicating that the name for which he or she was looking isn't present. If the search is successful, the `search` function displays the data in the `Families` object.

Listing 14.14   Using the binary search functions

```
void arrayMgr::search ()
{
    char which, dummy[2];
    Families * found;
    string25 iname;

    cout << "\nSearch by father or mother (m/f)? ";
    cin >> which;
//  gets (dummy); // my favorite kludge
    cout << "\nName: ";
    gets (iname);

    if (toupper(which) == 'F')
        found = searchFather (iname);
    else
        found = searchMother (iname);
    if (found == 0)
        cout << "\nThat family isn't here.";
    else
        found->display();
}
```

Programming Challenge Number 13

In this programming challenge, your job is to add a member function to the arrayMgr class to delete a family from the array of Families objects. The easiest way to do this is to first find the object you want to delete, using the existing search functions developed for the last version of the Families program in this chapter. Once you have found the object to remove, move each pointer below the deleted object up one position in the array. After you've finished moving the contents of the array, don't forget to decrement the count of the number of items in the array.

Data Structures: Linked Lists

15

In addition to arrays, object-oriented programs also work with other types of data structures. In this chapter we'll be looking at linked lists, where multiple objects are chained together using pointers from one to the other. Linked lists provide one alternative to arrays to handling multiple objects. Like Chapter 14, this chapter doesn't introduce any new language elements but instead discusses some new ways to use things you already know.

To begin, we'll be looking at a demonstration program that will show you the basics of inserting objects into a linked list and accessing those objects once they are part of the list. Then we'll look at how a linked list can be implemented in the Checkbook program to manage the transactions that are related to a checking account.

How a Linked List Works

A *linked list* is a chain of objects connected by pointers that indicate the object that comes next in the list. The list is managed by a special object designed just for that purpose, very much like the array manager object to which you were introduced in Chapter 14.

The figures in Figure 15.1 represent objects in a linked list. The list manager object is the largest figure. It points to the first object in the list, which in turn points to the next object, which points to the next object, and so on. The last object in the list points nowhere (usually a pointer with a value of 0).

Figure 15.1   A linked list

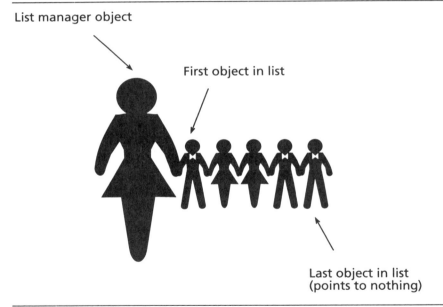

List manager object

First object in list

Last object in list
(points to nothing)

Because a linked list is made up of pointers from one object to the next, you access objects by following the chain. The list manager object begins the access by giving a program the pointer to the first object in the list. Then the program accesses each object in order, using the pointer stored in the object to find the next object. In its simplest form, a linked list gives you access from the first object to the next object to the next object, and so on, all the way to the end of the list.

If you want to be able to go backward in the list (from the last object, to the previous object, and so on), you must include additional pointers. The list manager object must include a pointer to the last object in the list. Then each object must include a pointer to the object that precedes it in the list. It's up to the programmer to determine whether access to previous objects is necessary.

To add an object to a linked list, you must move some pointers. Assume, for example, that you want to insert a new element between the second and third elements in Figure 15.1. You will need to move two pointers. As you can see in Figure 15.2, you must change the second object so that it points to the new object. The new object must then be initialized to point to the object that was previously third. (It will now be fourth.)

Figure 15.2   Inserting an object into a linked list

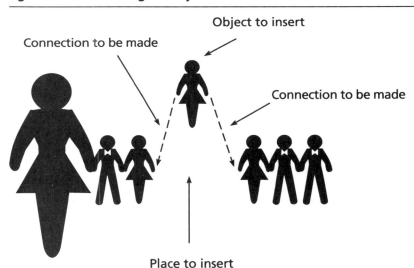

Although the preceding illustrations show the objects in the linked list as being next to one another, in actuality the objects in a linked list can be scattered anywhere in memory. The structure of the list is maintained just by the pointers between the objects.

Linked List Classes

A linked list manager class takes care of inserting elements into the list, deleting elements from a list, and providing access to the members of the list. To explore how a linked list works, we'll be looking at a sample program that handles a list of objects that store and retrieve people's birthdates. First, we'll look at the class being managed by the list, with special attention to the class features that are designed for its participation in the list. Then we'll look at the list manager class in detail.

THE CLASS BEING MANAGED

The class whose objects are part of the list—birthday (in Listing 15.1)— stores a person's first and last names, the person's birthdate using the date class that was introduced in Chapter 13, and a pointer to the next birthday object in the list. The most important thing you need to keep in mind when writing classes whose objects are going to be part of a linked list is that you have to plan for linked list membership by including the required pointer variables. In this case, we're providing for "next" access only. (If we wanted "previous" access as well, we'd need a second pointer variable.)

Listing 15.1   Header file for the linked list demo program

```
class birthday
{
    private:
        string25 first, last;
        date * b_day;
        birthday * next;
    public:
        birthday (string25, string25, date_string);
        birthday (ifstream &);
        void display ();
        birthday * getNext();
        char * getLast();
        char * getFirst();
        void setNextPtr (birthday *);
        date getDate();
        void write (ofstream &);
};
```

NOTE

The date class used in the linked list demonstration program has been modified to include the changes suggested by the programming challenges in Chapter 13. The class can handle days and months of one or two digits; it can also handle two- or four-digit years. The integer-to-ASCII conversion routine is also written so that it will handle an integer of any size. If you attempted the programming challenges, you might want to take a look at the date.cpp file in the linked list demo program folder to see one way of implementing those features.

The `birthday` class's member functions include the following:

- Two constructors (one for interactive input and one for input from a file)
- A display function to show all data in an object (`display`)
- A function to return the pointer to the next object in the linked list (`getNext`)
- Functions to return pointers to the first name and last name class variables (`getFirst` and `getLast`)
- A function to set the value in the pointer to the next object (`setNextPtr`)
- A function to return the birthdate (`getDate`)
- A function to write an object's data to a text file (`write`)

The member functions for the `birthday` class can be found in Listing 15.2. As you can see, there is nothing unusual or complicated in these functions. (This program exists only to demonstrate the management of a linked list, so the object being managed really doesn't need to do very much.) Pay special attention, however, to the `getNext` and `setNextPtr` functions. These two functions are essential to making the linked list work.

The `getNext` function returns the contents of the `next` class variable. To move from one element in the list to another, the list manager object can ask the current object to retrieve the contents of its pointer. For example, if a pointer to the current object in the list is named `current`, a program can travel to the next object in the list with:

```
current = curent->getNext();
```

The `setNextPtr` function inserts a value into the `next` variable. If a pointer to a new object is stored in `newObject`, you can make the current object point to the new object with:

```
current->setNextPtr(newObject);
```

Listing 15.2   Member functions for the birthday class

```
#include <iostream.h>
#include <fstream.h>
#include <string.h>
#include <stdio.h>
#include "date.h"
#include "linked list.h"

birthday::birthday (string25 ifirst, string25 ilast, date_string idate)
{
    strcpy (first, ifirst);
    strcpy (last, ilast);
    b_day = new date (idate);
    next = 0;
}

birthday::birthday (ifstream & fin)
{
    date_string idate;

    fin.getline (first,80,'\0');
    fin.getline (last,80,'\0');
    fin.getline (idate,80,'\0');
    b_day = new date (idate);
    next = 0;
}

void birthday::display()
{
    date_string sDate;

    cout << "\n" << first << " " << last << endl;
    cout << "Birthday: " << b_day->showDate(sDate);
}

birthday * birthday::getNext()
    { return next; }

char * birthday::getLast()
    { return last; }

char * birthday::getFirst()
    { return first; }

void birthday::setNextPtr (birthday * newNext)
    { next = newNext; }

date birthday::getDate()
    { return *b_day; }
```

Continued on next page

Listing 15.2 (Continued)   Member functions for the birthday class

```
void birthday::write (ofstream & fout)
{
    date_string sDate;

    fout << first << '\0';
    fout << last << '\0';
    fout << b_day->showDate(sDate) << '\0';
}
```

By the same token, you can make the new object point to the current object with:

```
newObject->setNextPtr(current);
```

THE LINKED LIST MANAGER CLASS

An object-oriented linked list is managed by a special object designed for that task. In Listing 15.3, for example, you can see the class declaration and constructor for the linked list manager that handles the list of birthday objects. This class (linkedList) has just two class variables: a pointer to the first object in the list it manages and a count of the number of items in the list.

The linkedList class has the following member functions:

- A constructor that simply initializes both class variables to 0
- A function to load data from disk and recreate the linked list in main memory (load)
- A function to write the entire list to disk (unload)
- A function to insert new objects into the list (insert)
- Two functions to search the list: one by a person's name, the other by birthdate
- A function to list all the objects in the list (list)

In the following sections of this chapter we'll be looking at exactly how the linkedList class manages the list using these functions.

Listing 15.3   A linked list manager class

```
class linkedList
{
    private:
        birthday * firstPerson;
        int numb_people;
    public:
        linkedList ();
        int load ();
        void unload ();
        void insert (birthday *);
        birthday * find (string25, string25); // find by name
        int find (date_string, birthday * []); // find by date
        void list (); // list all
};

// constructor for the list manager object
linkedList::linkedList()
{
    firstPerson = 0;
    numb_people = 0;
}
```

Inserting Elements

As you saw at the beginning of this chapter, inserting an object into a linked list means first finding the place in the list where the new object should go and then moving pointers to connect the new object. You have several choices as to where a new object is inserted. You might, for example, decide that all new objects go at the end of the list or that new objects always go at the beginning of the list. However, you might also decide to keep the list in some sorted order (chronological, alphabetical, or numerical).

For this particular example, we're going to be keeping the list in alphabetical order by the person's last name. This means that whenever we want to insert a new object into the list, we need to scan the existing list to find the correct place for the new object. Once the place is found, we can move pointers to connect the new object.

The linkedList class's insert member function in Listing 15.4 begins by looking to see whether the list is empty (the firstPerson variable contains 0). If so, there's no need to do anything else but make the new object the first element in the list by placing the new object's pointer in firstPerson.

Listing 15.4   Inserting an element into a linked list

```
void linkedList::insert(birthday * newB_day)
{
    char * newLast, * currentLast;
    birthday * previous, * current;
    int count = 0;

    if (firstPerson == 0) // simply insert first one
    {
        firstPerson = newB_day;
        numb_people = 1;
        return;
    }
    newLast = newB_day->getLast();
    int first = TRUE;
    current = firstPerson;
    currentLast = current->getLast();
    while (strcmp (newLast, currentLast) > 0 && count++ < numb_people)
    {
        first = FALSE; // not first in last
        previous = current; // save where we were
        current = current->getNext(); // move to next person
        if (current != 0)
            currentLast = current->getLast();
    }
    // set previous transaction to point to new transaction except when
    // new transaction is first in the list
    if (!first)
        previous->setNextPtr (newB_day);
    else
        firstPerson = newB_day; // new one is first in list
      // set new person to point to following person
    newB_day->setNextPtr (current);
    numb_people++;
}
```

However, if there is at least one element in the list, the function must search for the correct insertion location. To begin the search, the function initializes the `cur-rent` pointer to the first object in the list and retrieves the last name for the new object and the current object. Then it enters a `while` loop that compares the two last names. If the new last name alphabetically precedes the current last name, the new object precedes the current object in the list. In that case, the `while` loop stops and list insertion occurs.

Notice that the function maintains a variable called `first` that signals when a new object should be first in the list. If the new object should precede the object that is currently first (in other words, the function never enters the `while` loop), `first` retains its initial value of TRUE; it is set to FALSE inside the while. As you will see shortly, this signals the function to move pointers in a special way.

If the new object *isn't* first in the list, the function enters the while loop. The body of the loop sets first to FALSE and then saves the pointer to the current object in a variable named previous. This is essential because when we break the links in the list to insert the new object, we must set the pointer in the previous object to point to the new object. In other words, the new object will follow the "previous" object; the "current" object will follow the new object.

After saving the previous pointer, the insert function moves to the next object in the list by retrieving the current object's pointer to the next object. If the address just retrieved isn't 0 (in other words, we're not at the end of the list), the function gets the last name of the person in the next object, preparing it to be evaluated at the top of the loop.

Notice that this while loop also counts the number of objects in the list as they're being accessed, stopping the loop when all objects in the list have been examined. If you don't do this and the new object should go at the end of the list, two nasty things will probably happen. First, you'll enter an infinite loop because the condition in the while will always be true. Second, your program will eventually crash, bomb box and all, because the getNext and getLast functions will be accessing memory that doesn't belong to objects. You'll be reaching beyond the end of the list.

NOTE

One of the most common causes of crashes in Macintosh programs is pointers that don't point to valid data. If your program is crashing, look for uninitialized pointer variables (for example, you forget to issue a new statement) or pointer variables that are pointing to nonexistent data.

To perform the list insertion, the insert function looks at the first variable. If the new object isn't first, the previous object, whose address is stored in previous, is set to point to the new object. However, if the new object is first, the firstPerson variable in the linkedList class object is set to point to the new object. In either case, the new object is set to point to the current object (address in current). The final step is to increment the count of the number of objects in the list.

Accessing All Elements

Once your linked list has been created, you can use it to visit all objects that are part of the list. To do so, you begin at the first element, whose pointer can be found in the list manager object. Then you repeatedly call getNext to gain access to the pointers of successive elements.

To see how this works, consider the list function in Listing 15.5. The function begins by initializing the current variable to firstPerson and then enters a for loop. The loop displays the data from the current object by calling the birthday class's display member function and then moves to the next object. The loop counts objects as it goes, stopping when all objects in the list have been displayed.

Listing 15.5   Navigating the linked list

```
void linkedList::list ()
{
    birthday * current;

    current = firstPerson;
    for (int i = 0; i < numb_people; i++)
    {
        current->display();
        cout << endl;
        current = current->getNext();
    }
}
```

NOTE

Keep in mind when looking at the preceding function that all access to a linked list is sequential. In other words, you must always start at the first object in the list, move to the next, to the next, and so on. It's the only way you can access the list's elements.

Finding Elements

The procedure you have just seen for traversing all the elements in a linked list forms the basis for all search routines written for linked lists. In Listing 15.6, for example,

Listing 15.6   Searching a linked list

```
birthday * linkedList::find (string25 ifirst, string25 ilast)
{
    birthday * current;
    char * currentFirst, * currentLast;
    int count = 0;

    current = firstPerson; // start at beginning
    currentFirst = current->getFirst();
    currentLast = current->getLast();
    while ((strcmp (currentFirst,ifirst) != 0 ||
        strcmp (currentLast,ilast) != 0) && count++ < numb_people)
    {
        current = current->getNext();
        currentFirst = current->getFirst();
        currentLast = current->getLast();
    }
    return current; // will be 0 if not found
}

int linkedList::find (date_string idate, birthday * found[])
{
    birthday * current;
    date searchDate (idate), currentDate (idate);

    current = firstPerson;
    currentDate = current->getDate();
    // Need an index variable just for the found array.
    // The number of matches found will certainly be less than the
    // the number of elements in the array.
    int j = -1;
    for (int i = 0; i < numb_people; i++)
    {
        if (currentDate == searchDate)
            found[++j] = current; // save the object found
        current = current->getNext();
        currentDate = current->getDate();
    }
    return j; // return last index used in found array
}
```

you will find two find member functions that search for items in the linked list of birthday objects.

The first find function searches for someone who matches a specific first and last name. The assumption is that no two people in the list have exactly the same name. Therefore, the function stops when it either finds a match or reaches the end of the list. As you can see in Listing 15.6, the function begins at the first object in the list and then enters a `while` loop that compares the values in its `first` and `last` variables with the function's two input parameters. As soon as a match is found, the function returns a pointer to the current object. If no match exists, `current` will be **0** (the `next` pointer in the last object is 0). The program function calling this `find` function can then use a result of 0 to determine that the search was unsuccessful.

What can you do if you want a search that returns more than one value? The second `find` function does exactly that. The calling function passes in the birthdate for which the function should search and the address of an array to hold the pointers of all matches that are found. The function uses the `return` statement to send back the number of matches.

Because there may be more than one matching object, the second `find` function uses a `for` loop that accesses every object in the linked list. If a match is found, a pointer to the current object is placed in the result array (called `found` in this case). The index to that array represents a count of the number of found items and is returned to the calling function just before the `find` function terminates. There is no need to worry about "returning" the `found` array. Because it is an array, it is passed by reference; any changes made to the array in the `find` function are made to the original in main memory and are therefore accessible to the calling function.

Linked Lists and Data Files

A linked list is a data structure that exists in main memory. Although you can store the list's data in a file, you can't store the pointers. Why? Because each time you run the program, the list probably ends up in a different location in memory. The pointers that were valid the last time you ran the program aren't valid now. This means that you need to traverse the list when you write data, but you should store only the data, not the pointers. When you read the data in from a file, you must recreate the list.

WRITING THE DATA

Listing 15.7 contains the `linkedList` class's `unload` function. This function opens the data file, stores the number of items in the linked list, and then enters a `for` loop that traverses the entire list, beginning with the first element. The body of the `for` loop writes a `birthday` object's data by calling the object's `write` function. (If you look back at Listing 15.2, you'll notice that this function writes a first name, last

Listing 15.7   Writing linked list objects

```
void linkedList::unload()
{
    birthday * current;

    ofstream peopleOut ("Friends&Family");
    if (!peopleOut)
    {
        cout << "Couldn't open output file.";
        return;
    }
    peopleOut << numb_people << ' ';
    current = firstPerson;
    for (int i = 0; i < numb_people; i++)
    {
        current->write (peopleOut);
        current = current->getNext();
    }
}
```

name, and birthdate, but *doesn't* write the contents of the next variable.) The loop then moves to the next item in the list, using the getNext function.

READING THE DATA

Listing 15.8 contains the linkedList class's load function. Like other functions you have seen that read data from a text file, it opens the file and begins by reading the number of items in the file. It then enters a for loop that reads object data from the file, one object at a time. The body of the loop creates a new birthday object and then calls the insert function to place it in the list. As you begin to work with linked lists, keep in mind that when you read data that are part of data structures from files, you must recreate the data structure as you read the data.

NOTE

The load function uses a temporary count variable rather than reading the number of objects from the file into the numb_people. If you look back at the insert function, you'll see that the insert function counts objects as they are added to the list. Attempting to use numb_people to control the for loop doing the reading therefore wouldn't work.

Listing 15.8   Reading linked list objects

```
int linkedList::load()
{
    char yes_no, dummy;
    birthday * newB_day;
    int count;

    ifstream peopleIn ("Friends&Family");
    if (!peopleIn)
    {
        cout << "Couldn't open input file. Continue? ";
        cin >> yes_no;
        if (toupper(yes_no) == 'N')
            return FALSE; // couldn't read--quit
        else
            return TRUE; // couldn't read but OK
    }
    peopleIn >> count;
    peopleIn.get (dummy); // skip over blank
    for (int i = 0; i < count; i++)
    {
        newB_day = new birthday (peopleIn);
        // using the insert function recreates the list
        insert (newB_day);
    }
    peopleIn.close();
    return TRUE;
}
```

Making It Work

Now that we've looked at the member functions used by an object that manages a linked list of other objects, let's look at a program that uses the list manager class. In Listing 15.9 you can find a program that uses a linked list of birthday objects. From the user's point of view, the program does three things: adds new people, finds people, and lists people. The program also reads and writes a text file.

THE MAIN FUNCTION

The main function is relatively simple. The important thing to notice is that it declares a pointer variable to hold a linkedList object and then uses the new

Listing 15.9   Main program for the linked list demo program

```
void newPerson (linkedList *);
void findPeople (linkedList *);
int menu ();
void main ()
{
    linkedList * myList; // create one linked list object
    int option = 0;
    myList = new linkedList();
    int result = myList->load();
    if (result == FALSE)
        return;

    while (option != 9)
    {
        option = menu();
        switch (option)
        {
            case 1:
                newPerson(myList);
                break;
            case 2:
                findPeople(myList);
                break;
            case 3:
                myList->list();
                break;
            case 9:
                myList->unload ();
                break;
            default:
                cout << "\nUnavailable option" << endl << endl;
        }
    }
}

int menu()
{
    int choice;

    cout << "\n\nChoose an option:" << endl << endl;
    cout << "  1. Add a new person" << endl;
    cout << "  2. Find people" << endl;
    cout << "  3. See all people" << endl;
    cout << "  9. Quit" << endl << endl;
    cout << "Choice: ";
    cin >> choice;
    return choice;
}
```

Continued on next page

Listing 15.9 (Continued)   Main program for the linked list demo program

```
void newPerson(linkedList * myList)
{
     birthday * newB_day;
     string25 ifirst, ilast;
     date_string idate;
     char dummy[2];
//   gets (dummy); // my favorite kludge
     cout << "\nFirst name: ";
     gets (ifirst);
     cout << "Last name: ";
     gets (ilast);
     cout << "Birthdate: ";
     gets (idate);
     newB_day = new birthday (ifirst, ilast, idate);
     myList->insert (newB_day);
}

void findPeople (linkedList * myList)
{
     string25 ifirst, ilast;
     date_string idate;
     birthday * found[MAX_FOUND], * onePerson;
     int numb_found;
     char dummy[2];
//   gets(dummy); // my favorite kludge
     cout << "\nWhat birthdate? ";
     gets (idate);
     if (strlen (idate) > 0)
     {
          numb_found = myList->find (idate, found);
          if (numb_found >= 0)
               for (int i = 0; i <= numb_found; i++)
               {
                    found[i]->display();
                    cout << endl;
               }
     }
     else
     {
          cout << "FIrst name: ";
          gets (ifirst);
          cout << "Last name: ";
          gets (ilast);
          onePerson = myList->find (ifirst, ilast);
          if (onePerson == 0)
               cout << "No one was found.";
          else
               onePerson->display();
     }
}
```

statement to create the object. Why use dynamic binding in this case? Because the program function that adds items to the list modifies the linkedList object. If you use a pointer to the object as a parameter to the program function, you pass the linkedList object by reference; you don't need to return the modified object, because all changes are made to the original in main memory. In this case, it is much easier just to use a pointer than to worry about returning the object.

The newPerson program function collects data for a new birthday object, creates the object with the new operator, and uses the pointer returned by new to insert the object into the linked list. It's a toss-up whether this function is really necessary. The program could have placed the code to collect the data for the new object and to create the object in a linkedList member function. That function could then have called insert. Either organization will work. (You'll see an example of the alternative organization when we look at a linked list for the Checkbook program.)

On the other hand, the findPeople function is necessary: The linkedList class has two find functions, and the program needs to determine which one the user wants to use. It does this by asking the user for a birthdate to match. If the user presses Enter without typing anything, the length of the idate variable is 0, and the function knows that the user isn't interested in matching by date. It can then go on to ask for a first name and last name to match.

The way in which the findPeople function displays the results of a search is, of course, determined by which search is being performed. In the case of a search by date, the output code uses the number of matches returned by the find member function to control a for loop that displays data for each of the retrieved objects. However, a search by first and last names produces only one result, a pointer to which is returned by the function call. The display therefore needs only to check to see whether the search was successful.

Programming Challenge Number 14

Removing an item from a linked list is almost the opposite of inserting a new item. First, you find the object you want to delete. Then you set the previous object (the one preceding the object to be deleted) to point to the next object (the object following the object to be deleted). Because there are no longer any pointers to the object being removed, it is no longer part of the list.

For this programming challenge, add a member function to the linked list demonstration program's `linkedList` class to remove an item from the list. Once the object is deleted, remove it from memory with the `delete` command:

```
delete objectPtr;
```

Here `objectPtr` is a pointer variable containing the address of the object being removed from memory.

Provide a menu option to let the user delete items. Use one or both of the existing `find` functions to locate the object. Then remove it from the list. Use the program's `list` capabilities to verify that your function works. (Hint: Don't forget to decrement the `numb_people` variable each time you delete an object!)

Modifying the Checkbook Program

Rather than allocating an array of 10,000 pointers for transactions in the Checkbook program, why not use a linked list of transaction objects? If you do so, the program allocates both objects and pointers to those objects as needed. This makes more efficient use of memory than even an array of pointers to dynamically created objects.

Much of what has been implemented in the Checkbook program is identical to what you just saw in the linked list demonstration program. We therefore won't examine every facet of the Checkbook program's linked list implementation, but instead will focus on what makes the Checkbook program unique so that you can see another example of a how linked list is coded.

THE LIST MANAGER CLASS

The linked list for the Checkbook program is somewhat different from that in the linked list demonstration program, because the Checkbook program needs one linked list for each checking account. In the demonstration program, the `linkedList` object was handled by the main program. However, in the Checkbook program the `linkedList` object is handled by an `Account` object. (As you will see shortly, the `Account` class must therefore contain a pointer to its linked list manager object.)

The `linkedList` class for the Checkbook program, in Listing 15.10, contains class variables for a pointer to the first transaction in the list, a pointer to the `Account` object that owns the list, and a count of the number of transactions in the list. The member functions include a function to collect data for a new transaction (`newTrans`). The remaining member functions are similar to those found in the linked list demonstration program.

Listing 15.10   A linked list class for the Checkbook program

```
class linkedList
{
    private:
        Trans * firstTrans;
        Account * owner;
        int transCount;
    public:
        linkedList (Account *, int);
        void newTrans ();
        // insert into list; used by newTrans and file constructor
        void insert (Trans *);
        Trans * find (char *); // find by check/reference numb
         // find by date and Payee/Source
        Trans * find (date_string, string80);
        // list transactions in date range
        void byDate (date_string, date_string);
        Trans * next (Trans *); // pass in last one processed
        int gettransCount ();
};

linkedList::linkedList (Account * iowner, int icount)
{
    firstTrans = 0;
    owner = iowner;
    transCount = icount;
}
```

CREATING NEW TRANSACTIONS

For the Checkbook program, all processing needed to create a new transaction is handled by the `linkedList` object. The `newTrans` member function (Listing 15.11) collects the data needed for a new transaction and then creates the `Trans`

Listing 15.11 Creating new transactions for a linked list

```
void linkedList::newTrans() // for interactive use
{
    char icheck_numb[6], iType[8];
    date_string itrans_date;
    string80 iPayeeSource, iNote;
    float iAmount;
    Trans * newTrans;

    cout << "\nCheck or other reference #: ";
    cin.getline (icheck_numb,6);
    cout << "\nTransaction type (check, deposit, ATM, service): ";
    gets (iType);
    cout << "\nTransaction date: ";
    cin.getline (itrans_date,80);
    cout << "\Payee or source:" << endl;
    cin.getline (iPayeeSource,80);
    cout << "\nTransaction note (up to 80 characters):" << endl;
    cin.getline (iNote,80);
    cout << "\nAmount of the transaction: ";
    cin >> iAmount;
    newTrans = new Trans (owner, icheck_numb, itrans_date, iPayeeSource,
        iNote, iAmount, iType);
    insert (newTrans);
    transCount++;
}
```

object. Once it has a pointer to the new transaction, the function calls insert to make the new object a part of the list.

NOTE

The newTrans object knows the account to which this new transaction belongs because the linkedList object stores a pointer to the account that owns it in its "owner" variable.

The Checkbook program maintains transactions in reverse chronological order. This means that the latest date comes first. As you can see in Listing 15.12, the decision of where to insert a new object is made by comparing the date in the new object with the date in each object in the list. When the date in the new object is greater than the date in the current object, the function knows to insert the new object prior to the current object. Other than the change in the ordering of the objects, the list insertion process is the same as that used in the linked list demonstration program.

Listing 15.12　Inserting into the linked list of transactions

```
void linkedList::insert (Trans * newTrans)
{
    Trans * current, * previous;
    date * newDate, * currentDate;
    int count = 0;

    // order is in descending chronological order (latest date first)
    if (firstTrans == 0)
        firstTrans = newTrans; // simply insert first one
    else
    {
        newDate = newTrans->getDate();
        int first = TRUE;
        current = firstTrans; // start at first transaction
        currentDate = current->getDate();
        while (*newDate < *currentDate && count++ < transCount)
        {
            first = FALSE;
            previous = current; // need to save where we were
            current = current->getNext(); // move to next transaction
            if (current != 0)
                currentDate = current->getDate();
        }
        // set previous transaction to point to new transaction except when
        // new transaction is first in the list
        if (!first)
            previous->setNextPtr (newTrans);
        else
            firstTrans = newTrans; // new transaction is first in list
        // set new transaction to point to following transaction
        newTrans->setNextPtr (current);
    }
}
```

ACCESSING THE LIST

In Listing 15.13 you will find the Account class member functions that search for transactions. These functions look very much the originals in which the transactions were stored in an array. The major difference is that rather than moving to the next element in an array of transactions, the functions use a getNext function to step through the linked list.

These functions use a slightly different method of controlling the loop that steps through the list. Rather than checking a count of the number of objects that have been processed, the loops look for an object pointer of 0. This is based on the knowledge that the pointer to the next object in the last object in the list is 0. Which is

Listing 15.13   Accessing data in the linked list of transactions

```
Trans * linkedList::find (char * icheck_numb) // find by check number
{
    Trans * current;
    current = firstTrans;
    while (current != 0)
    {
        if (strcmp(current->getCheck_numb(),icheck_numb) == 0)
            return current;
        current = current->getNext();
    }
    return 0;
}

Trans * linkedList::find (date_string idate, string80 iPS)
{
    Trans * current;
    date cDate (idate), iDate (idate);

    current = firstTrans;
    while (current != 0)
    {
        cDate = *current->getDate();
        if (cDate == iDate && strcmp (current->getPS(),iPS) == 0)
            return current;
        current = current->getNext();
    }
    return 0;
}

void linkedList::byDate (date_string start, date_string end)
{
    date sDate (start), eDate (end), tDate (start);
    Trans * current;

    current = firstTrans;
    tDate = *current->getDate();
    while (tDate > eDate && current != 0) // find first one
    {
        current = current->getNext();
        if (current != 0)
            tDate = *current->getDate();
    }
    while (tDate >= sDate && current != 0) // now display
    {
        current->displayTrans();
        current = current->getNext();
        if (current != 0)
            tDate = *current->getDate();
    }
}
```

better: counting the objects or looking for a pointer of 0? It doesn't matter. Counting objects will work as long as you faithfully increment the object counter whenever a new object is created. Looking for a pointer of 0 will work as long as you make sure that the next pointer is always initialized to 0 whenever an object is created.

MODIFICATIONS TO THE ACCOUNT CLASS

The Account class needs to be modified slightly to deal with a linked list of transactions rather than an array of transactions. The class declaration (top of Listing 15.14) must include a variable (transList) that points to the linkedList object that manages the account's transactions. In addition, the declaration must provide a member function to return a pointer to that list manager object (getList).

The bulk of the other changes come in the class's two constructors (also found in Listing 15.14). The interactive constructor creates a linkedList object for a new Account object. The file input constructor must create the list manager object, read transaction data from the file—creating Trans objects as it goes—and also insert each Trans object into the linked list.

FINDING THE LIST MANAGER

When the Account class used an array of transactions, all a program needed to do to gain access to those transactions was to find the account in which the transactions were stored. However, now that there's a list manager object between an account and its transactions, access to the transactions requires finding the linkedList object.

To see how this works, take a look at the modified program function to enter a new transaction (Listing 15.15). This function collects the bank name and account number and uses them to find the account, just like it did in previous versions of this program. However, once the function has a pointer to an account, it must use the Account class's getList function to retrieve the pointer to the account's linkedList object. Once the program function has a pointer to the list manager object, it can use that pointer to call the member function that creates a new transaction. All of the program functions that work with transactions directly must use this two-step process to access the linked list: Find the account and then find the account's linked list manager.

Listing 15.14   Modifications to the Account class

```
class Account
{
    private:
        string25 acc_numb;
        string50 bank_name;
        float balance;
        linkedList * transList; // list manager object
        int lastTrans_numb;
    public:
        Account (string25, string50, float); // interactive constructor
        Account (ifstream &); // constructor for file input
        int nextTrans_numb ();
        void Reconcile();
        void write (ofstream &); // write to file
        char * getAcc_numb ();
        char * getBank_name();
        void setBalance (int, float); // change balance
        linkedList * getList (); // return pointer to transaction list
};

// interactive constructor
Account::Account (string25 iAcc_numb, string50 iBank_name, float iBalance)
{
    strcpy (acc_numb, iAcc_numb);
    strcpy (bank_name, iBank_name);
    balance = iBalance;
    transList = new linkedList (this, 0); // create list manager object
    lastTrans_numb = 0;
}

// file input constructor
Account::Account (ifstream & fin)
{
    Account * owner;
    Trans * newTrans;
    char dummy;
    int transCount;
    fin.getline (acc_numb,80,'\0');
    fin.getline (bank_name,80,'\0');
    fin >> balance;
    fin >> lastTrans_numb;
    fin >> transCount;
    transList = new linkedList (this, transCount); // create list manager
    for (int i = 0; i < transCount; i++)
    {
        newTrans = new Trans (fin); // create transaction object
        transList->insert(newTrans); // insert it into linked list
    }
    fin.get (dummy); // skip over blank between accounts
}
```

Listing 15.15   Program function to enter a new transaction

```
void enterTrans (arrayMgr accountArray)
{
    Account * whichAccount;
    linkedList * whichList;

    whichAccount = accountArray.findAccount();
    if (whichAccount == 0)
    {
        cout << "\nThat account isn't in the database." << endl;
        return;
    }
    whichList = whichAccount->getList();
    whichList->newTrans ();
}
```

Programming Challenge Number 15

It's not uncommon to have linked lists where new objects are always inserted either at the beginning of the list or at the end of the list. For this challenge, you'll be modifying the Checkbook program to explore both types of ordering. Start with a fresh copy of the folder *Checkbook (Chapter 15)* each time. Be sure to delete the *Checkbook* data file as well. When you reorder the linked lists, the data in the file won't work properly.

First, modify the Checkbook program so that new transactions are always inserted first. Use the View Transactions menu selection to help you look at your data so that you know your modifications are working properly.

Second, modify a new copy of the Checkbook program so that new transactions are always inserted last. As you get ready to do this, consider whether there is a change you could make to the `linkedList` class that would make it possible to find the last element in the list without traversing the entire list. (If you make this change, you'll also have to make some modifications to the `insert` function.) Once again, be sure to check your code to make sure it works.

Linked Lists Versus Arrays

Given that you can choose between arrays and linked lists to manage a group of objects of the same class, which should you use? Because there are advantages and disadvantages to each, there is no straightforward answer.

Arrays are random access data structures. You can access any element by simply supplying its array index; you don't need to start at the beginning of the array. An array can therefore be used for fast search techniques like the binary search you saw in Chapter 14. However, the number of elements you can place in array is limited by the size declared in the program. If you need to expand an array, you must modify the program's source code and recompile it. In addition, an array always takes up as much space as is declared for the array, regardless of whether you place data in every array element. An array therefore isn't terribly efficient in its use of memory.

On the other hand, the number of elements you can add to a linked list is limited only by available main memory. You don't need to allocate a large array and tie up memory before you need it. The major drawback to a linked list is that it is a sequential data structure; you can access its elements only in order, beginning with the first one and moving to the next. Fast search techniques, such as the binary search, can't be used and therefore, as the linked list gets large, searching may be slow.

Inheritance

16

The one remaining major feature of object-oriented C++ that we haven't explored to this point is inheritance. As you will remember from Chapter 2, inheritance is a mechanism through which classes can use variables and member functions declared in other classes, providing a way to avoid duplication when a program uses several similar, but not quite identical, classes.

In this chapter you will learn more about situations in which inheritance is appropriate. You will also learn how to implement an inheritance hierarchy and how to use something called *polymorphism* to get objects in the same hierarchy to respond differently to the same message.

Where Inheritance Makes Sense

Inheritance can save you a lot of work: It often means that you can avoid duplicating variables and member functions. It can also make programming easier because related classes can be handled in the same way. However, there are some very specific circumstances under which inheritance is applicable.

To help you understand when inheritance can be used, let's take a look at some of the classes that might be used in a program that manages realty listings. (This program will be used as an example throughout this chapter.) The company that uses this program handles homes, farms, and businesses. All of these might be classified as pieces of property, but the data that describe them are somewhat different. For example, when listing a home, the program should store information about the number of bedrooms and bathrooms; when listing a farm, the program should include the number of acres that can be planted. However, all pieces of property have an owner and an asking price.

When you have a situation in which classes share some but not all variables, then the use of inheritance may be helpful. The iron test of whether you are looking at inheritance, however, is the relationship between the classes. If you look at Figure 16.1, for example, you can see that the words we use to talk about the relationship between a generic class that describes a piece of property and specific types of properties are "is a." In other words, a house "is a" piece of property, just like a farm "is a" piece of property and an office "is a" piece of property. Houses, farms, and offices are more specific instances of the generic class property. When you can express the relationship between two classes using "is a"—when one class is a more specific instance of another—then you are looking at inheritance.

If you look again at Figure 16.1, you'll notice that you read the "is a" relationship up the diagram. However, the inheritance of variables and member functions travels down the hierarchy. In this case, the property class is a *base* class, a class from which other classes inherit. The classes for homes, farms, and offices are *derived* classes because their declarations are derived from the declaration of another class. The derived classes share all the variables and many of the member functions of their base class.

There are other types of relationships between classes that occur within an object-oriented program. For example, if the Realty Listings program were to include a class for the owner of properties that were listed, you might say that an owner "owns" a piece of property (see Figure 16.2). Although the property class will need to contain

Figure 16.1 Inheritance in the Realty Listings program

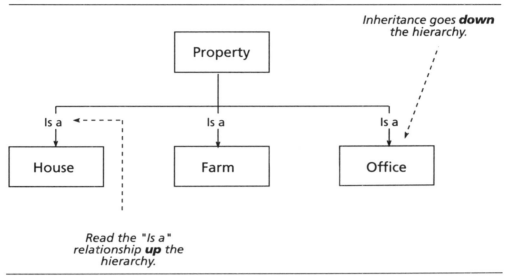

Figure 16.2 A relationship between classes that doesn't constitute inheritance

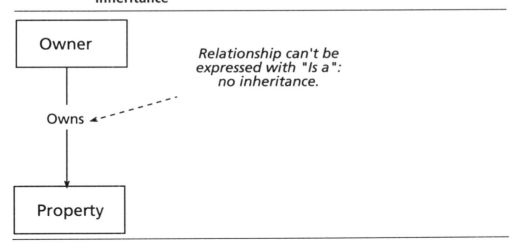

at least an owner's name, inheritance isn't applicable here, because a piece of property isn't a more specific example of an owner.

Examining a Base Class

The Realty Listings program contains four classes: the base class property and three derived classes (residential, agricultural, and commercial). The declaration of the base class (Listing 16.1) initially looks very much like any other class. There are, however, some important differences.

Listing 16.1   Base class for the Realty Listings program

```
typedef char string80[81];
typedef char string25[26];

const MAX_PROPERTIES = 25;
const float HOUSE_COM = .0625;
const float FARM_COM = .03;
const float BUS_COM = .075;

class property
{
    protected:
        int propertyID;
        double asking_price;
        string80 owner_name;
        string25 owner_phone, type;
        char * switchBoolean(int); // change TRUE/FALSE to a string
    public:
        property (string25);
        property (ifstream &, string25);
        void setPrice (double); // change asking price
        int getID ();
        char * getType ();
        double getPrice ();
        virtual void display () = 0; // display all data
        virtual float computeCommission () = 0; // compute commission
        virtual void write (ofstream &) = 0; // write to text file
};
```

First, notice that the class variables are protected, not private. When a base class's variables are private, derived classes can't access them, effectively preventing the derived classes from inheriting (sharing) the base class variables. However, if you make the base class variables protected, all classes in the inheritance hierarchy can access the base class variables, but classes outside the hierarchy can't. In other words, protected variables are essentially private to classes not part of the hierarchy.

MEMBER FUNCTIONS FOR INHERITANCE: VIRTUAL FUNCTIONS

A derived class inherits many of its base class's member functions. However, constructors, overloaded operators, and friend functions aren't inherited. In Listing 16.1 the `setPrice`, `getID`, `getType`, and `getPrice` functions are inherited directly by derived classes, which can call the base class functions by simply using their names. This means that you don't need to duplicate the functions in the derived classes. Their source code needs to appear only once, as part of the base class.

However, because the derived classes are going to add their own variables, there are some base class functions whose source code can't be inherited. These include the `display` function (displays data about a property), `computCommission` (compute how much commission a property will generate for the realty firm, different for each derived class because the commission rates vary), and `write` (writes data to a text file). Nonetheless, the same three functions should be part of each derived class.

When you have a situation in which the same function should appear in classes derived from the same base class but the function bodies are different, you are looking at *polymorphism*. Polymorphism means that classes derived from the same base contain functions with the same signature, although the classes act differently when the functions are called.

NOTE

Don't get polymorphism confused with function overloading. Function overloading occurs when one class has multiple functions with the same name, each with a different signature. Polymorphism occurs when different classes derived from the same base class each have a function with the same signature.

Polymorphism is implemented using *virtual functions*. A virtual function—declared by placing the keyword `virtual` in front of the function prototype—is a function that can be redefined in a derived class. If a derived class contains source code for a virtual function, calling the function uses the derived class's function. However, if the derived class doesn't redefine the function, calling the function uses the base class's implementation.

A base class doesn't need to provide an implementation of a virtual function. In the case of the Realty Listings program, for example, there's no way to provide an implementation of the virtual functions that can be used by any of the derived classes. (Writing a function that would never be used is a waste of code.) The base class therefore contains only a prototype for the virtual functions.

To indicate that a virtual function will have no body and that it will definitely be redefined in derived classes, follow its prototype with = 0. A function of this type is known as a *pure function*. In turn, any base class that contains at least one pure function is an *abstract base class*, a class from which no objects can be created. An abstract base class therefore functions as a generic starting point for an inheritance hierarchy. (It has another important use to which you will be introduced shortly.)

> **NOTE**
> *If you forget the =0 at the end of a pure function, your program will compile, but will generate a linker error that begins with "_vt_".*

Once a virtual function has been declared as virtual, it remains virtual all the way down the inheritance hierarchy. However, the keyword virtual isn't necessary anywhere except in the base class where the function first becomes virtual.

Examining Derived Classes

Derived classes also look very much like classes that aren't part of an inheritance hierarchy. Listing 16.2, for example, contains the three classes derived from the property class. There is one additional element that you haven't seen before: the indication of the base class from which a class is derived.

To indicate the base class, you follow the name of the derived class with a colon, the type of inheritance, and the name of the base class:

```
class class_name : type_of_inheritance base_class_name
```

There are two types of inheritance, public and private, although private inheritance is rarely used. When inheritance is private, all of the base class's elements (variables and functions) are private to the derived class. In other words, the derived class won't be able to access anything in the base class, a situation that, in most cases, defeats the purposes of inheritance. Under public inheritance, the derived class inherits the base class's protected elements as protected and public members as public. Private elements, if there are any, remain private.

Unfortunately, private inheritance is the default. Although you will use public inheritance in virtually every case, if you happen to leave off the public keyword,

Listing 16.2   Derived classes for the Realty Listings program

```
class residential : public property
{
    private:
        int numb_bedrooms, fireplace, family_room;
        float sq_ft, numb_bathrooms;
    public:
        residential (string25);
        residential (ifstream &, string25);
        void display ();
        float computeCommission ();
        void write (ofstream &);
};

class commercial : public property
{
    private:
        int numb_offices, numb_floors, elevator;
        float sq_ft;
    public:
        commercial (string25);
        commercial (ifstream &, string25);
        void display ();
        float computeCommission ();
        void write (ofstream &);
};

class agricultural : public property
{
    private:
        float acreage, house_sq_ft, barn_sq_ft;
        int house, barn;
    public:
        agricultural (string25);
        agricultural (ifstream &, string25);
        void display ();
        float computeCommission ();
        void write (ofstream &);
};
```

you'll discover that your derived classes won't be able to access anything from their base classes.

As you look at Listing 16.2, notice that the classes don't contain the variables that are part of the base class. Nonetheless, when a program creates objects from one of these derived classes, those objects will include the base class variables. In addition, the derived classes don't include the nonvirtual functions that are part of the base class. When functions are bound to objects created from the derived classes, the nonvirtual member functions of the base class are bound along with any functions defined in the derived classes.

Base Class Pointers

One of the most useful features of inheritance is the ability to use a pointer to a base class object to reference any object of any class derived from that base class. Consider, for example, the problem facing the Realty Listings program. Because the objects that represent the listings are from three different classes, there is no immediately obvious way to reference them together, to place them in the same array or linked list. If you must keep groups of listings objects in different data structures, searching through those listings will be very cumbersome.

However, because the three listings classes are all derived from the same base class, you can declare data structures that hold pointers to objects created from the base class rather than any of the individual derived classes. This does not mean that you will ever create objects from the base class. Instead, it means that when you assign a pointer to an object from a derived class to the base class data structure, the computer will typecast the derived class object's pointer to a base class pointer. The beauty of this is that you can handle objects from different but related classes together.

The Realty Listings program does exactly that with its array that manages objects of listings. As you can see in Listing 16.3, the declaration of the `arrayMgr` class, the `listed` array is declared to hold pointers to `property` objects. Although no object is ever created from the `property` class—it can't be, as `property` is an abstract base class—the `listed` array can hold pointers to homes, farms, and businesses.

In addition, notice that the `arrayMgr` class's member functions (Listing 16.4) work on base class pointers. For example, the `insert` function, which places a new piece of property into the array, expects a pointer to a `property` object. This means that it will accept a pointer from any object created from any class derived from `property`. The first `find` function returns a pointer to a `pointer` object, which will be a pointer to an object from one of the three derived classes. The second `find` function also returns pointers to any of the three derived classes through an array declared to hold `property` class pointers.

Although the array deals with all three derived classes in the same way when inserting them into the array or searching for a property, the structures of the three classes are still different. This means that when the program creates an object for a new piece of property, it must create an object of one specific type. To see the

Listing 16.3   Array manager class from the Realty Listings program

```
class arrayMgr
{
    private:
        int numb_properties;
        property * listed[MAX_PROPERTIES];
    public:
        arrayMgr ();
        int load (); // read from file
        void insert (property *);
        property * find (int); // find by property ID
        int find (property * [], string25); // find by type of property
        void unload (); // write entire array to file
};
```

implications of this issue, look at the load function in Listing 16.4, the function that controls reading data from the text file. Notice that the function reads the type of object from the data file first. It then uses that value to decide what type of object to create with the new operator.

On the other hand, the unload function, which controls writing data to the text file, doesn't need to be concerned explicitly with the type of object. The computer knows the type of object to which a given pointer in the array is pointing. When the load function calls a derived object's write function, it calls the write function from the correct class.

Base Class Member Functions

Two types of member functions are defined in base classes. The first is member functions that can be used by most or all of the functions derived from the base class. The second is member functions that can't be inherited but that can be called by derived classes. Constructors fall into the latter classification.

In Listing 16.5 you will find the member functions for the property class. The first two functions are constructors: one for interactive input and the other for file input. The third function is a private function that converts the integer used to store yes/no values into a string. The fourth is a function that sets a new asking price, and the final three are functions that return private data to a calling function. Because the constructors are somewhat different from ones you have seen before, we'll look at them in a bit more depth.

Listing 16.4   Array manager member functions

```
arrayMgr::arrayMgr()
{
    numb_properties = 0;
    for (int i = 0; i < MAX_PROPERTIES; i++)
        listed[i] = 0;
}

int arrayMgr::load ()
{
    char yes_no, dummy;
    string25 itype;
    int count;
    ifstream fin ("Properties");
    if (!fin)
    {
        cout << "\nCouldn't open input file. Continue? ";
        cin >> yes_no;
        if (toupper(yes_no) == 'N')
            return FALSE;
        else
            return TRUE;
    }
    fin >> count;
    fin.get (dummy); // skip over blank
    for (int i = 0; i < count; i++)
    {
        fin.getline (itype,80,'\0');
        if (strcmp (itype,"house") == 0)
            listed[i] = new residential (fin, itype);
        else if (strcmp (itype,"farm") == 0)
            listed[i] = new agricultural (fin, itype);
        else
            listed[i] = new commercial (fin, itype);
        insert (listed[i]);
    }
    fin.close();
    return TRUE;
}

void arrayMgr::insert (property * newPlace)
    { listed[numb_properties++] = newPlace; }
property * arrayMgr::find (int propID)
{
    for (int i = 0; i < numb_properties; i++)
        if (listed[i]->getID() == propID)
            return listed[i];
    return 0;
}
```

Continued on next page

Listing 16.4 (Continued)   Array manager member functions

```
int arrayMgr::find (property * found[], string25 itype)
{
    int j = 0;

    for (int i = 0; i < numb_properties; i++)
        if (strcmp(listed[i]->getType(),itype) == 0)
            found[j++] = listed[i];
    return j;
}

void arrayMgr::unload ()
{
    ofstream fout ("Properties");
    if (!fout)
    {
        cout << "\nCouldn't open output file.";
        return;
    }
    fout << numb_properties << ' ';
    for (int i = 0; i < numb_properties; i++)
        listed[i]->write(fout);
}
```

THE INTERACTIVE CONSTRUCTOR

In most of the programs you have seen to this point that use dynamic binding, data are collected by a program function and then passed into a constructor. However, in this case the data are collected by the constructor. The advantage to this strategy is that data can be input directly into class variables. Doing so significantly reduces the volume of the data that must be passed from one function to another and thus simplifies function signatures.

The drawback to doing this is that the user interface—the code that collects the data—is part of the class. This means that if you move the program from one computing platform to another (for example, from the Macintosh to Windows), you must modify the class when you make the change. However, if all the user interface code is part of the main program, classes can be transported without significant modification.

NOTE

This doesn't mean that user interface code should never be a part of classes. In fact, when you get into ToolBox programming and in particular begin to use Metrowerks's application framework (PowerPlant), you'll see that elements of the Macintosh user

Listing 16.5   Base class member functions

```
property::property (string25 itype)
{
    char dummy[2];

    strcpy (type, itype);
    cout << "\nProperty ID: ";
    cin >> propertyID;
    cout << "Asking price: ";
    cin >> asking_price;
//  gets (dummy); // kludge
    cout << "Owner's name: ";
    cin.getline (owner_name,80);
    cout << "Owner's phone: ";
    cin.getline (owner_phone,80);
}

property::property (ifstream & fin, string25 itype)
{
    char dummy;

    strcpy (type, itype);
    fin >> propertyID >> asking_price;
    fin.get (dummy);
    fin.getline (owner_name,80,'\0');
    fin.getline (owner_phone,80,'\0');
}

// Private function to translate integer storage into strings for
// output.
char * property::switchBoolean (int Boolean)
{
    static char yes[] = "Yes", no[] = "No";
    if (Boolean == TRUE)
        return yes;
    return no;
}

void property::setPrice (double newPrice)
    { asking_price = newPrice; }

int property::getID ()
    { return propertyID; }

char * property::getType ()
    { return type; }

double property::getPrice ()
    { return asking_price; }
```

interface, such as windows and menus, are represented as objects. However, the classes that support the interface are generally separate from classes that manipulate data. Whether you code your user interface inside classes or leave it in the main program is up to you, based on your judgment on how likely you think it is that you'll be modifying that interface code in the future.

The `property` class's interactive constructor has only one input parameter: the type of property. As you saw in Listing 16.4, the array manager object needs to know the type of property so that it can create the correct type of derived class object. The type of property therefore becomes the only variable that it is essential to collect before creating an object and calling a constructor.

Notice that this constructor collects data for the variables that are declared in the base class. Each of the derived classes can then call this constructor, sharing this code, which is common to all three of them. The major benefit here is the avoidance of unnecessarily duplicated code.

NOTE

Although you normally cannot explicitly call a constructor, a derived class constructor can call its base class's constructor. You will see how to do so shortly.

THE FILE INPUT CONSTRUCTOR

As you would expect, the file input constructor requires a file input stream as an input parameter. It also, however, accepts the type of property, which is read from the input file by the array manager object.

Why is this read by the array manager and not by the derived class's constructor? Because the array manager must know which type of object to create when it issues a `new` statement. Since the type of object has already been read, it can simply be passed into the constructor.

As you look at this constructor, keep in mind that the order in which the values are read must match the derived class's `write` functions exactly. The constructors and the `write` functions were therefore coded at the same time, ensuring the correct ordering of data values.

Derived Class Member Functions

The member functions for the three derived classes look very similar to one another. Nonetheless, they have been tailored to the specific variables used by each derived class. In this section we'll look at each type of member function and examine how they differ among the three classes.

THE INTERACTIVE CONSTRUCTORS

The interactive constructors for the derived classes can be found in Listing 16.6. The first thing you should notice is that the function headers are somewhat different from what you have seen before: Each header is followed by a colon and a call of the base class constructor. This is the only way in which you can explicitly call a constructor.

The call to the base class constructor occurs immediately after the computer enters the function. Once execution of the base class constructor is complete, the computer executes the body of the derived class constructor.

The body of all three functions is completely different. The data that are collected by each derived class constructor reflect the specific variables that a derived class has added to the variables inherited from the base class.

Consider what would be needed in the main program (or the array manager object, should you choose to put it there) if the I/O to collect input data weren't part of the constructors. Regardless of where the rest of the data are collected, the main program needs to know which type of object the user wants to create. If the rest of the I/O is in the constructor, once the main program knows the type of object, it can use the correct class name with the new operator. However, if the I/O isn't in the constructor, the main program must contain all of the code found in the three constructors, one set of I/O statements for each type of object. As you can see, there is a significant trade-off between the simplicity of placing the I/O inside the constructors and the cross-platform flexibility you gain by keeping the user interface out of data classes.

THE FILE INPUT CONSTRUCTORS

Like the interactive constructors, the function headers for the file input constructors (Listing 16.7) contain calls to the base class constructor. The base class constructor

Listing 16.6 **Interactive constructors for the derived classes**

```
residential::residential (string25 itype)
    : property (itype) // call base class constructor
{
    char yes_no;

    cout << "Square footage: ";
    cin >> sq_ft;
    cout << "Number of bedrooms: ";
    cin >> numb_bedrooms;
    cout << "Number of bathrooms: ";
    cin >> numb_bathrooms;
    cout << "Does it have a fireplace? ";
    cin >> yes_no;

    // store Booleans as integers
    if (toupper(yes_no) == 'Y')
        fireplace = TRUE;
    else
        fireplace = FALSE;

    cout << "Does it have a family room? ";
    cin >> yes_no;
    if (toupper(yes_no) == 'Y')
        family_room = TRUE;
    else
        family_room = FALSE;
}

commercial::commercial (string25 itype)
    : property (itype)
{
    char yes_no;

    cout << "Square footage: ";
    cin >> sq_ft;
    cout << "Number of offices: ";
    cin >> numb_offices;
    cout << "Number of floors: ";
    cin >> numb_floors;
    cout << "Elevator? ";
    cin >> yes_no;

    // store Booleans as integers
    if (toupper(yes_no) == 'Y')
        elevator = TRUE;
    else
        elevator = FALSE;
}
```

Continued on next page

Listing 16.6 (Continued)   Interactive constructors for the derived classes

```
agricultural::agricultural (string25 itype)
    : property (itype)
{
    char yes_no;

    cout << "Arable acreage: ";
    cin >> acreage;
    cout << "Is there a house? ";
    cin >> yes_no;
    if (toupper(yes_no) == 'Y')
    {
        house = TRUE;
        cout << "Square footage of house: ";
        cin >> house_sq_ft;
    }
    else
    {
        house = FALSE;
        house_sq_ft = 0;
    }
    cout << "Is there a barn? ";
    cin >> yes_no;
    if (toupper(yes_no) == 'Y')
    {
        barn = TRUE;
        cout << "Square footage of barn: ";
        cin >> barn_sq_ft;
    }
    else
    {
        barn = FALSE;
        barn_sq_ft = 0;
    }
}
```

initializes the `type` variable and reads data that are common to all three derived classes. When execution of the base class constructor has finished, the computer executes the constructor specific to the derived class.

Data for all three derived classes are intermixed in the text file used by the Realty Listings program. As long as all objects for a given class are written and read consistently, this mingling of data layouts presents no problems. However, it will not work if the computer is unable to correctly identify the type of object that it will be reading from the file.

Listing 16.7   File input constructors for the derived classes

```
residential::residential (ifstream & fin, string25 itype)
    : property (fin, itype)
{
    char dummy;
    fin >> sq_ft >> numb_bedrooms >> numb_bathrooms >> fireplace
        >> family_room;
    fin.get (dummy);
}

commercial::commercial (ifstream & fin, string25 itype)
    : property (fin, itype)
{
    char dummy;
    fin >> sq_ft >> numb_offices >> numb_floors >> elevator;
    fin.get (dummy);
}

agricultural::agricultural (ifstream & fin, string25 itype)
    : property (fin, itype)
{
    char dummy;
    fin >> acreage >> house >> house_sq_ft >> barn >> barn_sq_ft;
    fin.get (dummy);
}
```

Displaying Data

The display function is a pure virtual function that has no body in the base class. Separate implementations of that function therefore appear in each of the derived classes (Listing 16.8).

As an alternative, the program could make display a nonpure virtual function in the base class by not following the prototype with = 0. In that case, the base class would contain an implementation of the function containing code that was common to all three derived classes. The derived classes could call the base class function using the scope resolution operator to tell the compiler where to find the function:

```
property::display();
```

This is a good strategy when the derived classes share some of the function code but not all, much like what happens with the constructors. However, in this case the code is similar, but not identical, for each derived class. It therefore isn't feasible to

Listing 16.8   Displaying data for the derived classes

```cpp
void residential::display()
{
    cout << "\nProperty #" << propertyID << " (House):" << endl;
    cout << "   " << sq_ft << " square feet" << endl;
    cout << "   " << "Asking $" << asking_price << endl;
    cout << "   " << "Current owner: " << owner_name << " ("
        << owner_phone << ")" << endl;
    cout << "   " << "Bedrooms: " << numb_bedrooms << "  Bathrooms: "
        << numb_bathrooms << endl;
    cout << "   " << "Fireplace: " << switchBoolean(fireplace)
        << "  Family room: " << switchBoolean(family_room) << endl;
}

void commercial::display ()
{
    cout << "\nProperty #" << propertyID << " (Office):" << endl;
    cout << "   " << sq_ft << " square feet" << endl;
    cout << "   " << "Asking $" << asking_price << endl;
    cout << "   " << "Current owner: " << owner_name << " ("
        << owner_phone << ")" << endl;
    cout << "   " << "Number of offices: " << numb_offices << " on "
        << numb_floors << "floors" << endl;
    cout << "   " << "Elevator: " << switchBoolean (elevator) << endl;
}

void agricultural::display ()
{
    cout << "\nProperty #" << propertyID << " (Farm):" << endl;
    cout << "   " << "Asking $" << asking_price << endl;
    cout << "   " << "Current owner: " << owner_name << " ("
        << owner_phone << ")" << endl;
    cout << "   " << "Total arable acreage: " << acreage;
    cout << "   " << "House? " << switchBoolean (house) << " ("
        << house_sq_ft << " square feet)" << endl;
    cout << "   " << "Barn? " << switchBoolean (barn) << " ("
        << barn_sq_ft << " square feet)" << endl;
}
```

separate some of the code into a base class function that is called at the beginning of the derived class function.

COMPUTING THE ANTICIPATED COMMISSION

The computeCommission function is also a pure virtual function in the base class. A complete implementation therefore appears in all three derived classes (Listing

16.9). The individual functions are necessary only because the commission rate is different for each type of derived object.

Listing 16.9 Computing the anticipated commission for the derived classes

```
float residential::computeCommission ()
     { return asking_price * HOUSE_COM; }

float commercial::computeCommission ()
     { return asking_price * BUS_COM; }

float agricultural::computeCommission ()
     { return asking_price * FARM_COM; }
```

WRITING THE DATA TO A TEXT FILE

Writing data to a text file (Listing 16.10) presents the same choices as does displaying data: You could code three separate functions or place the common code in a base class function that the derived class functions could call. In this case, there is much more common code than found in the display function. However, the duplication is minimal, and it is logically simpler to place all the output code in one function.

The Main Program

Because so much of the work in the Realty Listings program is done in the member functions, the main program is relatively simple. As you can see in Listing 16.11, the main function declares a pointer variable to hold a pointer to an arrayMgr object and then creates the object and calls the array manager's load function to read the data stored in the text file. The rest of the main function is switch logic that calls program functions based on the user's menu choice.

The program functions called by the main function can be found in Listing 16.12. Look first at the newProperty function. As mentioned earlier, this function needs to collect at least one piece of data about a piece of property—its type—so that it knows which type of object to create. However, once the program knows the type, it can use the new operator to create the function and turn the rest of the data collection over to the object's constructor. After the constructor initializes the object, the newProperty function inserts it into the arrayMgr object's array.

Listing 16.10   Writing data to a text file for the derived classes

```
void residential::write (ofstream & fout)
{
     fout << type << '\0';
     fout << propertyID << ' ';
     fout << asking_price << ' ';
     fout << owner_name << '\0';
     fout << owner_phone << '\0';
     fout << sq_ft << ' ';
     fout << numb_bedrooms << ' ';
     fout << numb_bathrooms << ' ';
     fout << fireplace << ' ';
     fout << family_room << ' ';
}

void commercial::write (ofstream & fout)
{
     fout << type << '\0';
     fout << propertyID << ' ';
     fout << asking_price << ' ';
     fout << owner_name << '\0';
     fout << owner_phone << '\0';
     fout << sq_ft << ' ';
     fout << numb_offices << ' ';
     fout << numb_floors << ' ';
     fout << elevator << ' ';
}

void agricultural::write (ofstream & fout)
{
     fout << type << '\0';
     fout << propertyID << ' ';
     fout << asking_price << ' ';
     fout << owner_name << '\0';
     fout << owner_phone << '\0';
     fout << acreage << ' ';
     fout << house << ' ';
     fout << house_sq_ft << ' ';
     fout << barn << ' ';
     fout << barn_sq_ft << ' ';
}
```

The remaining program functions (other than the one that manages the menu) all require searching the array manager's array of properties to find one or more of them. The checkCommission function asks the user for the property ID number and then uses the array manager find function that expects an integer as an input parameter. (The searches in this program are sequential just to keep the code as short

Listing 16.11   The main function for the Realty Listings program

```cpp
#include <iostream.h>
#include <string.h>
#include <stdio.h>
#include <iomanip.h>
#include "realty.h"

int menu();
void newProperty (arrayMgr *);
void findProperty (arrayMgr *);
void checkCommission (arrayMgr *);
void setPrice (arrayMgr *);

void main ()
{
    arrayMgr * listings;
    int result, option = 0;

    listings = new arrayMgr ();

    result = listings->load(); // read text file
    if (result == FALSE)
        return; // exit program

    while (option != 9)
    {
        option = menu ();
        switch (option)
        {
            case 1:
                newProperty (listings);
                break;
            case 2:
                findProperty (listings);
                break;
            case 3:
                checkCommission (listings);
                break;
            case 4:
                setPrice (listings);
                break;
            case 9:
                listings->unload (); // write to text file
                break;
            default:
                cout << "You've entered an unavailable option.";
        }
    }
}
```

Listing 16.12   Program functions for the Realty Listings program

```
int menu ()
{
    char dummy[2];
    int choice;
    cout << "\n\nPick an option:" << endl;
    cout << "  1. Add a new property" << endl;
    cout << "  2. Find properties" << endl;
    cout << "  3. Check commissions" << endl;
    cout << "  4. Change aksing price" << endl;
    cout << "  9. Quit" << endl << endl;
    cout << "Choice: ";
    cin >> choice;
//  gets (dummy); // kludge
    return choice;
}

void newProperty (arrayMgr * listings)
{
    string25 itype;
    property * newParcel;
    cout << "\nWhat type of property (house, farm, business): ";
    cin.getline (itype,80);
    if (strcmp(itype,"house") == 0)
        newParcel = new residential (itype);
    else if (strcmp (itype,"farm") == 0)
        newParcel = new agricultural (itype);
    else
        newParcel = new commercial (itype);
    listings->insert (newParcel);
}

void checkCommission (arrayMgr * listings)
{
    property * whichPlace;
    int ID;

    cout << "\nProperty ID#: ";
    cin >> ID;
    whichPlace = listings->find (ID);
    if (whichPlace == 0)
    {
        cout << "That property isn't listed.";
        return;
    }
    cout << setprecision (2) << setiosflags (ios::fixed);
    cout << "\nThe projected commission is $"
         << whichPlace->computeCommission();
}
```

Continued next page

Listing 16.12 (Continued)   Program functions for the Realty Listings program

```cpp
void findProperty (arrayMgr * listings)
{
    int ID, how_many;
    string25 itype;
    property * whichPlace, * found[MAX_PROPERTIES];

    cout << "Which type of property (house, farm, business)? ";
    gets (itype);

    if (strlen(itype) > 0)
    {
        how_many = listings->find (found, itype);
        if (how_many > 0)
            for (int i = 0; i < how_many; i++)
                found[i]->display();
        return;
    }
    cout << "Property ID#: ";
    cin >> ID;
    whichPlace = listings->find (ID);
    if (whichPlace == 0)
    {
        cout << "That property isn't listed.";
        return;
    }
    whichPlace->display();
}

void setPrice (arrayMgr * listings)
{
    int ID;
    float newPrice;
    property * whichPlace;

    cout << "\nProperty ID#: ";
    cin >> ID;
    whichPlace = listings->find (ID);
    if (whichPlace == 0)
    {
        cout << "\nThat property isn't listed.";
        return;
    }
    cout << "\nThe current asking price is $" << whichPlace->getPrice();
    cout << "\nNew asking price: ";
    cin >> newPrice;
    whichPlace->setPrice(newPrice);
}
```

as possible). Using the base class pointer returned by find, it places the base class function getPrice in a cout statement to call the function, computes the anticipated commission, and displays the result.

The setPrice program function lets the user change the asking price of a property. The function must first find the property (in this case, also by property ID). It then uses the base class pointer to call the base class function setPrice.

> **NOTE**
>
> *There's a program function named setPrice and a base class function named SetPrice. Doesn't the compiler get confused? No, it doesn't get confused at all. A function's signature includes the class (if any) to which it belongs, along with its parameter list. Even if these two functions had the same parameter list, the fact that one belongs to a class and one doesn't is enough to make them distinct.*

The findProperty program function uses both the array manager's find functions. The second find, which expects a property type as an input parameter, returns multiple values in an array whose address is passed into the function. Notice that this array (found) has been declared to hold base class pointers. Like the other data structures used by this program, it therefore can hold pointers to objects created from any or all of the three classes derived from property.

Introducing the ToolBox

17

As you read in the Preface, writing a Macintosh application involves both knowing the language in which you are writing the program and being able to implement the Macintosh user interface. Fortunately for Macintosh programmers, the elements of the Macintosh user interface, along with many other aspects of the Macintosh environment, are supported by a large group of functions that make up the Macintosh ToolBox, much of which is stored in the Macintosh ROM.

NOTE

One of the things that has prevented Macintosh clones from being developed independently of Apple is the complexity of the ToolBox ROM. Without the ROMs to support ToolBox calls, it is virtually impossible to run existing Macintosh software (both the operating system and application software). Only now that Apple is licensing the Tool-Box have clones become feasible.

The Macintosh ToolBox is a powerful, complex set of functions. Although it is beyond the scope of this book to teach you ToolBox programming, this chapter will give you a flavor of what is involved in adding the Macintosh user interface to your program. You will see some sample ToolBox routines and be introduced to the way in which programs that use the ToolBox are structured. Finally, you'll find some suggestions of where you can go to extend your programming knowledge once you're comfortable with the C++ concepts covered in this book.

Macintosh Application Structure

A Macintosh program is *event-driven*. An *event* is anything that occurs in the Macintosh environment, such as moving the mouse pointer, pressing a key on the keyboard, making a choice from the menu bar, or inserting a floppy disk. An event-driven program, therefore, is one that bases its actions on the types of events that occur.

Events are initially trapped by the Macintosh operating system. If the event is something that the operating system should handle (for example, making a choice from a Finder menu), the operating system takes care of the event without involving any programs. However, if the event relates to a program that is running, the operating system places the event in a waiting list known as the *event queue*.

Each Macintosh program contains in its `main` function a loop that calls a ToolBox routine named `waitNextEvent`. Whenever an event for the program is in the event queue, `waitNextEvent` returns information about the event. The program figures out the type of event that has occurred and then uses `switch` logic to branch to a part of the program that handles that specific event.

The programs we have written throughout this book are event-driven only in a very simplistic manner. The single event that these programs trap is entering a choice from a text-based menu. Once the menu is displayed on the screen, the program uses `cin` to wait until the user enters a choice. After the choice has been entered, however, our programs have used `switch` logic to call functions that process each menu choice individually. This is exactly the structure an event-driven program uses to identify and respond to events.

ToolBox Calls

The Macintosh ToolBox debuted with the first Macintosh in 1984. At that time there were two languages you could use to program the Mac: Pascal and assembly language. Even today the ToolBox distinctly reflects its Pascal roots.

The ToolBox routines are both Pascal functions (routines that return a value in a manner similar to the C++ `return` statement) and procedures (routines that either don't return any values or return values through a pass by reference). C++ programmers can handle all routines as functions. However, you must still deal with some of the subtle differences between the languages, including the way in which strings are stored.

Documentation for the ToolBox is contained in a set of books known collectively as *Inside Macintosh*, published by Addison-Wesley. The books are available through major bookstores and APDA, an Apple subsidiary that sells materials of interest to software developers:

NOTE
To reach APDA, write to:

> *APDA*
> *Apple Computer Inc.*
> *P.O. Box 319*
> *Buffalo, NY 14207-0319*

Or call (800) 282-2732 and ask for a catalog.

TOOLBOX ORGANIZATION

The Macintosh ToolBox isn't just an amorphous collection of functions. The functions are grouped into *managers*, functions that support a specific aspect of the Macintosh environment. Among the many managers provided by the ToolBox are the following:

- Control Manager: routines to handle controls, such as buttons, scroll bars, and sliders, that appear in windows
- Dialog Manager: routines to handle dialogs and alerts
- Event Manager: routines to handle event trapping
- Font Manager: routines to handle font type and style

- File Manager: routines to handle care of working with files
- Menu Manager: routines to provide support for menus
- Printing Manager: routines to handle printing
- QuickDraw: graphics drawing routines
- Sound Manager: routines to support the recording and playback of sound
- TextEdit: routines to perform basic text editing functions, such as cut, copy, and paste
- Window Manager: routines to support windows

One of the benefits of the concept of managers is that new ones can be added to the ToolBox whenever needed. New managers appear with new releases of the Macintosh operating system and are available on disk to Macintoshes that were produced before the managers were created. (New managers are incorporated into the ROMs of new Macintosh models, but Apple has a history of not updating the ROMs on older machines: thus the technique of using disk-based ToolBox routines to expand the ToolBox for older Macintoshes.)

ToolBox Data Structures

The ToolBox is not object-oriented. Classes for portions of the Macintosh user interface, such as windows and menus, are the responsibility of the programmer. This means that although you may be writing an object-oriented program, you nonetheless must deal with the non-object-oriented data structures used by many of the ToolBox routines.

The primary type of data structure used by ToolBox routines is a Pascal *record* (known as a *structure* in C and C++). A structure is somewhat like a class without member functions and without restrictions on variable access. In other words, it's a way of grouping variables of different types under a single name.

To reference the elements of a structure, you can use dot notation, the same notation you have been using to access variables and functions of objects that are created for use with static binding. For example, assume that you have the following structure:

```
struct Account
{
    int ID_numb;
    float Amt_Owed;
    date * Date_Due;
};
```

A program would declare a variable that holds the structure with:

```
Account myAccount;
```

Then the variables would be referenced with:

```
myAccount.ID_numb
myAccount.Amt_Owed
*(myAccount.Date_Due)
```

The ToolBox makes extensive use of structures to represent many items within the Macintosh environment, including windows, menus, and files. Even if you are writing an object-oriented program, you must work with non-object-oriented structures, because they are the format in which ToolBox routines return much of their information.

NOTE

The ToolBox routines also rely on a large number of data types created with the Pascal equivalent of the typedef statement.

TOOLBOX HEADER FILES

CodeWarrior supports the ToolBox routines by providing C-style prototypes for each of the ToolBox routines. These prototypes can be found in the Universal Headers folder. However, if you set up CodeWarrior properly, you never need worry about including the correct ToolBox header file.

The ToolBox headers have been precompiled. You can therefore make them available automatically to all programs you write by including the name of the precompiled header file as a prefix to your project. To do so, go to the Preferences window and click on the Languages icon. Make sure that MacHeadersPPC (if you're working on a Power Mac) or MacHeaders68K (if you're working on a 68K Mac) appears in the Prefix File box, as in Figure 17.1. (This is the default setup for CodeWarrior, so in most cases you shouldn't have to do anything.)

Figure 17.1   Using precompiled headers

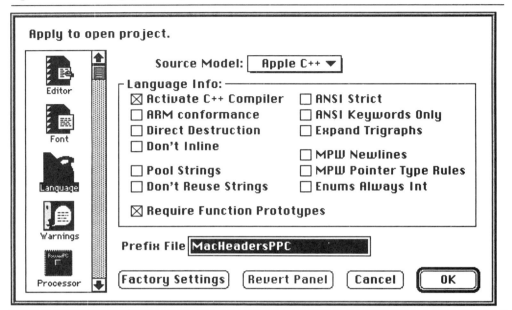

Sample ToolBox Calls

To give you an idea of what is involved in using ToolBox routines, we'll be adding some simple ToolBox calls to the Realty Listings program that you read about in Chapter 16. First, we'll add support for the Open File and Save File dialog boxes so that users can choose the files in which data should be stored. Then we'll add to the program some alerts that tell users when a search for property is unsuccessful.

GETTING STARTED: INITIALIZING THE MANAGERS

The first thing any Macintosh program that uses the ToolBox must do is initialize the managers. In most cases, you simply initialize all of them so you don't need to worry about exactly which ones your program will be using. A program function to do the initialization appears in Listing 17.1. The first manager initialized is QuickDraw (InitGraf). This routine takes one parameter, which is a global variable that is part

Listing 17.1   Initializing the ToolBox managers

```
void startToolBox ()
{
    // qd.thePort is a global Mac variable initialized by InitGraf
    InitGraf (&qd.thePort);
    InitFonts ();
    InitWindows ();
    InitMenus ();
    TEInit ();
    InitDialogs (nil);
    InitCursor ();
}
```

of a structure named qd. Because this structure is declared in the MacHeaders file, you needn't define it yourself. The only other initialization routine that requires a parameter is the one that initializes the dialog manager. In this case, you pass it the constant nil, which has been predefined to represent a null.

CHOOSING FILES: THE STANDARD FILE PACKAGE

Along with the large groups of routines clustered in managers, the ToolBox also has smaller groups of specialized routines known as *packages*. One of the oldest packages is the Standard File Package, which takes care of the Open File and Save File dialog boxes.

NOTE

Users call these dialog boxes Open File and Save File, but the ToolBox documentation has always referred to them as Get File and Put File.

NOTE

Although the Standard File Package has been part of the ToolBox since 1984, it has been significantly revised over the years. If you aren't running System 7, the Standard File Package calls that have been added to the realty program won't work!

Choosing a File to Open

To display the Get File dialog box, a program uses the `standardGetFile` function:

```
void StandardGetFile (FileFilerProcPtr fileFilter,
     short numTypes, SFTypeList typeList,
     StandardFileReply *replyPtr);
```

Although the data types in this parameter list look very strange, keep in mind that these are structures and user-defined data types that have been declared in the Mac-Headers file.

The first parameter—`fileFilter`—is a pointer to code that can be used to filter the types of files that appear in the dialog box. In most cases, you can just pass `nil`. The second parameter—`numTypes`—is the number of types of files that you will allow to appear. To allow all types, as we will do in this case, you can pass -1.

The `typeList` is an array of four character file types. The number of types in the list is contained in the `numTypes` parameter. If you are allowing all types of files, the computer ignores the `typeList`.

The final parameter is a pointer to a structure in which the Macintosh will return information about the user's interaction with the Get File dialog box. The structure has the following elements:

```
struct StandardFileReply
{
     Boolean      sfGood;
     Boolean      sfReplacing;
     OSType       sfType;
     FSSpec       sfFile;
     ScriptCode   sfScript;
     short        sfFlags;
     Boolean      sfIsFolder;
     Boolean      sfIsVolume;
     long         sfReserved1;
     short        sfReserved2;
};
```

For our simple example, two of the elements of the structure are of particular importance. The first is the Boolean `sfGood`. This tells a program whether the user chose the Open button (either by clicking on it or by pressing Enter) or the Cancel button. If `sfGood` is `TRUE`, the user chose Open; it it's `FALSE`, the user chose Cancel.

The second important element is sfFile. This structure, embedded within the StandardFileReply structure, contains the name of the chosen file. When you are working with File Manager routines, you can pass the entire FSSpec structure as a parameter. However, to use stream I/O, we need to extract the file name from the structure so that it can be used when creating a file stream object.

The FSSpec structure has the following elements:

```
struct FSSpec
{
        int         vRefNum;
        long        parID;
        Str63       name;
};
```

If we have declared a StandardFileReply structure using the name reply-Struct, we can access the name with:

```
replyStruct.sfFile.name
```

The problem that the preceding presents is that the name of the file isn't stored as a C++ string; it's stored as a Pascal string. Pascal strings begin with a length byte and have no terminating null. In this case, the data type Str63 indicates a 64-byte string (63 characters plus the leading length byte). As it stands, the file name can't be used as a parameter when creating an I/O stream object. It must first be translated into a C++ string.

The Realty Listings program does the conversion with a short function of its own. As you can see in Listing 17.2, the function accepts two parameters: the Pascal string and a pointer to where the C++ string will be stored. The function retrieves the length of the Pascal string by copying the contents of the first byte into an integer variable. It then uses that to determine how many characters to copy, one at a time, from the Pascal string to the C++ string. The final step is to explicitly add the terminating null to the C++ string.

With the string conversion routine in place, the Realty Listings program is ready to use a Get File dialog box. The code modifications occur in the arrayMgr class, which is responsible for loading data from the text file. The new version of the load member function can be found in Listing 17.3.

The first addition to this function is the variables needed for the call to StandardGetFile. These include the replyStruct, a typeList (although unused, it

Listing 17.2   Converting a Pascal string to a C++ string

```
void convertPascalStr (Str63 Pascalstring, char * Cstring)
{
    int length;

    length = Pascalstring[0]; // get length byte
    for (int i = 0; i < length; i++)
        Cstring[i] = Pascalstring[i+1];
    Cstring[i] = '\0'; // don't forget the terminating null
}
```

must be present), and numTypes. The function must also include a string variable to hold the file name after it has been converted from the Pascal format (fileName).

Once the variables have been declared, the function calls the ToolBox routine:

```
StandardGetFile (nil, numTypes, typeList, &replyStruct);
```

The next step is to figure out which button the user chose to dismiss the dialog box. The following logic checks the sfGood element:

```
if (!replyStruct.sfGood)
```

As you will remember from earlier discussion, if the value is FALSE, the user chose Cancel. In that case, the load function returns without any further processing.

When sfGood is TRUE, the load function must then convert the Pascal file name into a C++ string by calling the function you saw in Listing 17.2:

```
convertPascalStr (replyStruct.sfFile.name, fileName);
```

At that point, load can pass fileName when creating the ifstream object. The rest of the function remains unchanged from what you saw in Chapter 16.

With this code in place, the first thing the user sees when the program runs is the dialog box in Figure 17.2. If the user clicks the Cancel button, the program proceeds without opening a file, allowing the user to enter completely new data. If the user chooses a file, the program attempts to open it.

Listing 17.3   The arrayMgr class's load function, using the Get File dialog box

```
int arrayMgr::load ()
{
    char yes_no, dummy;
    string25 itype;
    int count;


    // Data structures and variables for call to StandardGetFile

    StandardFileReply replyStruct;
    SFTypeList typeList; // we're going to allow all file types
    short numTypes = -1; // allow all types of files
    char fileName[64];

    StandardGetFile (nil, numTypes, typeList, &replyStruct);
    if (!replyStruct.sfGood)
        return TRUE; // user cancelled but continue anyway

    convertPascalStr (replyStruct.sfFile.name, fileName);
    ifstream fin (fileName);
    if (!fin)
    {
        cout << "\nCouldn't open input file. Continue? ";
        cin >> yes_no;
        if (toupper(yes_no) == 'N')
            return FALSE;
        else
            return TRUE;
    }
    fin >> count;
    fin.get (dummy); // skip over blank
    for (int i = 0; i < count; i++)
    {
        fin.getline (itype,80,'\0'); /
        if (strcmp (itype,"house") == 0)
            listed[i] = new residential (fin, itype);
        else if (strcmp (itype,"farm") == 0)
            listed[i] = new agricultural (fin, itype);
        else
            listed[i] = new commercial (fin, itype);
        insert (listed[i]);
    }
    fin.close();
    return TRUE;
}
```

Figure 17.2   The Get File dialog box produced by the code in Listing 17.3

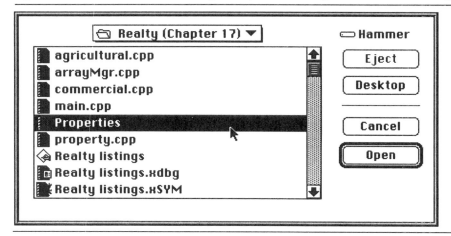

Choosing a File to Save

Producing a Put File dialog box is even easier than generating a Get File dialog box. The StandardPutFile dialog box has the following prototype:

```
void StandardPutFile (Str255 prompt, Str255 defaultName,
    StandardFileReply *replyPtr);
```

The prompt parameter is the text that appears above the box where the user enters a file name. As you might guess, defaultName is the file name that appears highlighted in that box. Both of these parameters are Pascal strings (one length byte followed by up to 255 characters.)

In Listing 17.4 you will find the arrayMgr class's modified load function. Notice first that the two string parameters are initialized as Pascal strings by placing the escape sequence \p at the beginning of each string. The \p isn't compiled as part of the string but instead is interpreted as requiring a length byte at the beginning of the string rather than a terminating null.

The load function calls StandardPutFile, producing a dialog box like that in Figure 17.3. The function then checks to see whether the user has clicked the Save or Cancel buttons (recorded in sfGood) and bases its decision whether to write the file on the user's choice. If the user has clicked Save, the function converts the name of the file to a C++ string, creates an ofstream object, and then writes to the file.

Listing 17.4   The arrayMgr class unload function, using a Put File dialog box

```
void arrayMgr::unload ()
{
    // \p tells the compiler to make a Pascal string
    Str255 prompt = "\pSave file as:";
    Str255 default_name = "\pProperties";
    // create a standard reply structure
    StandardFileReply replyStruct;
    char fileName[64];

    StandardPutFile (prompt, default_name, &replyStruct);
    if (!replyStruct.sfGood)
        return; // user cancelled; don't save

    convertPascalStr (replyStruct.sfFile.name, fileName);
    ofstream fout (fileName);
    if (!fout)
    {
        cout << "\nCouldn't open output file.";
        return;
    }
    fout << numb_properties << ' ';
    for (int i = 0; i < numb_properties; i++)
        listed[i]->write(fout);
}
```

Figure 17.3   The Put File dialog box produced by the code in Listing 17.4

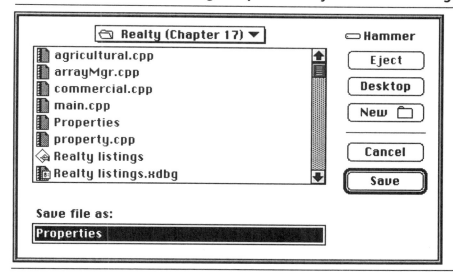

DISPLAYING ALERTS: WORKING WITH RESOURCES

Alerts are the windows that appear to give you a warning that something you might not want is about to happen or that something unexpected has occurred. For example, in most Macintosh programs an alert appears when you attempt to close a document that has unsaved changes. The Realty Listings program can use alerts to inform a user that a search for properties has been unsuccessful.

The modified Realty Listings program uses two alerts. The first (Figure 17.4) appears whenever a search by property ID is unsuccessful. The second (Figure 17.5) appears whenever a search by property type is unsuccessful. Notice that both alerts have a caution icon, some text that indicates the nature of the problem, and a button to dismiss the alert.

Figure 17.4   An alert that indicates that a search by property ID has been unsuccessful

Figure 17.5   An alert that indicates that a search by property type has been unsuccessful

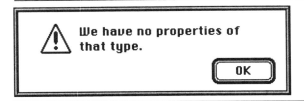

The only action a user can take with an alert is to click a button. Because an alert is relatively simple—it has no editable text fields, no scrolling lists, no checkboxes, no radio buttons—the ToolBox routine to create and manage an alert is also relatively simple. However, before a program can display an alert, it needs to know what text and what buttons should appear in the alert window.

Creating the Resources

The data that a program uses to construct an alert are known as *resources*. Resources contain information such as the initial size of a window, its initial place on the screen, and its contents (for example, buttons, editable text boxes, scrolling lists of items, pop-up menus, radio buttons, and checkboxes). An alert is described by two types of resources: one that describes that boundaries of the alert window and one that describes its contents. Although there are several ways to create resources, many programmers use a program called ResEdit, a freeware utility from Apple that is shipped with most Macintosh development software (including CodeWarrior).

While resources are under development, they are typically stored in a separate file with a *.rsrc* extension. If you add such a file to your CodeWarrior project, the C++ compiler will automatically use the resources in that file when compiling your program.

ResEdit lets you creates resources by drawing the look of a window, menu, or other element of the Macintosh user interface. To implement its alerts, the Realty Listings program needs two types of resources: ALRT for the alert windows and DITL for the lists of items that are in the alert windows. Because there are two different alert windows, the program needs to ALRT resources and a DITL resource for each.

Resources of a given type are numbered. In Figure 17.6, for example, you can see that the two ALRTs are numbered 128 and 129. (You can also give resources names to make them easier to work with, but internally the Macintosh uses the numbers.)

Figure 17.6   ALRT resources for the Realty Listings program

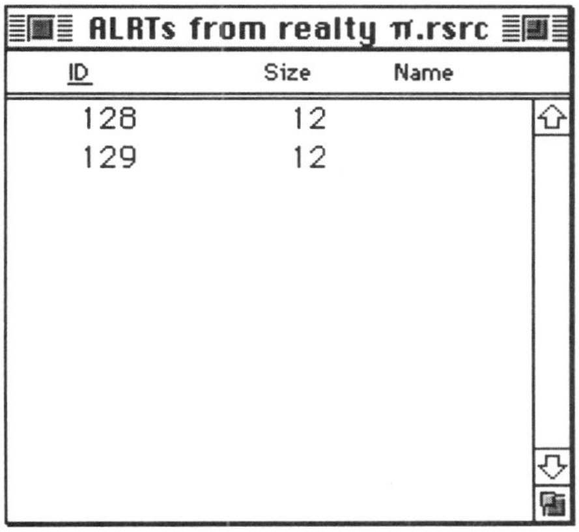

To create an ALRT resource, you tell ResEdit that you want to create a new resource and then choose the type. ResEdit displays a dialog box that lets you draw the size and shape of the alert window; you can also set the alert's initial position on the screen by dragging it into position. In Figure 17.7 you can see the alert as it would appear on the Macintosh's start-up monitor (in this case, a 14" monitor). Because the alert in Figure 17.7 has a list of items, those items also appear, letting you see what your alert looks like.

Figure 17.7   Drawing an alert

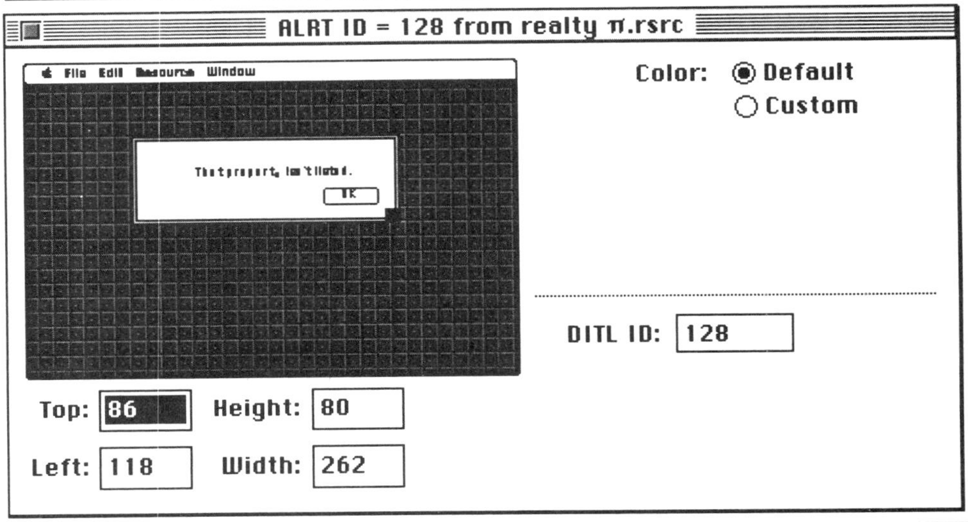

A DITL resource contains all the items that appear on the alert. (You're right; the caution icon isn't there. You'll see where it comes from in a bit.) As you can see in Figure 17.8, you choose the types of possible items from a list and then drag them into the window you created for the ALRT resource.

When you've finished creating the resources, ResEdit gathers all resources of a single type under one icon. For example, in Figure 17.9 you can see that there are two types of resources in this file. Double-clicking on any single type of resource brings up the list of individual resources that you saw in Figure 17.6. This gives you easy access to your resources while your program is under development.

Figure 17.8   Creating items for an alert

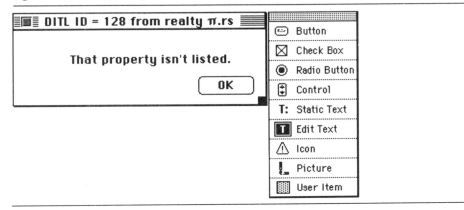

Figure 17.9   Completed resources for the Realty Listings program

NOTE

If you want to learn more about ResEdit, pick up a copy of ResEdit Complete, *by Peter Alley and Carolyn Strange (Addison-Wesley, 1991).*

Writing the Alert Management Code

Once the resource file has been saved and added to the Realty Listings project, we can add code to the program that uses those resources. To make it easy to reference the two alerts, the program first defines macros that assign names to the resource IDs:

```
#define NotOne 128
#define NotAny 129
```

The `NotOne` alert will be used whenever a search for a property ID fails; the `NotAny` alert will be used whenever a search for a type of property fails.

There are three functions that produce alerts, one for each type of icon that might appear at the left of the alert window:

```
int StopAlert (int alertID, ModalFilerPtr filerProc);
int NoteAlert (int alertID, ModalFilerPtr filerProc);
int CautionAlert (int alertID, ModalFilerPtr filerProc);
```

The `alertID` parameter is the number by which the alert's resource is known. The second parameter is a pointer to a procedure that can filter events generated by working with the alert. In most cases, you can just pass `nil` for this parameter. The alert's return value is an integer that corresponds to the number of the button click by the user (relevant when there is more than one button in the window).

To call an alert, you simply call the function that corresponds to the type of icon you want to see:

```
itemHit = CautionAlert (NotOne, nil);
```

The Macintosh takes care of displaying the alert, accepting user input (a click on a button), and returning the button chosen to the program. As you can see in Listing 17.5 (the Realty Listing program's `find` function), the primary change this makes to the code is to replace the error message formerly generated with `cout` with a call to `CautionAlert`. Because there is only one button in the alert, the program doesn't need to use the `itemHit` return value.

Where to Go from Here

Now that you know the basics, where can you go to learn more about programming the Macintosh? First, if you're going to be working with the ToolBox, you should

Listing 17.5   Modified find function that displays alerts for unsuccessful searches

```
void findProperty (arrayMgr * listings)
{
    int ID, how_many;
    string25 itype;
    property * whichPlace, * found[MAX_PROPERTIES];
    int itemHit; // for alert

    cout << "Which type of property (house, farm, business)? ";
    gets (itype);
    if (strlen(itype) > 0)
    {
        how_many = listings->find (found, itype);
        if (how_many > 0)
            for (int i = 0; i < how_many; i++)
                found[i]->display();
        else
            itemHit = CautionAlert (NotAny, nil); // display an alert
        return;
    }
    cout << "Property ID#: ";
    cin >> ID;
    whichPlace = listings->find (ID);
    if (whichPlace == 0)
    {
        itemHit = CautionAlert (NotOne, nil); // display an alert
        return;
    }
    whichPlace->display();
}
```

consider purchasing *Inside Macintosh* (at least those volumes that contain documentation of the ToolBox calls you'll be using).

Tutorial material can be found in several books, including the following:

- May, John, and Judy Whittle. *Programming Primer for the Macintosh*. AP Professional, 1995.
- Mark, Dave, and Cartwright Reed. *Macintosh C Programming Primer*. Volume 1, second edition. Addison-Wesley, 1992.
- Mark, Dave. *Macintosh C Programming*. Volume II. Addison-Wesley, 1990.

Glossary

Abstract base class: A base class from which no objects are created.

Address: A number given to identify a byte in main memory.

American Standard Code for Information Interchange: The binary code used to represent characters in most microcomputers.

Array: A group of objects or data values stored under the same name and referenced by their position in the group.

Array bounds checking: Checking the limits of an array to make sure that the array doesn't overflow.

Array element: One member of an array.

Array index: A number that represents the position of an element in an array.

ASCII: The abbreviation for American Standard Code for Information Interchange.

Assembly language: A programming language in which a two- to five-letter mnemonic code is substituted for a binary instruction code.

Assignment operator: The operator used to assign a value to a variable (=).

Base class: A class from which other classes are derived in an inheritance hierarchy.

Binary: Base 2; the system used to represent everything in a computer, including program instructions and data.

Binary file: A file that contains an unformatted stream of bits that are not understandable by most humans.

Binding: Creating a link between an object and the member functions of its class.

Bit: One binary digit (0 or 1).

Bubble sort: A sorting method that works by comparing successive pairs of values in an array and swapping those pairs that aren't in the correct order.

Byte: Eight bits.

Call (a function): To issue a command to execute a function.

Calling function: A function that places a call to another function.

Class: Used by an object-oriented program, a description of an entity containing variables used to store data that describe objects created from the class and declarations of the member functions that objects of the class know how to perform.

Clear (a bit): To set the bit's value to 0.

Comment statement: Text added to a source code file to document parts of the code.

Compiler directive: A command that a compiler executes during compilation.

Concatenation: Combining two strings to form a larger string by pasting one onto the end of the other.

Conditional operator: An operator used to return one of two values based on a logical condition, as in a < b ? a : b, which returns a if a < b is true and b if a < b is false.

Console: The default computer "terminal," or window, used by ANSI C++ for stream output.

Constant: A value that doesn't change during the run of a program.

Constructor: A member function that runs automatically when an object is created.

Control condition: A logical expression used to determine when a loop should stop iterating.

Control variable: A variable whose value changes inside a loop to control when the loop will stop iterating.

Cross-compiler: A compiler that generates machine language for a CPU other than the one on which the program is being written.

Data structure: A program structure that organizes data.

Debugger: A program used to help find logic errors in programs.

Dereference (a pointer): To precede a pointer variable name with an * to obtain the contents of the location pointed to by the pointer variable.

Derived class: A class that is created from another class in an inheritance hierarchy.

Destructor: A member function that is executed automatically when an object is removed from main memory.

Dynamic binding: Binding functions to objects while a program is running.

Element (of an array): One member of an array.

Escape character: A character preceded by \ and used to format an output stream.

Event: Anything that occurs in the Macintosh environment, such as moving the mouse pointer, pressing a key on the keyboard, making a choice from the menu bar, or inserting a floppy disk.

Event queue: A waiting list of events that a program must handle.

Event-driven: A program that bases its actions on the type of events that occur.

Floating point unit (FPU): Circuitry designed to speed operations on floating point numbers.

Force quit: The key combination Command-Option-Esc, which forces an executing program to terminate.

Forward declaration: A statement that identifies a class to the compiler by name without defining the class.

Formal parameters: Data passed into a function through the function's signature.

Friend function: A function that has access to all the private elements of a class in which the friend isn't a member function.

Function overloading: Defining two or more functions in the same class with the same name but different signatures.

Function prototype: A statement of a function's signature used to verify that function calls are made correctly.

Function: A self-contained block of code that returns at most one value.

G or Gb: Abbreviations for gigabyte.

Gigabyte: Approximately one billion bytes; exactly 1,073,741,824 bytes.

Header file: A file that contains data definition statements, including constants, classes, and function prototypes.

Hexadecimal: Base 16.

High-level language: An English-like programming language that is relatively portable among types of comptuers.

Infinite loop: A loop that never stops.

Information hiding: Keeping class variables and the details of member function execution private to a class, hidden from functions that use the class.

Inheritance: A hierarchical relationship between classes in which classes lower in a hierarchy inherit, or share, the variables and member functions of classes above them in the hierarchy.

Instruction set: The instructions that a computer knows how to execute without translation.

Iteration: Repeating groups of statements in a computer program.

K: An abbreviation for kilobyte.

Kilobyte: Approximately 1,000 bytes; exactly 1,024 bytes.

Library: A collection of precompiled programs that can be called from an application program.

Linked list: A chain of objects connected by pointers that indicate the object that comes next in the list

Linking: Combining the parts of an application into a runable program.

Local variable: A variable declared in a function that is accessible only within that function.

Logical expression: An expression that produces a result of true or false.

Logical operators: Operators used to formulate logical expressions.

Logicial OR: An operation that works on two bits. If either bit is 1, the result is 1; if both bits are 0, the result is 0.

Loop: A block of code that is repeated in a program.

Looping: Repeating actions in a program.

Mb or Meg: Abbreviations for megabyte.

Machine language: A computer language made up of the binary codes in a computer's instruction set.

Macro: A small block of code that is copied into source code wherever its name appears during compilation.

Manager: A group of ToolBox routines that supports one specific aspect of the Macintosh envrionment.

Manipulator: A function of the ios class, used to format a input or output stream.

Mb: An abbreviation for megabyte.

Megabyte: Approximately one million bytes; exactly 1,048,576 bytes.

Member function: A function that is part of a class.

Message: A command sent to an object to execute one of the object's member functions.

Method: A member function.

Modulo division: An integer division operation that returns the remainder of the division.

Object: An instance of a class.

Object code: A program made up of the binary codes that form a computer's instruction set.

One-dimensional array: An array made up of a single list of values.

Package: A small, specialized group of ToolBox routines.

Pass by reference: Passing a parameter by sending its address to a function. Changes to the parameter are made directly in main memory so that changes are available to the calling function.

Pass by value: Passing a value into a function as an input value only. Changes made to the parameter in the function aren't returned to the calling function.

Persistent object: An object that can read itself from and write itself to a file.

Pointer: The address at which some form of data storage begins in main memory.

Pointer arithmetic: An operation that modifies the contents of a pointer variable.

Pointer variable: A variable that is declared to hold a pointer to some specific type of data.

Polymorphism: The ability of different classes to respond differently to the same message.

Postdecrement: To decrease the value in a variable by 1 after evaluating the rest of the expression.

Postincrement: To increment the value in a variable by 1 after completing evaluation of the rest of the expression.

Precedence of operations: The order in which arithmetic and logical operations are performed within an expression.

Predecrement: To decrease the value in a variable by 1 before performing other operations in an expression.

Preincrement: To increase the value in a variable by 1 before performing other operations in an expression.

Project: A CodeWarrior file that specifies all the object code files that should be linked to make an executable application.

Pure function: In a base class, a function that has only a prototype but no implementation; a function whose prototype is followed by =0.

Reference parameter: A parameter passed by sending its address to a function. Changes to the parameter are made directly in main memory so that changes are available to the calling function.

Resource file: A file that contains definitions of portions of the Macintosh user interface

Resources: Data used to construct aspects of the Macintosh user interface, such as the contents of windows and menus.

Scope (of a variable): The portion of a program in which a variable exists.

Scope resolution operator: Two colons (::) used with a class name to indicate the class to which a function belongs.

Sequential search: A search of a group of items that begins at the first item and looks through all items, in order.

Set (a bit): To give a bit the value of 1.

Signature (of a function): A function's name and input parameters.

Source code: The text of a program, created using a text editor and containing statements in either assembly language or a high-level language.

Static binding: Binding functions to objects during program compilation.

Storage class (of a variable): An expression of how the variable should be stored in main memory (auto = destroyed when function ends; static = always resident; register = stored in CPU register).

Stream extraction operator: An operator (>>) used to accept input from the keyboard.

Stream insertion operator: The operator used to insert values into an output stream (<<).

String: A collection of characters (a word or sentence) handled as a unit.

Structure: A C and C++ data structure in which variables of different data types are grouped together under the same name.

Structured programming: Program logic derived from three simple structures: sequence, selection, and iteration.

Syntax error: An error detected by an assembler or compiler indicating a mistake in constructing language statements.

Terabyte: Approximately one trillion bytes (1,099,511,627,776 bytes)

Text file: A file containing readable characters that can be viewed with any word processor or text editor.

Trucate: To drop the fractional portion of a number.

Two-dimensional array: An array that stores data in a grid made up of columns and rows.

2's complement: The binary format used for storing integers.

Unary operator: An operator that operates on only one value at a time.

Value parameter: A value passed into a function as an input value only. Changes made to the parameter in the function aren't returned to the calling function.

Variable: A label for a main memory storage location used by a program.

Virtual function: A function that can be redefined in a derived class through polymorphism.

Index

SOFTWARE LICENSE

PLEASE READ THIS LICENSE CAREFULLY BEFORE USING THE SOFTWARE. BY USING THE SOFTWARE, YOU ARE AGREEING TO BE BOUND BY THE TERMS OF THIS LICENSE. IF YOU DO NOT AGREE TO THE TERMS OF THIS LICENSE, PROMPTLY RETURN THE UNUSED SOFTWARE TO THE PLACE WHERE YOU OBTAINED IT AND YOUR MONEY WILL BE REFUNDED.

1. License. The application, demonstration, system and other software accompanying this License, whether on disk, in read only memory, or on any other media (the "Software") the related documentation and fonts are licensed to you by Metrowerks. You own the disk on which the Software and fonts are recorded but Metrowerks and/or Metrowerks' Licensor retain title to the Software, related documentation and fonts. This License allows you to use the Software and fonts on a single Apple computer and make one copy of the Software and fonts in machine-readable form for backup purposes only. You must reproduce on such copy the Metrowerks copyright notice and any other proprietary legends that were on the original copy of the Software and fonts. You may also transfer all your license rights in the Software and fonts, the backup copy of the Software and fonts, the related documentation and a copy of this License to another party, provided the other party reads and agrees to accept the terms and conditions of this License.

2. Restrictions. The Software contains copyrighted material, trade secrets and other proprietary material. In order to protect them, and except as permitted by applicable legislation, you may not decompile, reverse engineer, disassemble or otherwise reduce the Software to a human-perceivable form. You may not modify, network, rent, lease, loan, distribute or create derivative works based upon the Software in whole or in part. You may not electronically transmit the Software from one computer to another or over a network.

3. Termination. This License is effective until terminated. You may terminate this License at any time by destroying the Software, related documentation and fonts and all copies thereof. This License will terminate immediately without notice from Metrowerks if you fail to comply with any provision of this License. Upon termination you must destroy the Software, related documentation and fonts and all copies thereof.

4. Export Law Assurances. You agree and certify that neither the Software nor any other technical data received from Metrowerks, nor the direct product thereof, will be exported outside the United States except as authorized and as permitted by the laws and regulations of the United States. If the Software has been rightfully obtained by you outside of the United States, you agree that you will not re-export the Software nor any other technical data received from Metrowerks, nor the direct product thereof, except as permitted by the laws and regulations of the United States and the laws and regulations of the jurisdiction in which you obtained the Software.

5. Government End Users. If you are acquiring the Software and fonts on behalf of any unit or agency of the United States Government, the following provisions apply. The Government agrees: (i) if the Software and fonts are supplied to the Department of Defense (DoD), the Software and fonts are classified as "Commercial Computer Software" and the Government is acquiring only "restricted rights" in the Software, its documentation and fonts as that term is defined in Clause 252.227-7013(c)(1) of the DFARS; and (ii) if the Software and fonts are supplied to any unit or agency of the United States Government other than DoD, the Government's rights in the Software, its documentation and fonts will be as defined in Clause 52.227-19(c)(2) of the FAR or, in the case of NASA, in Clause 18-52.227-86(d) of the NASA Supplement to the FAR.

6. Limited Warranty on Media. Metrowerks warrants the diskettes and/or compact disc on which the Software and fonts are recorded to be free from defects in materials and workmanship under normal use for a period of ninety (90) days from the date of purchase as evidenced by a copy of the receipt. Metrowerks' entire liability and your exclusive remedy will be replacement of the diskettes and/or compact disc not meeting Metrowerks' limited warranty and which is returned to Metrowerks or a Metrowerks authorized representative with a copy of the receipt. Metrowerks will have no responsibility to replace a disk/disc damaged by accident,abuse or misapplication. ANY IMPLIED WARRANTIES ON THE DISKETTES

AND/OR COMPACT DISC, INCLUDING THE IMPLIED WARRANTIES OF MERCHANTABILITY AND FITNESS FOR A PARTICULAR PURPOSE, ARE LIMITED IN DURATION TO NINETY (90) DAYS FROM THE DATE OF DELIVERY. THIS WARRANTY GIVES YOU SPECIFIC LEGAL RIGHTS, AND YOU MAY ALSO HAVE OTHER RIGHTS WHICH VARY BY JURISDICTION.

7. Disclaimer of Warranty on Apple Software. You expressly acknowledge and agree that use of the Software and fonts is at your sole risk. Except as is stated above, the Software, related documentation and fonts are provided "AS IS" and without warranty of any kind and Metrowerks and Metrowerks' Licensor(s) (for the purposes of provisions 7 and 8, Metrowerks and Metrowerks' Licensor(s) shall be collectively referred to as "Metrowerks") EXPRESSLY DISCLAIM ALL OTHER WARRANTIES, EXPRESS OR IMPLIED, INCLUDING, BUT NOT LIMITED TO, THE IMPLIED WARRANTIES OF MERCHANTABILITY AND FITNESS FOR A PARTICULAR PURPOSE. ACADEMIC PRESS DOES NOT WARRANT THAT THE FUNCTIONS CONTAINED IN THE SOFTWARE WILL MEET YOUR REQUIREMENTS, OR THAT THE OPERATION OF THE SOFTWARE WILL BE UNINTERRUPTED OR ERROR-FREE, OR THAT DEFECTS IN THE SOFTWARE AND THE FONTS WILL BE CORRECTED. FURTHERMORE, ACADEMIC PRESS DOES NOT WARRANT OR MAKE ANY REPRESENTATIONS REGARDING THE USE OR THE RESULTS OF THE USE OF THE SOFTWARE AND FONTS OR RELATED DOCUMENTATION IN TERMS OF THEIR CORRECTNESS, ACCURACY, RELIABILITY, OR OTHERWISE. NO ORAL OR WRITTEN INFORMATION OR ADVICE GIVEN BY ACADEMIC PRESS OR AN ACADEMIC PRESS AUTHORIZED REPRESENTATIVE SHALL CREATE A WARRANTY OR IN ANY WAY INCREASE THE SCOPE OF THIS WARRANTY. SHOULD THE SOFTWARE PROVE DEFECTIVE, YOU (AND NOT ACADEMIC PRESS OR AN ACADEMIC PRESS AUTHORIZED REPRESENTATIVE) ASSUME THE ENTIRE COST OF ALL NECESSARY SERVICING, REPAIR OR CORRECTION. SOME JURISDICTIONS DO NOT ALLOW THE EXCLUSION OF IMPLIED WARRANTIES, SO THE ABOVE EXCLUSION MAY NOT APPLY TO YOU.

8. Limitation of Liability. UNDER NO CIRCUMSTANCES INCLUDING NEGLIGENCE, SHALL ACADEMIC PRESS BE LIABLE FOR ANY INCIDENTAL, SPECIAL OR CONSEQUENTIAL DAMAGES THAT RESULT FROM THE USE OR INABILITY TO USE THE SOFTWARE OR RELATED DOCUMENTATION, EVEN IF ACADEMIC PRESS OR AN ACADEMIC PRESS AUTHORIZED REPRESENTATIVE HAS BEEN ADVISED OF THE POSSIBILITY OF SUCH DAMAGES. SOME JURISDICTIONS DO NOT ALLOW THE LIMITATION OR EXCLUSION OF LIABILITY FOR INCIDENTAL OR CONSE-

QUENTIAL DAMAGES SO THE ABOVE LIMITATION OR EXCLUSION MAY NOT APPLY TO YOU.

In no event shall Metrowerks' total liability to you for all damages, losses, and causes of action (whether in contract, tort (including negligence) or otherwise) exceed that portion of the amount paid by you which is fairly attributable to the Software and fonts.

9. Controlling Law and Severability. This License shall be governed by and construed in accordance with the laws of the United States and the State of California, as applied to agreements entered into and to be performed entirely within California between California residents. If for any reason a court of competent jurisdiction finds any provision of this License, or portion thereof, to be unenforceable, that provision of the License shall be enforced to the maximum extent permissible so as to effect the intent of the parties, and the remainder of this License shall continue in full force and effect.

10. Complete Agreement. This License constitutes the entire agreement between the parties with respect to the use of the Software, the related documentation and fonts, and supersedes all prior or contemporaneous understandings or agreements, written or oral, regarding such subject matter. No amendment to or modification of this License will be binding unless in writing and signed by a duly authorized representative of Metrowerks.

Become a CodeWarrior Now!

To order the full version of Metrowerks CodeWarrior, fill out and fax this order form.

Fax: (419) 281-6883
Voice: (800) 377-5416 (USA only)
          (419) 281-1802 (outside USA)

For sales and site licensing information:

Voice: (512) 305-0400
Fax: (512) 305-0440
Internet: sales@metrowerks.com

Please print clearly	Qty	Cost each	Total
Name			
Company or educational institution			
Address			
Address			
City State/Province ZIP/Postal code			
Telephone number Fax number			
E-mail address			

	Qty	Cost each	Total
CodeWarrior Gold		$399.00	
CodeWarrior Bronze		$99.00	
CodeWarrior Academic		$99.00	
Academic Lab Pack 10		$650.00	
Academic Lab Pack 25		$1450.00	
CodeWarrior Magic/MPW		$299.00	
		Total	
	Applicable tax(es), shipping & handling		
		Total payment	

☐ VISA   ☐ Master Card   ☐ American Express

Credit card number   Expiry date (MM/YY)

Cardholder's signature

About the CD-ROM

The **CD-ROM** that accompanies this book contains a fully-functional copy of **CodeWarrior**™ **C++**. It is, however, limited in a significant way: It will only compile and run the projects that are on the CD-ROM. You will therefore find two types of projects. The first type includes all the sample code from the book. You will be using those projects and their source code files for the book's programming challenges.

The second type of project are two "blank" projects. In other words, empty files have been added to the projects so that you can add your own code to those files. The first blank project is for use in the exercises i n Chapter 3. The second is for you to use to create your own programs from scratch. Because each blank project only has two source code files (one for the main program and one for the class functions), they are only suitable for very small programs that you can use to practice.